BEYOND CANDLESTICKS

学問に近道なし

"Learning is Like Rowing Upstream; Not to Advance is to Fall Back"

BEYOND CANDLESTICKS

New Japanese Charting Techniques Revealed

STEVE NISON

JOHN WILEY & SONS, INC.

New York • Toronto • Chichester • Brisbane • Singapore

This text is printed on acid-free paper.

© 1994 by Steve Nison
Published by John Wiley & Sons, Inc.

All rights reserved. Published simultaneously in Canada.

Reproduction or translation of any part of this work beyond
that permitted by Section 107 or 108 of the 1976 United
States Copyright Act without the permission of the copyright
owner is unlawful. Requests for permission or further
information should be addressed to the Permissions Department,
John Wiley & Sons, Inc., 605 Third Avenue, New York, NY
10158-0012.

This publication is designed to provide accurate and
authoritative information in regard to the subject
matter covered. It is sold with the understanding that
the publisher is not engaged in rendering legal, accounting,
or other professional services. If legal advice or other
expert assistance is required, the services of a competent
professional person should be sought.

Library of Congress Cataloging in Publication Data:
Nison, Steve.
    Beyond candlesticks: New Japanese charting techniques revealed/Steve
Nison.
      p.   cm.—(Wiley finance editions)
    Includes bibliographical references.
    ISBN 0-471-00720-X
    1. Stocks—Prices—Charts, diagrams, etc. 2. Stock price
forecasting. 3. Stocks—Prices—Japan—Charts, diagrams, etc.
I. Title. II. Series.
HG4638.N568 1994
332.63'222'0952—dc20   94-4290
                                 CIP

Printed in the United States of America

10 9 8 7 6 5 4 3 2 1

WILEY FINANCE EDITIONS

The New Technical Trader / Chande and Kroll
Trading on the Edge / Deboeck
Forecasting Financial and Economic Cycles / Niemira and Klein
Trader Vic II / Sperandeo
Genetic Algorithms and Investment Strategies / Bauer
Understanding Swaps / Marshall
Fractal Market Analysis / Peters
Trading Applications of Japanese Candlestick Charting / Wagner and
  Matheny
Fixed-Income Arbitrage / Wong
Trading for a Living / Elder
The Day Trader's Manual / Eng
The Mathematics of Money Management / Vince
Intermarket Technical Analysis / Murphy
The Foreign Exchange and Money Markets Guide / Walmsley
Chaos and Order in the Financial Markets / Peters
Portfolio Management Formulas / Vince
Financial Statement Analysis / Fridson
Money Management Strategies for Futures Traders / Balsara
Dynamic Asset Allocation / Hammer
Relative Dividend Yield / Spare
Inside the Financial Futures Markets, 3rd Edition / Powers and
  Castelino
Option Market Making / Baird
Fixed-Income Synthetic Assets / Beaumont
Selling Short / Walker
The New Technology of Financial Management / Chorafas
Managed Futures in the Institutional Portfolio / Epstein
Analyzing and Forecasting Futures Prices / Herbst
Forecasting Financial Markets / Plummer
A Complete Guide to Convertible Securities Worldwide / Zublake
Corporate Financial Risk Management / Wunnicke and Wilson
Investing in Intangible Assets / Parr
Treasury Operations and the Foreign Exchange Challenge / Chorafas
Trading and Investing in Bond Options / Wong

ACKNOWLEDGMENTS

....

三人寄れば文珠の知恵

"You Cannot Clap With One Hand"

A Japanese book that I had translated said that: "Japanese charts are frequently considered secretive. The number of people who know the essentials of these charts are few and reference material is scarce."[1] This paucity of material was particularly true with some of the new techniques revealed in the second part of this book. However, thanks to the help of some important individuals, I was able to uncover many previously hidden aspects of Japanese technical analysis.

Without the assistance of the translating done by Richard Solberg, it would have been almost impossible to write this book—or my first one! Not only did Richard ably do the translating, but equally important was his tenacity in finding and obtaining the Japanese books I needed for my basic research. Richard has been one of my most vital resources.

As with my first book, I had the help of knowledgeable Japanese traders who helped refine my knowledge by sharing valuable insights obtained from their years of experience.

Mr. Hiroshi Okamoto, Director at Nomura Investment Trust, Mr. Yasuhi Hayashi, Senior Trader at Sumitomo Life Insurance, Mr. Nori Hayashi, Investment Manager at Barclays Trust, and other members from the Nippon Technical Analysts Association (NTAA) in Japan were all very gracious. I am sure many of my questions may have seemed very rudimentary to them, but they were patient and open about sharing their knowledge. Without their insights, this book would be much less detailed.

Mr. Kiyohiko Yoshizawa, vice president at Paine Webber, provided valuable new facts and insights about the candles during our numerous meetings.

One of my most important contacts was Mr. Yoji Inata, a correspondent for Reuters. Mr. Inata's assistance was critical for the new tools addressed in this book; we spent many hours together. Not only did he take his valuable time to review some of the new techniques to make sure I correctly understood the ideas, but he also took the extra step of conferring with his Japanese colleagues on points about which he was not 100% sure. Mr. Inata said that he enjoyed our studying together. I think he was being polite. Although I may have contributed to his knowledge in some respects, for the most part I was the student. I was fortunate to have had a gracious, knowledgeable, and friendly teacher.

Thanks again goes to my friend, Bruce Kamich. A true professional, he continues to provide me with a stream of insightful and helpful ideas.

The editor of this book, Susan Barry, was also the editor of my first book. Susan had the foresight to see how brightly the interest in the candles would burn. She was a major factor in my choice of John Wiley & Sons to publish this book. I hope Susan does not decide to move to a publishing firm in the Antarctic. If I ever do a third book, I would have to follow her.

As an English poet said: "Where ignorance is bliss, wisdom is folly." Before writing my first book, I was blissfully ignorant of all the time and effort that goes into such a project. That book, made me aware of how difficult the process is. Because of this, I had no desire to go through it all again. However, Dodge Dorland, Chief Investment Officer of Landor Investment Management (New York, NY), gave me the push to do this second book. Dodge uses candles to trade stocks on an intra-day basis and has been one of the earliest proponents of candles. Anyone who has dealt with Dodge can vouch for his amiability and for his knowledge.

Many of the charts in this book are from the MetaStock software by EQUIS International (Salt Lake City, UT). Without their assistance in providing me with the new software to draw the kagi, three-line break, and renko charts, this book would be much less detailed. Their excellent software, and helpful and knowledgeable staff makes MetaStock a pleasure to use. For those interested in finding out more about the MetaStock software, there is a coupon included at the back of this book. The data used for the Metastock charts was from Dial-Data (Brooklyn, NY). I found their data accurate and easily accessible.

I would like to thank Shahrokh Nikkhah whose early appreciation of my work and desire to make available the many advantages of candlestick analysis to his clients brought about my joining his team where we offer advisory and brokerage services at Daiwa Securities America. I would also thank my colleague, Mark Tunkel for taking the time to help proofread this book.

In this, as in my first book, you will see many CQG charts (Glenwood Springs, CO). They are a real-time graphics charting service. CQG was among the first services in the West to offer candle charts to their clients. I have used their service for many years. The accuracy of their data and their support personnel, such as Steve Onstad in New York, make this a premier real-time charting service. Their excellent worldwide reputation is well justified.

Reuters Ltd. (New York, London, and Tokyo) have also provided charts for this project. Their RTA technical analysis real-time charting product offers some unique capabilities. I have had the pleasure of giving a series of seminars for them throughout Europe. The fact that Reuters has gone through the time, effort, and expense to send me to Europe for these seminars shows how committed they are in meeting the educational needs of their clients.

My first book, *Japanese Candlestick Charting Techniques*, was written around the same time as the birth of my son, Evan. (At the time of Evan's birth, I frightened my wife, Bonnie, when I said I was going to name him "Candlesticks Nison.") Evan is now four, and he enjoys "typing" on my keyboard. I tell you this so that if there are typos, I now have an excuse. My daughter, Rebecca, is eight and very bright. I have jokingly said that I wanted this book easy enough for a child to understand, so I think I'll ask her to proofread these pages (yet another excuse if you find any mistakes!). Finally, there is my loving and patient wife, Bonnie, who understands that it is great to have written, but most difficult to write.

Final thanks go to those who provided another incentive for writing this book—the credit card companies and the bank that has my mortgage.

Note

[1]Oyama, Kenji, p. 51.

CONTENTS

....

PART ONE: CANDLES

Chapter 3   THE PATTERNS   55

Chapter 4   CANDLES AND THE OVERALL TECHNICAL PICTURE   129

PART 2: THE DISPARITY INDEX AND NEW PRICE CHARTS

PART 1

CANDLES

十人十色

"Let Every Bird Sing its Own Song"

INTRODUCTION

$\mathbf{A}$ chart is like a map, the more information each one provides, the better the chance of reaching your destination safely. Candle charts display a more detailed and accurate map of the market than do bar charts. A Japanese book that I had translated stated, ''It is not an exaggeration to say that candlesticks are the best in the world and a very exquisite creation for charts.''[1] This is because, as detailed below, candle charts open new avenues of analysis and offer many advantages over bar charts:

1. Candle charts will pictorially display the supply–demand situation by showing who is winning the battle between the bulls and the bears. Bar charts do not.
2. Like bar charts, candle charts will show the trend of the market, but candle charts add another dimension of analysis by revealing the force behind the move.
3. Bar chart techniques can often take weeks to transmit a reversal signal. However, candle charts will often send out clues of imminent reversals in one to three sessions. The result is that candle charts often provide the opportunity for more timely trades.

These are just some reasons why the flames of interest in candle charts grow ever brighter. In just a few years, candle charts have joined bar charts and point and figure charts as a basic charting technique.

Candle charts are drawn using the same data as bar charts (the open, high, low, and close), so they send all the same signals that can be found on bar charts. Yet, as just discussed, the candles offer many advantages over bar charts, so using candle charts instead of bar charts is a win–win situation. When you use bar charts you only get bar chart signals. But, with candle charts you get all the bar chart signals, plus you gain the unique and powerful insights provided by the candles. So, why use a bar chart?

Because the Japanese are major players in most of the world's markets, there is strong interest in how the Japanese use their technicals to trade. Candles are the most popular form of technical analysis in Japan. The importance of the candles for the Japanese trading community is illustrated in the following quote from the European magazine, *Euroweek*. This article quotes an English trader who works at a Japanese bank. He states: "All the Japanese traders here—and that's in the foreign exchange, futures and equities markets—use the candles. It might be difficult to work out the billions of dollars traded in London on interpretations of these charts each day, but the number would be significant."[2]

Think about it: Although billions are traded every day based on the candle chart signals, until recently we had no knowledge of how the Japanese viewed the market with their technicals. This is hard to believe. Knowing the candles and their other technical tools discussed in this book may help answer the question, "What are the Japanese going to do next?."

Years ago, I met with the head of technical analysis for one of Japan's largest life insurance companies (this Japanese trader wanted to meet with me to learn how I used western technicals to trade). When he walked into my office, he saw I had candle charts on my desk. In a surprised voice, he asked: "You know about the candles?." I responded that I did. I then asked if he used them. He told me that his company's top management would meet each Monday to discuss the world markets. At these meetings, he would bring his candle charts to offer his technical views. Then he pointed to my candle charts and asked: "How many other Americans know about this?." I said no one (this was before the publication of my first book). He looked relieved. I then continued, "But I will soon have a book out about it." "So, many others will know about this?," he asked in a disappointed tone. The point of the story is that the Japanese trader came to me to learn about how we, in the West, use technicals. The Japanese have learned from us and they know almost all of our technical methods. In most of the candlestick books and articles I have had translated from Japanese to English, there was at least some reference to western technical techniques. A quote from one of the books I had translated stated, "To understand stocks it is not enough to know the Japanese chart methods . . . one must absorb the best parts of western technicals: and on top of that using the best parts of Japanese charts to make for a progressive outlook which is necessary for stock analysis."[3] We can see from this statement how the Japanese have used our methods to enhance their own. One of the purposes of this book is to do the same for Western traders—to show how to use the techniques implemented by the Japanese to enhance our market knowledge.

An article about my work appeared in the *Japan Economic Journal*. In it, the reporter states: ''Japan, which has been in the position to learn many things from the West in the investments area, may be in the position to teach something.''[4] We now have access to a wealth of technical information refined by generations to use; we are learning from the Japanese.

Chapter 2 shows how to draw the basic candle line, and delves into some history of the candle charts. Later in that chapter, I show how a single candle line can provide important market insights. Chapter 3 discusses the basic candle patterns. With the detailed descriptions of these patterns, those new to candles *and* candle experts can discover new market perspectives. The last chapter in this section, Chapter 4 focuses on how the overall technical picture is more important than a single candle pattern.

Notes

[1] Hoshii, Kazutaka, p. 18.
[2] *Euroweek*, August 30, 1991.
[3] Yasui, Taichi, p. 95.
[4] *The Japan Economic Journal*, July 23, 1991.

CHAPTER 1

OVERVIEW

••

仏作って魂入れず

"The Buddha is Complete, But the Eyes Are Not in Yet"
(The Job is Not Yet Done)

THE EXPLOSIVE INTEREST IN THE CANDLES

There is a Japanese saying, "A clever hawk hides its claws." For over a century, the claws of Japanese technical analysis, that is candlestick charts, were a secret hidden from the western world.

For those new to the exciting field of candlestick charts, *candlestick* is the term used for Japan's most popular and oldest form of technical analysis. They are older than Western point and figure and bar charts. Amazingly, candlestick charting techniques, used for generations in the Far East, were virtually unknown to the West until I revealed them in my first book, *Japanese Candlestick Charting Techniques*.

I am pleased and proud that my first book has been credited with revolutionizing technical analysis by igniting the flames of interest in the candles. Before its publication, few people in the West had ever heard of a candle chart. Now, candle charting techniques are among the most discussed form of technical analysis in the world!

Interest in candle charts has become so intense that the World Bank in Washington, DC asked me to address them on the subject. The worldwide interest in these previously secret techniques are reflected in the financial headlines below:

Institutional Investor—"Revealed! Ancient Japanese Trading System"

Wall Street Journal—"Japan's Candlesticks Light Traders' Path"

Euroweek—"Candlestick Charting Comes of Age"

Equity International—"Candlestick Charting—A New Language for the West"

Reuters—"Candlesticks Light New Path for Western Chartists"

For over 70 years, the standard charting tools in the West have been bar charts and point and figure charts. Yet, within a short time, candle charts have now joined these as a basic charting tool. The rapidity with which this has happened is a direct reflection of the candle's popularity and value.

The groundswell of interest in the candlestick charting has become a topic in the media. A TV show, *Tech Talk*, on the business news cable station CNBC is hosted by the famous technician, John Murphy. John told me that a viewer once called and asked him, "What are those charts that look like hot dogs?" What an interesting and amusing idea, I thought, to Americanize these charts by referring to them as hot dog charts. But I guess the term "candle chart," thankfully, is here to stay.

I have had many wonderful compliments from famous traders and analysts. However, the most endearing compliment came from a woman who wrote, "If you ever have a down day, just remember there's a nice little grandmother in Missouri who's in awe of your accomplishments." This letter, besides being so gracious, illustrates the universal appeal of candles—from traders at the World Bank to a grandmother in Missouri.

The reason for the popularity of candlestick analysis is easy to understand. They can be melded with any other form of technical analysis, they are applicable to any of the markets to which technical analysis is applied, and they provide market insights not available anywhere else.

Why this book? A renowned 16th-century samurai swordsman stated that "learning is the gate, not the house. You first have to go through the gate to get to the house."

My other book, *Japanese Candlestick Charting Techniques*, took you to the gate. This book takes you to the house and has many new, exciting, and effective techniques to improve your trading, investing, or hedging.

Japanese charting was considered a secret. However, I have managed to pry open the "secrets of the Orient" by exchanging ideas with many Japanese traders who use candles and by having many hundreds of pages translated from Japanese into English. Lin Yutang, a noted Chinese philosopher, sagely noted that one gets a different flavor from reading the same book at different stages in life. Therefore, he says, all great books can be read with profit and pleasure a second time; I have found this to be true.

In the time since the publication of my first book, I have reread my original candlestick documents and have gleaned new insights. In addition, I have obtained and translated new Japanese material, have expanded my dialogue with more Japanese technicians and, of course, have continued to learn from my use of candles. I reveal these new and valuable insights in this book.

My first book focused on the futures markets. The candles have now become so important that their popularity has spilled over from futures into stock, bond, and foreign exchange markets from around the world. As a result, this book will have many more of the charts than did my other book.

At times, a single candle line can be important. The Japanese have a saying, "With the fall of one leaf we know that autumn has come to the world." In this sense, a single candle line may be the first sign of a market turn. In this book, I will show how to use individual candle lines to obtain clues about the market's health.

It has been very exciting to see the intense interest sparked by the candles. However, it is often forgotten that the emergence of a candle pattern is but one aspect of trading. Other aspects, such as the risk and reward ratio of a potential trade and monitoring where the candle pattern appears in the overall technical picture, must also be considered. This is so important that I have devoted a chapter to these aspects.

In my continuing studies of Japanese trading techniques, I have uncovered three charting methods that are very popular in Japan, yet are unknown to the West. These charting techniques are called three-line break charts, kagi charts, and renko charts. They are revealed in Part 2 of this book.

In the days of fur trading in the United States, there was a company called the Hudson Bay Trading Company. They were known for taking risks and for careful preparation. Trading journeys were undertaken with much excitement, but in case the fur traders forgot anything, they would camp out the first night just a few miles away from the company's headquarters. In other words, careful preparation spared the travelers potential difficulties.

In Chapters 2 and 3, I too provide careful preparation by providing a primer on basic candle theory and patterns. For those new to candle charts, these chapters will provide the groundwork for your candle chart analysis.

Many of you are probably already familiar with the basics of candle charts. With this in mind, Chapters 2 and 3 will also offer a deeper knowledge of the candles by revealing new candle theories, techniques, and tools. As a result, even those knowledgeable about candles will gain new insights and perspectives into the power of the candle charts. For example, when I describe the candle patterns in Chapter 3, I will provide a unique visual glossary of candle patterns. This method of drawing the patterns will provide a dimension of candle pattern analysis that was never before available. After you explore with me the beauty and power of the candle charts, you will never be able to go back to a bar chart.

This book will be a self-contained unit. I will not go over all the candle patterns; that is done in my first book. However, I will sometimes make references to the more obscure or rare patterns discussed in my first book. This is for the benefit of those who are familiar with all the candle patterns. Do not worry if you have not heard of the pattern before; it will not detract from the discussion of the chart.

Numerous charts and exhibits will quickly and clearly make evident how candles can enhance your trading, timing, and investing. As shown throughout the book, candles can be merged with any other form of technical analysis. Consequently, I have included charts that show how to fully utilize the candles' power alone, or when joined with other technical tools.

Just as important as the recognition of candle patterns is an understanding of the relationship of the candle patterns to the overall technical picture. Chapter 4 focuses on this vital, but often neglected, aspect. In this chapter, I will address how trading with the candles must take into account the risk and reward of a potential trade, the stop-out level, and the overall trend. I will also address the value of adapting to changing market conditions.

Before I discuss trading with candles, I want to clarify a few points. In the futures market, selling short is as common as buying long. This is not true in the stock market; most equity traders look to buy. Consequently, throughout this book when I use the term ''bearish'' or ''selling'' when discussing a stock, you should not think of necessarily going short. Instead, view it as an area to protect existing longs by such means as selling covered calls, moving up protective stops, or offsetting all or some longs.

But this book is about more than candles. In Part II I reveal the disparity index, the three-line break, renko charts, and kagi. These techniques, popular in Japan, are virtually unknown in the West and, unlike candle charting, little has been written about these techniques, even in Japan.

The disparity index compares the close to a moving average. It is used in the same manner as dual moving averages, but it has an interesting wrinkle to it. The three-line break, kagi charts, and renko charts are popular among Japanese traders. They are excellent technical tools for determining the trend of the market.

Whether you use the techniques discussed in this book individually or in combination with one another, you will discover that they provide dynamic advantages for those who make use of their tremendous potential.

Note to Reader: Many charts in this book, especially in Part II, were drawn using technical analysis software from Metastock by EQUIS International (Salt Lake City, UT). A coupon for Metastock Software is included at the end of the book.

CHAPTER 2

THE BASICS

∙∙

小事が大事

"Inattention is Fatal"

HISTORY OF THE CANDLE CHARTS

THE Japanese were the first to use technical analysis to trade one of the world's first futures markets—rice futures. The Japanese started trading in this market in the 1600s. Interestingly, the birth of the Japanese rice futures market was a consequence of the country's military history.

After a century of internal warfare among the daimyo (Japanese feudal lords), General Tokugawa Ieyasu, who ruled from Edo (the ancient name of Tokyo), won the famous battle at Sekigahara in 1600. This was the battle that helped unify Japan. Tokugawa thereafter became Shogun of all Japan. After his victory over the daimyo, General Tokugawa cleverly required that all the feudal lords live in Edo with their families. When the lords returned to their respective provinces, the entire family stayed at Edo as hostage. The feudal lord's main source of income was rice that was collected as tax from the peasants who worked their land. Since this rice could not be transported from the daimyo's provinces all the way to Edo, they set up warehouses in the port city of Osaka to store their rice.

Because all these powerful daimyo lived so close to each other in Edo, they attempted to outdo one another in lavish dress, mansions, and other luxuries. This was reflected by a popular saying at the time, ''The Edoite will not keep his earnings overnight.'' This showed that the daimyo in Edo were seen as spendthrifts with an expensive lifestyle. To maintain this lifestyle, the daimyo sold rice from their warehouse in Osaka; sometimes they even sold rice from future harvests. The warehouse would issue receipts for this future rice. These were called empty rice contracts ("empty rice" since the rice was not in anyone's physical possession) and they were sold in the secondary market. This was the beginning of one of the world's first futures market.

Trading in rice futures engendered much speculation, and it was from this speculation that Japanese technical analysis was born. The most famous trader in the rice futures market was Homma. Homma traded in the rice futures markets in the 1700s. He discovered that although there was a link between the supply and demand of rice, the markets were also strongly influenced by the emotions of the traders. Because of this, there were times when the market perceived a harvest as different from the actual. He reasoned that studying the emotions of the market could help in predicting prices. In other words, he understood that there was a difference between the value and the price of rice. This difference between price and value is as valid today with stocks, bonds, and currencies, as it was with rice centuries ago.

In the material I had translated, candle charts are often called Sakata charts in reference to the port city of Sakata, where Homma lived. However, based on my research, it is unlikely that Homma used candle charts. As will be seen later, when I discuss the evolution of the candle charts, it was more likely that candle charts were developed in the early part of the Meiji period in Japan (in the late 1800s).

Whether or not Homma invented charting is open to question. But determining whether one person, in this case Homma, created charts or used them to trade is not too important. There is a tendency in the West to be preoccupied with imposing authorship to one person. It is more likely that the candle charts we know today and all the techniques associated with them tended to be a process of cumulative authorship by several people over many generations. Even if he did not invent candle charts, Homma understood that the psychological aspect of the market was critical to his trading success. And it appears that the earliest forms of technical analysis in Japan dealt more with the psychology of the market rather than charts.

In the book, *The Fountain of Gold—The Three Monkey Record of Money*, purportedly written by Homma, the author states: "After 60 years of working day and night I have gradually acquired a deep understanding of the movements of the rice market." The book then goes on to say: "When all are bearish, there is cause for prices to rise. When everyone is bullish there is cause for the price to fall." This phrase echos what is now called contrarian opinion, a tool important to so many traders. Yet, *The Fountain of Gold—The Three Monkey Record of Money*, was written in 1755. It is amazing that before America was a nation, the Japanese were trading with contrarian opinion! The title had me perplexed for some time. I did not understand the reference to the "three monkeys" in the title. Then in some of my translated material, it said something about comparing successful trading to being like the three monkeys we all knew as children—see, hear, and speak no evil. Then it dawned on me; the title of the book, *The Fountain of Gold—The Three Monkey Record of Money*, means that for traders to get to their "fountains of gold," they should have the characteristics of these three monkeys. Specifically:

1. "See no evil"—when you *see* a bullish (bearish) trend, do not get caught up in it; consider it an opportunity to sell (buy).

In the *Fountain of Gold*, it states that there is always a rotation of Yang (bullishness) and Yin (bearishness). This means that within each bull market, there is a bear market, and within a bear market, there is a bull market. This view may explain why Japanese candlestick techniques place so much emphasis on reversal, rather than continuation, patterns.

2. "Hear no evil"—when you *hear* bullish or bearish news, don't trade on it.

It may be safer to take a position after you determine how the market reacts to a news item rather than initiating a trade when the news is released. Bernard Baruch, the millionaire stock speculator and presidential advisor, stated that what is important in market fluctuations "are not the events themselves, but the human reactions to these events." Exhibit 2.1 shows that how the market reacts to the news may be just as important as the news itself.

The Iraqi War started in the first few days of August 1990. Yet, Exhibit 2.1 shows that gold stalled at $425. This $425 level was gold's high earlier in 1990. This failure to take out the prior high was in spite of the fact that there was a Mideast War. Gold's failure to rally on supposedly bullish news sent out volumes of information about the state of the market. To wit, be careful of a market that fails to rally on bullish news. Note that after this failure at $425, gold lost its luster as prices returned to their pre-Mideast crisis price near $360 within two months.

Also be aware of what the Japanese refer to as "whispering tactics." This is what they call the spreading of false news to trick others in the market. Try to keep out of rumor buffeted markets. Isaac Newton once said, "I can calculate the motion of heavenly bodies but not the madness of people." Why get involved with the madness of people?

3. "Speak no evil"—don't *speak* to others about what you are going to do in the market.

EXHIBIT 2.1.   Observing the Market's Reaction to Fundamental News, Gold—
December 1990, Daily

Has the following happened to you? Based on your analysis, you decide
to buy into a market. You tell someone else of this decision, but they say
something negative about that market. Because there is always a degree
of uncertainty, you get nervous and decide not to buy. Then, of course,
the market rallies.

   If you have carefully studied the market, it is safer not to speak to
anyone about what you plan on doing unless you believe they have better
insight than you. Look only to the market to give you direction. In one
of my favorite passages in *The Fountain of Gold*, it says that ''. . . to learn
about the market ask the market—only then can you become a detestable
market demon.'' Isn't that a wonderful phrase? Wouldn't you love to
become a *detestable market demon?* The colorful language used by the Japanese is just one reason their technical techniques are so exciting.

   Let us turn our attention to Exhibit 2.2, which illustrates the path that
ultimately led to the candle charts.

Evolution of the Candle Charts

   A. Stopping chart—Also referred to as a point, line, or star chart. This
was the earliest type of chart and was drawn by joining only closing

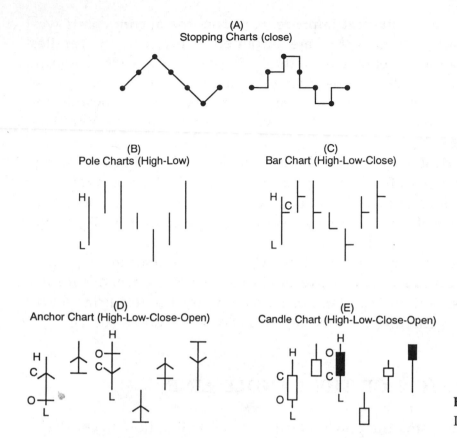

EXHIBIT 2.2. The Evolutionary Path to the Candlestick Charts

prices. They were named stopping charts because that was where the prices stopped by the end of the session. Stopping charts were drawn with either diagonal lines or horizontal lines connecting the closes.

B. Pole chart—Its name is derived from the fact that the lines resemble poles. This chart added the extra information imparted by showing the range between the high and the low of the session. These lines show not only the direction of the move, but the extent of the move for each session.

C. Bar chart—This is a combination of the stopping and pole charts.

D. Anchor chart—Named as such because it looks like an anchor. Based on legend, these charts originated in the Kyoho Era (from 1716) from the fact that the usual meeting place for rice traders was port cities.

The anchor chart was an important event in the evolution of charting. With this chart, the opening price was now added and created a chart with an open, high, low, and close. Just as important, and something unique to Japanese charts, was that the relationship between the open and close was pictorially displayed. The top and bottom of the anchor's vertical line are the high and low of that session. The horizontal line of the anchor line is the open. The arrow of the anchor line is the close. If the close is higher than the open, the arrow points up; if the close is lower, the arrow points down.

E. Candle chart—The next improvement from the anchor charts was the candle chart. Although they are shrouded in mystery, the candles probably started in the early part of the Meiji period (from 1868). As can be seen in Exhibit 2.2E, candle lines were a refinement of the anchor chart. The use of black and white real bodies made analyzing the underlying supply and demand situation visually easier to determine than with the anchor charts.

With the arrival of the candle charts, Japanese technical analysis flowered as people started thinking in terms of signals and trading strategies. Patterns were developed and market prediction became more important. Trying to forecast the market took on extra importance in the 1870s when the Japanese stock market opened.

As can be seen from Exhibit 2.2, bar charts were one of the ancestors of the more evolved and productive candle charts. In essence, this means that since most of the West is still using bar charts, it is also using a less evolved form of charting than the Japanese are with candle charts.

CONSTRUCTION OF THE CANDLE LINE

The first step in using the power of candles is learning how to construct the basic candle line. Exhibits 2.3. and 2.4 show that the candle line consists of a rectangular section and two thin lines above or below this section. We see why these are named candlestick charts; the individual lines often look like candles with their wicks. The rectangular part of the candlestick line is called the *real body*. It represents the range between the session's open and close. When the real body is black (e.g., filled in), it shows that the close of the session was lower than the open. If the real body is white (that is, empty), it means the close was higher than the open.

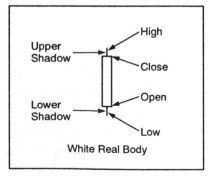

EXHIBIT 2.3. White Real Body

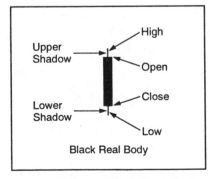

EXHIBIT 2.4. Black Real Body

The thin lines above and below the real body are the *shadows*. The shadows represent the session's price extremes. The shadow above the real body is referred to as the upper shadow and the shadow under the real body is the lower shadow. Accordingly, the peak of the upper shadow is the high of the session and the bottom of the lower shadow is the low of the session.

Candle charts can be used throughout the trading spectrum, from daily, to weekly, and intra-day charting. For a daily chart, one would use the open, high, low, and close of the session. For a weekly chart, the candle would be composed of Monday's open, then the high and low of the week, and Friday's close. On an intra-day basis, it would be the open, high, low, and close for the chosen time period (i.e., hourly).

Exhibit 2.3 shows a strong session in which the market opened near the low and closed near its high. We know that the close is higher than the open because of the white real body. Exhibit 2.4 illustrates a long black candlestick. This is a bearish session in which the market opened near its high and closed near its low.

The Japanese focus on the relationship between the open and close. This makes sense; probably the two most important prices of the day are the open and close. It is therefore surprising that American newspapers have openings for futures prices, but not for stocks. A member of the Nippon Technical Analysts Association told me that he found it unusual that U.S. newspapers do not have opening stock prices; the Japanese have the openings in their papers. He said that he did not know why the Americans disregard the openings.

I would expect that just as almost all technical software vendors now carry candle charts, so it may be that as candles become more popular in the equity market, newspapers may, by popular request, carry stock openings. Until then, in order to obtain the data needed to draw the candles (the open, high, low, and close) you need to use a data vendor service. These services furnish prices on disks or through modems. The data supplied from a data vendor are then transferred into a technical analysis software package that will draw the candles based on these data.

A note of caution: Some data vendors who do not have the actual opening price of a stock default to the prior session's close as today's open. This, in my opinion, is not valid. You must have the true open to draw an accurate candle line. Although an open on a stock will usually not be much different from the prior close, there are some candle patterns in which a higher or lower opening (compared to the prior close) gives valuable information. A data vendor that includes actual opens on stocks is Dial Data (Brooklyn, NY).

REAL BODY AND SHADOWS

While an individual candle usually should not be used alone to place a trade, the size and color of its real body and the length of its shadows can provide a wealth of information. Specifically, looking at a line's real body and shadows gives a sense of the supply and demand situation. This section will discuss this basic idea, and explain how to use real bodies and shadows to get clues about the market's underlying strength or weakness. By using the candle lines discussed below, you may be able to get an early and tentative indication of market direction.

THE REAL BODY

In Japanese charts, even an individual candle line has meaning, and one of the first clues about the vitality of the market is to look at the size and color of the real body. To the Japanese, the real body is the essence of the price movement. This is a critical and powerful aspect of candle charts; through the height and color of the real body, candle charts clearly and quickly display the relative posture of the bulls and the bears.

This section will be segmented according to the decreasing size of the real bodies. The first part of this section will consequently focus on long white and then long black real bodies. After these, attention is turned to candles with small real bodies called spinning tops. These diminutive real bodies display a market where the bulls and bears are in a tug of war.

This section will conclude with candles that have no real bodies. These candles have the same (or nearly the same) opening and closing. Such candles, called doji (pronounced dō-gee), reflect a market in a state of transition. Doji, as you will see later, can be an important market signal.

Long White Real Bodies

A long white real body is defined as a session that opens at or near the low of session, and then closes at or near the session's high. The close should be much higher than the open. For example, if a stock opens at $40 and closes at $40⅝, it would not be a long white candle since the opening and closing range were relatively close. For a long white candle to have meaning, some Japanese candlestick traders believe that the real body should be at least three times as long as the previous day's real body.

EXHIBIT 2.5.   Long White at a Low Price Level

Long White at a Low Price Level

A single candle by itself is rarely sufficient reason to forecast an immediate reversal. It could, however, be one clue that the prior trend may be changing. For instance, as shown in Exhibit 2.5, a long white real body at a low price range may be the first sign of a market bottom. A long white candle shows that the ability to rise is virtually unimpeded by the bears. The closer the close is to the high of the session, and the longer the white real body, the more important the candle line.

Exhibit 2.6 shows that in late 1991, this stock was stabilizing near $5. The first sign that the bulls were attempting to take control was the unusually long white real body at 1. Note how this real body was extended compared to the prior real bodies. However, an almost equally long, but black real body (for information on black real bodies, see page 29), on the week after candle 1 showed that the bears still had enough force to offset the bulls' advance. In early 1992, another unusually long white candle, shown at 2, appeared. This white candle opened on its low (since it does not have a lower shadow) and closed on its high (since it does not have an upper shadow). Such a candle is exceptionally strong, notably when it is so elongated as in candle 2. Candle 3 was another strong white candle that propelled prices to new multi-month highs. With the tall white candles 1 and 2 both appearing near $5, we can see the significance of that $5 support area. Consequently, when prices corrected back to this level in July and August 1992, it is not surprising that the selloff stopped near $5.

Long White Candle Confirms Support

As shown in Exhibit 2.7, the tall white candle that rebounds from support underscores the aggressiveness of the bulls. A long white candle that bounces off a support area such as a trendline, a moving average, or a retracement level gives extra confirmation of that support.

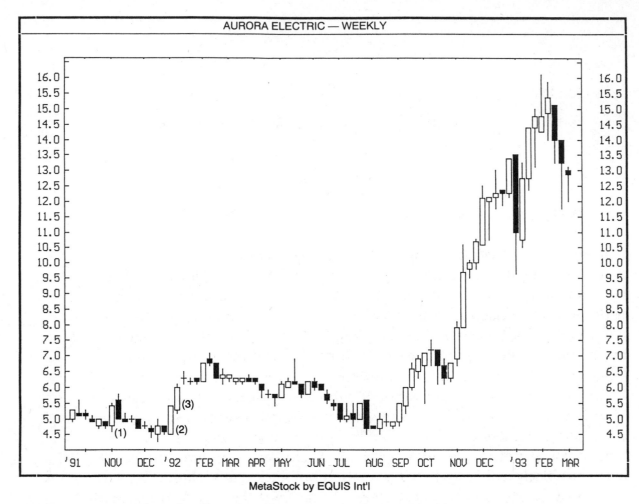

EXHIBIT 2.6. Long White Candle at Low Price, Aurora Electric—Weekly

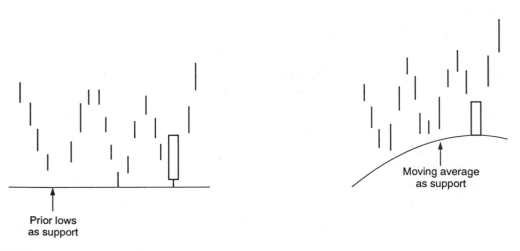

EXHIBIT 2.7. Long White Candle Confirms Support

EXHIBIT 2.8. Long White Candle Confirms Support, General Re—Daily

In Exhibit 2.8, we see how drawing a support line with a candle chart is done the same way as with a bar chart. In this case, we are looking at a support line that is obtained by connecting the lows of the session (that is, by connecting the bottom of the lower shadows). This upward sloping trendline was tested numerous times. In late January, a bounce from this support via a long white real body showed the eagerness of the bulls to buy near that support.

Long White Body Breaks Resistance

Exhibit 2.9 displays how the market can prove its mettle by piercing a resistance area with a tall white real body. As shown in Exhibit 2.10, the highs at areas A and B disclosed a resistance area near $44 and $45. In late November, an extended white real body gapped higher on the open-

EXHIBIT 2.9.   Long White Candle Breaks Resistance

ing and closed at the session's high. This tall white candle confirmed an important breakout from the aforementioned resistance band. Note how in early 1993 the gap before this white candle became a support area. We will look at the importance of gaps as support when windows are discussed in the next chapter.

Long White Real Bodies as Support

Exhibit 2.11 brings out one of the more exciting uses of long white candles, specifically, that long white candles can become support areas. I have found this to be an excellent tool since it serves to alert traders to support zones that are not available with bar charts. The depth of the reaction should find support at either the middle of the long white real body or the bottom of the entire white candle, including the lower shadow. The Japanese literature says that a long white real body should be support in a rising market. However, based on my experience, it can also be used as support in a falling market. The reason the market may fall back after an exceptionally tall white real body is that prices may become short-term overbought (that is, they rallied too far too fast). In this scenario, the market may have to retrace some of the prior rally to relieve this overbought condition.

In Exhibit 2.12, the huge white candle in early 1992 propelled prices from $10½ to about $15. Almost a 50% rise in one week! After such a move, it was not surprising that the market had to consolidate its gains. Based on the precept that a long white candle is support, the middle of the white real body (at the arrow), near $12½, should then be monitored as support. The power of the market is well reflected by the fact that for the rest of 1992, the market held above this support area.

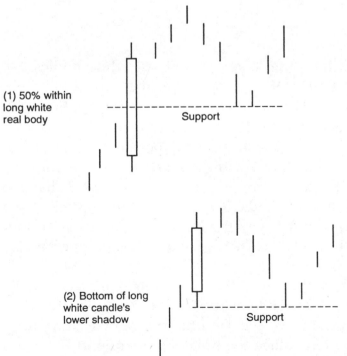

(1) 50% within long white real body

Support

(2) Bottom of long white candle's lower shadow

Support

EXHIBIT 2.11.   Long White Real Bodies as Support

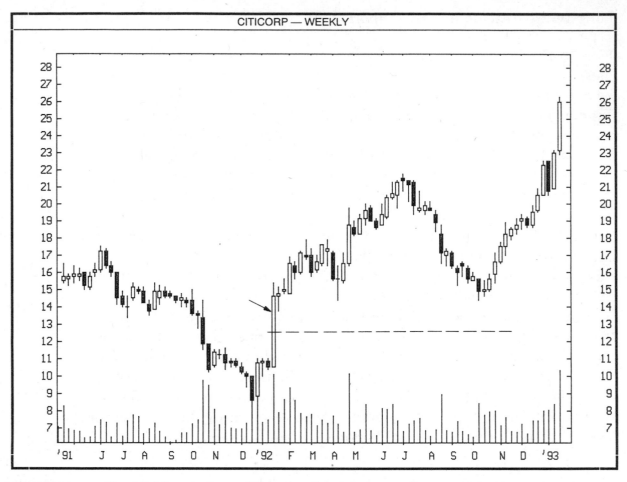

CITICORP — WEEKLY

EXHIBIT 2.12. The Middle of a Long White Candle as Support, Citicorp—Weekly

Exhibit 2.13 illustrates how the lower end of tall white bodies 1–4 became support on corrections. Of interest is that the support line obtained by extending the low of candle 3 was broken in September 1992. Observe, however, that the sell-off stopped near the support area from the low of candle 2. This chart also illustrates an important point. Candlestick traders should wait, if possible, for the market to close under support to confirm a break. In this example, we see in mid-1992 that the support level from the bottom of candle 3 was broken intra-weekly (see X on the chart), as was the support by the bottom of candle 4 (see Y). Because the weekly (i.e., the Friday) close held above these support areas, the support line was still in force.

Notice in Exhibit 2.14 how the low of the long white real body in early April (at the arrow) was 109–22. This means that area should provide a base on sell-offs. In this exhibit we see the importance of waiting for a close under a support area to confirm the breaking of support.

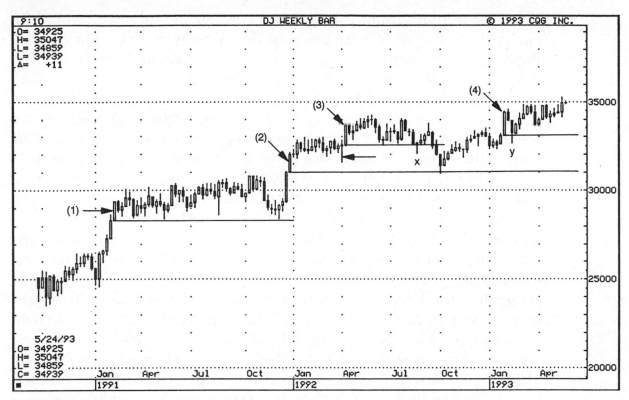

EXHIBIT 2.13. Bottom of Tall White as Support, Dow Jones—Weekly

EXHIBIT 2.14. Bottom of Tall White Candle as Support with Bond Futures—Daily

A method you could use with this concept of tall white candles as support is to buy on a correction near the midpoint of the white candle. From that level down to the bottom of the long white candle (this includes the bottom of the lower shadow) should be support. If the bottom end of the support zone (that is, the lows of the tall white candle) is penetrated on a close, then you should reconsider your long position. At times, these support areas are broken on an intra-session basis, but as long as the support holds on the close, I still view it as valid support.

One of our institutional clients told me he found that, at times, after a tall white candle, the market corrects. I advised him that such action is not surprising since after such a candle, the market may be overbought and hence vulnerable to a setback. I then suggested the use of a long while candle as a support area in which he could buy on a correction. Coincidentally, on November 23, at the time the trader and I were talking about this, the bond's first hour of trading had just ended. This first hour, as shown in area 2 in Exhibit 2.15, completed a tall white candle. Since he traded bonds, I informed the client that support should be from the halfway point of this white candle down to the bottom of the candle, including the lower shadow. I then pointed out that there was another long while candle from the preceding day's first hour of trading (see

EXHIBIT 2.15.   Using the Support Zone in a Tall White Candle December 1993 Bond Futures—Intra-Day

candle 1). The bottom of that tall white candle (including the shadow) was successfully defended as support with candle 2. Thus, there were two white candles (at 1 and 2) that reinforced the support near 114–16. Note how, after white real body 2, the market retraced about halfway into it before rallying.

Long Black Real Body at High Price Area

Just as a long white candle could be an early signal that the market may be trying to build a bottom, so it is that a distinctively long black real body at a high price may be a tentative warning of a top. The long black real body should be significantly longer than the candles preceding it. This is illustrated in Exhibit 2.16. Such a long black real body displays that the bears had grabbed control of the market. The longer the rally continued and the more overbought the market, the more reliable the cautionary signal of this long black real body becomes.

The long white candle (1) in Exhibit 2.17 echoes a vibrant market. However, there were a few warnings that Home Depot was overheating. The first was that the relative strength index (RSI) was above 70%. Such a high RSI figure is a clue that the market is overbought. Another sign that the bulls were losing their upside push was the series of small real bodies following the tall white candle at 1. These small real bodies showed that the supply–demand situation was more in balance as compared to tall white candle 1 (candle 1 showed that demand was overwhelming supply). Small real bodies are discussed in more detail later in this chapter.

Falling black real body at 2 showed that the bears had wrested control of this stock. Note how black real body 2 was the longest black real body since at least November 1992. This shouts out a warning that there is now something very different about the market, and that appropriate defensive action—such as selling covered calls, or offsetting some longs—should be undertaken. For those who are familiar with all the candle patterns, note how the tall white candle at 1 and the black real body at

EXHIBIT 2.16.   Long Black Real Body at High Price Area

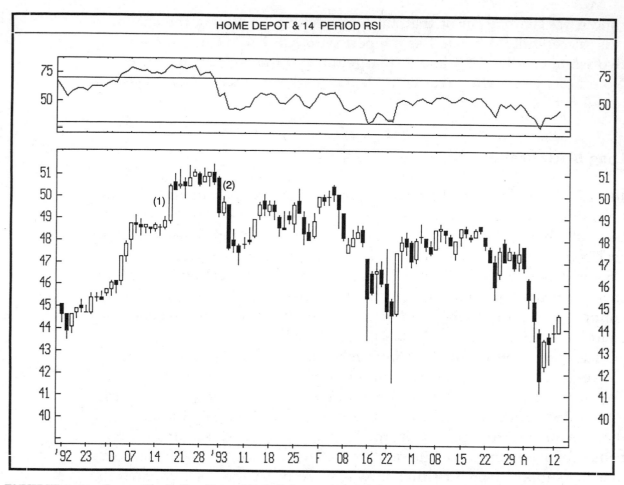

EXHIBIT 2.17.   Large Black Candle at High Price and the Relative Strength Index,
Home Depot—Daily

2 formed a bearish tower top, so named because the two long candles at
1 and 2 look like towers.

Long Black Confirms Resistance

If, as shown in Exhibit 2.18, the market backs off sharply from resistance
through a long black candle, it is extra confirmation of the resistance
area. This is because such a candle means that either the bulls have

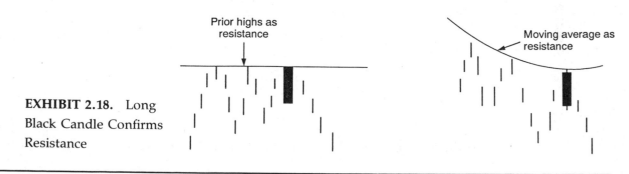

EXHIBIT 2.18.   Long
Black Candle Confirms
Resistance

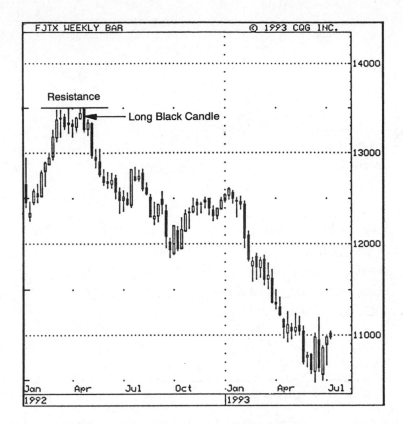

FJTX WEEKLY BAR © 1993 CQG INC.

Resistance

Long Black Candle

14000

13000

12000

11000

Jan   Apr   Jul   Oct   Jan   Apr   Jul
1992   1993

EXHIBIT 2.19. Long Black Candle at Resistance, Cash Yen—Weekly

retreated or that the bears have become aggressive enough to overwhelm the bulls. Either of these scenarios is potentially bearish. In Exhibit 2.19, there is an evident resistance area near 135 yen. This is shown by the horizontal trendline. The first long black candle at the arrow stalled at this resistance. With the retreat from this resistance through this unusually long black real body, there was a cause for caution. Two weeks later, the second, even longer black real body signified the capacity of the bears to drag prices lower.

Long Black Breaks Support

As shown in Exhibit 2.20, the way the market breaks a support area may indicate the seriousness of the break. For instance, a move under a support area by way of a long black candle should be viewed as a potentially more bearish scenario than if the market closes under a support area with a short black candle or a white candle.

A popular longer term moving average monitored by both Japanese and American stock market participants is the 200 day moving average. Exhibit 2.21 shows how this moving average was support throughout

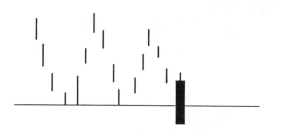
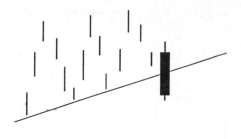

EXHIBIT 2.20.   Long Black Candle Breaks Support

late 1992 into January 1993. However, the first sign of a break of this support came by way of long black real body 1. Although this only broke the 200 day moving average line by a few cents, it was an early, but provisional, sign of trouble. Final proof of a decisive break of the support area came with long black candlestick 2.

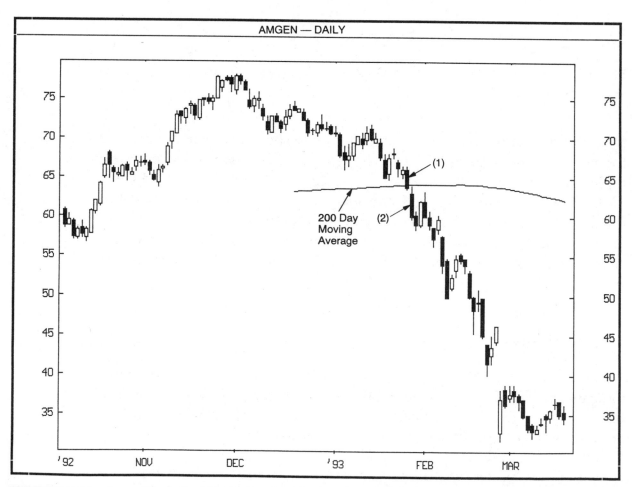

EXHIBIT 2.21.   Long Black Real Body Breaks Moving Average Support, Amgen—Daily

EXHIBIT 2.22. Long Black Candle as Resistance

Long Black as Resistance

As a long white real body acts as a support area, so a long black real body should act as resistance (see Exhibit 2.22). In Exhibit 2.23, long black real body 1 penetrated an uptrending support line. With the long black candle at 1 and the long black real body six weeks earlier (at X), there

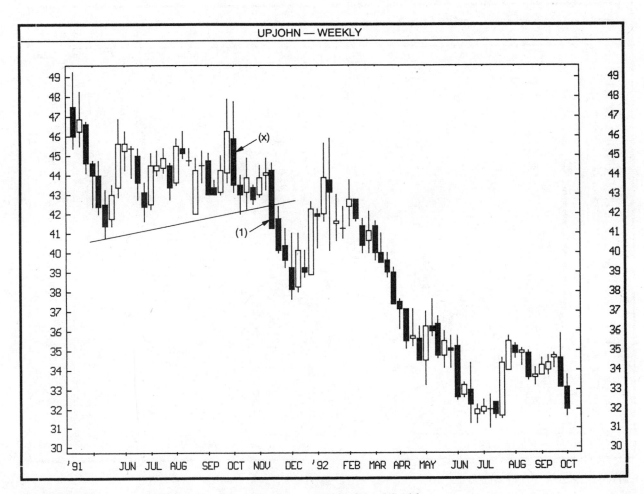

EXHIBIT 2.23. Long Black Candle as Resistance, Upjohn—Weekly

was now a resistance zone that could be used to exit longs or to go short, on a bounce to that resistance.

Exhibit 2.24 displays a price explosion via a long white candle in late 1991. Using the theory of long candles, let us see how one could have traded this market. A long white candle gives us a support area at 50% within its real body. Consequently, a pullback to near the 50% retracement of the long white could be used as an early buying zone. This could have been at areas 1 through 4. Now, we turn our attention to a price target. Notice the exceptionally bearish long black real body from September 1991 (at the arrow). As discussed above, we would expect a rally to stall as it approaches the top of this black candle. Although the bulls were finally able to gather enough force to breach this resistance of the long black candle, it took them over a year to accomplish this. Thus, buying on a pullback into the long white with a minimum target to September's long black real body could have been an effective trading strategy.

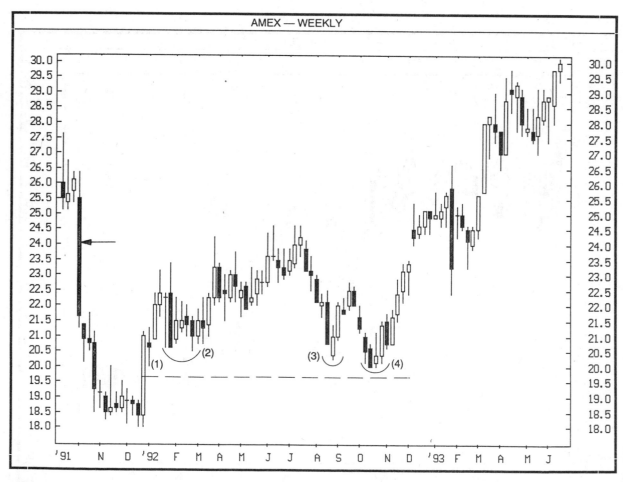

EXHIBIT 2.24. Long Black Candle as Resistance, Amex—Weekly

Size, Frequency, and Color of Real Bodies

The tone of the market can be gauged by comparing the relative height, frequency, and color of a group of candle lines. The first sign of trouble in Exhibit 2.25 came with the long black candle at 1. Note how this is the longest black candle in some time. Then, an appearance of an elongated black candle at 2 was an evident warning sign of trouble. The price descent continued until February's tall white candle at 3 arose. This was the loftiest white real body in many months, and relayed that the bulls had entered the market in force. Observe how the midpoint of February's white real body became a base for a minor rally.

In the boxed section in Exhibit 2.26, we see a period in which the market was trading laterally. With a bar chart, it would be difficult to glean information about the relative strength of the bulls or the bears in such an environment. With the candles, however, we can do this. In this trading range environment, we can see that there were eight black real

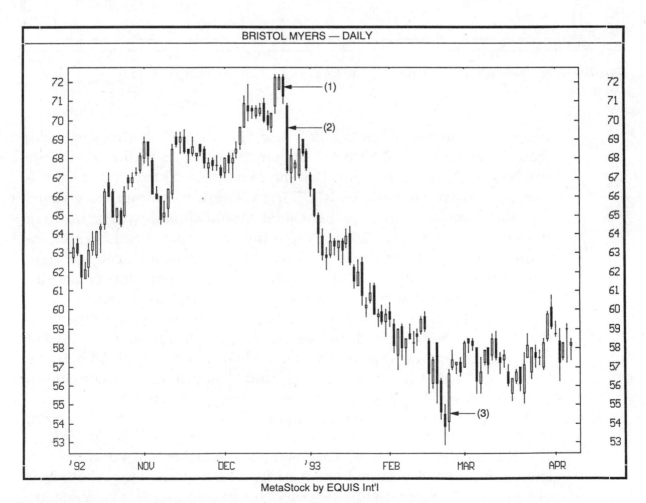

BRISTOL MYERS — DAILY

MetaStock by EQUIS Int'l

EXHIBIT 2.25.   Size and Color of Real Bodies, Bristol Myers—Daily

EXHIBIT 2.26.   Relative Size, Frequency, and Color of Real Bodies, August 1993 Crude Oil

bodies and only four white candles. Also, the black real bodies were taller than the white ones. With more and larger black real bodies than white real bodies, the candles tell us that the bears were taking a more aggressive stance than were the bulls. Classic Western technical theory stated that after a congestion band, the market's trend should have resumed in the same direction that it had before the congestion band. In this example, the preceding trend was down. Thus, the bearish candle action during the lateral range reinforced the classic Western theory and increased the odds of a continuation of the preceding downtrend.

In the next section, using information on how the open compares to the close will be discussed. But before that, I will discuss new ways of interpreting candle patterns. This methodology will help illuminate the theory and market action behind each candle pattern. Each candle pattern in this book will be illustrated four ways (refer to Exhibit 2.27).

Exhibit 2.27 (B) The blended candle—If the candle pattern has more than one candle line, you can combine them to make a single candle line, which I call a *blended candle*. This method is sometimes used in the Japanese candlestick literature to help clarify whether a pattern is bullish or bearish. The blended candle is an individual line that is a combination of the open, high, low, and close of all the candle lines in the pattern.

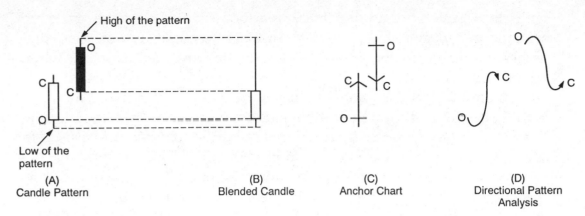

High of the pattern

Low of the pattern

(A)
Candle Pattern

(B)
Blended Candle

(C)
Anchor Chart

(D)
Directional Pattern
Analysis

EXHIBIT 2.27. Candle Pattern Analysis

As shown in Exhibit 2.27 (B), the blended candle is drawn using a four-step process:

1. Use the open of the first session of the candle pattern as the open of the blended candle.
2. Use the high of the candle pattern (in other words, the top of the highest upper shadow) as the high of the blended candle.
3. Use the low of all the sessions of that pattern (i.e., the bottom of the lowest lower shadow) as the low of the blended candle.
4. Use the close of the last session of the candle pattern as the close of the blended candle.

Based on the insight offered by the blended candle line in Exhibit 2.27, we can deduce that the two-candle combination in Exhibit 2.27 (A) is a bearish combination. This is because the blended candle shows the bearish aspects of a long upper shadow and small real body near the bottom of the range.

Exhibit 2.27 (C) Anchor charts—Those who draw the candle charts by hand and are tracking many markets or are restricted in time may find this task to be burdensome. One way to circumvent this (besides buying software) is to consider using anchor lines instead of candle lines. The anchor chart as previously discussed, is composed of the open, high, low, and close. If the anchor is pointing up, it means that the close is higher than the open (with the arrow part of the anchor representing the close). An anchor pointing down means that the close is lower than the open.

Although the anchor chart is less visual than the candle chart, it provides the same information and is faster to draw. The disadvantage to the anchor chart is that you don't have the quick color clue, as you do with the candle's white and black real bodies. But you can draw up sessions in red and down sessions in black (remember, however, that unless you have a color printer, all the anchor lines will be black when a hard copy is printed).

Exhibit 2.27 (D) Directional Pattern Analysis—To clarify the market's path that unfolds during the candle pattern, I will draw arrows reflecting the market's basic intra-session action. I call this *directional pattern analysis*. The path shown by the market's action in the directional pattern analysis can be used as a rough method to gauge the overall price action during the session. Although the arrow in the directional pattern analysis will show the path taken by the market during the session, it will not show the order of when these prices where touched.

For example, based on the relationship of the real body and shadows of the first white candle in Exhibit 2.27 (A), we know that, at some time during the session, prices moved under the opening price. However, we do not know when the price moved under the open. While the arrow in Exhibit 2.27 (D) may make it appear that the market immediately moved lower after the opening, it may not have unfolded that way. The market instead may have rallied after the open and later in the session fell under the opening price. Thus, it is important to keep in mind that the directional pattern analysis should be thought of as a visual clue about the relative price action of the open, high, low, and close compared to one another. However, it does not tell us the sequence of that price action.

Opening Compared to Prior Real Body

A disadvantage of candle charts is that they require the close to complete the candle line. There are some ways around this limitation. One method is to go to a shorter time. In other words, if you are looking at a daily chart, you can sometimes get a signal on the hourly chart before the close of the daily session. Another mechanism to bypass waiting for the close, and the one I will focus on here, is comparing the opening to the prior real body.

Exhibit 2.28 (A) illustrates that if the opening is under the midpoint of the previous white real body, it could be a bearish scenario. Conversely, if the next day's opening is above the black body's midpoint, as shown in Exhibit 2.28 (B), it could be viewed as a positive sign. This concept might be useful for those who are more aggressive and risk-oriented and would want to buy or sell on an opening rather than waiting for a close.

This technique is more important for stocks than for futures. This is because the futures market's higher volatility makes it more likely for the

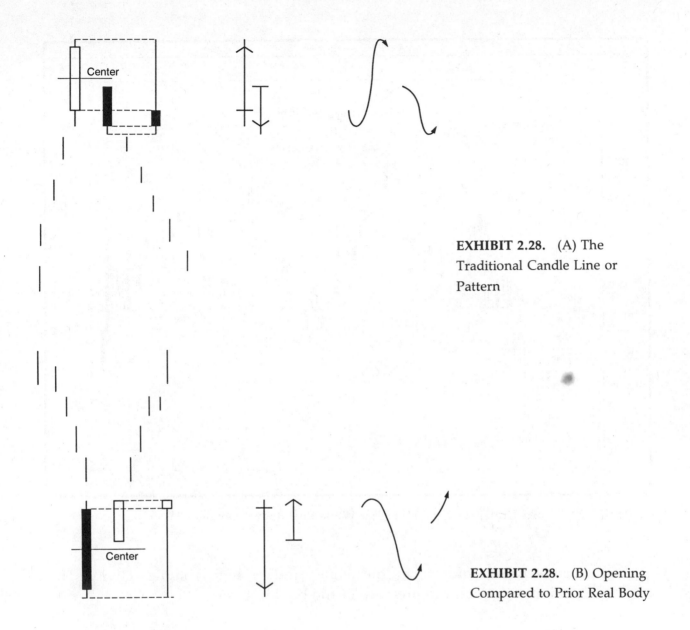

EXHIBIT 2.28. (A) The Traditional Candle Line or Pattern

EXHIBIT 2.28. (B) Opening Compared to Prior Real Body

price to open away from the prior close (remember that for prices to open above or below the prior real body's midpoint, it has to open away from the prior close). However, for a stock, such an occurrence is rarer, and as a consequence more significant.

The chart of Manville (Exhibit 2.29) gave three signals that it was in trouble in mid-1992. First was the long upper shadow candle at the arrow (shadows are discussed in detail in the next section of this chapter). This showed the market rejected the $11 zone. The next signal was when Manville opened under the center of the prior white real body. Final bearish confirmation came the following week when the market gapped lower.

In Exhibit 2.30, in the session marked by the arrow, the market opened above the midpoint of the prior black real body. This positive develop-

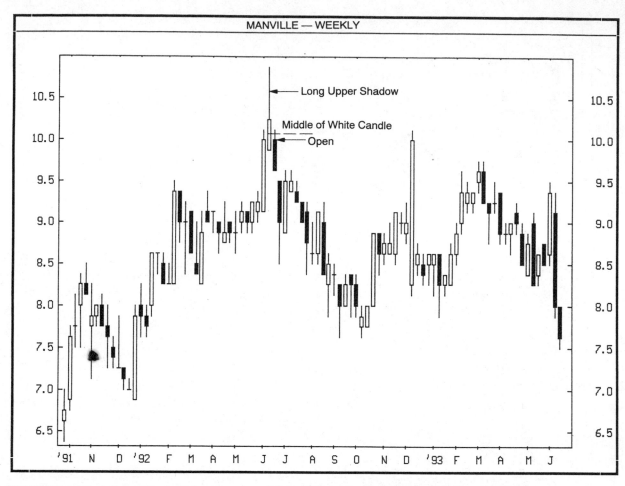

EXHIBIT 2.29.   Open Under the Center of Prior White Real Body, Manville—Weekly

ment was reinforced by the white candle's high volume activity. This volume showed the pressure of the buying force.

Spinning Tops

We have seen the power inherent in tall white or black real bodies. A tall white body reflects a strong session in which the bulls are in control, whereas a long black real body means that the bears are in charge. Now, what would it mean if, instead of tall real bodies, there were small real bodies? This would tell us that the bulls and bears are in a tug of war and that there is more of a balance between supply and demand. Such small real bodies, called spinning tops, tell us that the power to move up or down is lacking, or as the Japanese phrase it, the "market is losing its breath."

As shown in Exhibit 2.31, these are spinning tops even if the lower and/or upper shadows are large. It is the diminutive size of the real body

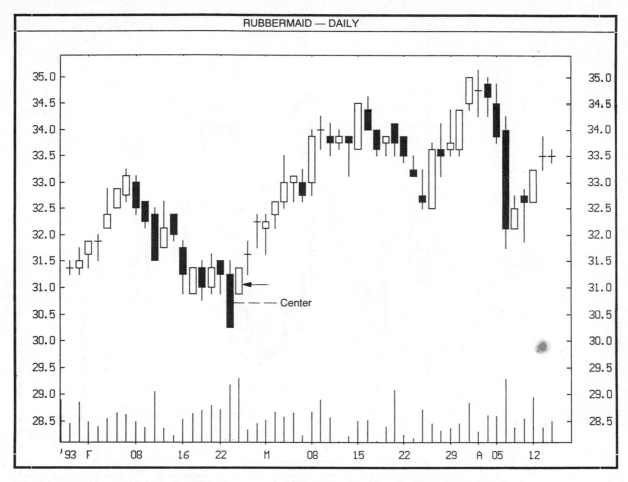

EXHIBIT 2.30. Open Above the Center of a Black Real Body, Rubbermaid—Daily

that defines a spinning top. A spinning top is a warning sign that the market is losing its momentum. For instance, if the market is at or near a new high—especially after a steep advance—the emergence of a spinning top could be a signal that the bulls are having trouble in continuing their ascent. This could be a cautionary signal that the prior move is stalling.

In Exhibit 2.32, the strong, long white real bodies at the end of July left no doubt about who had control of this market—the bulls. But the two spinning tops after these long white real bodies sent out a warning

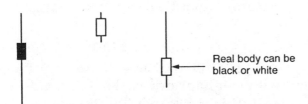

Real body can be black or white

EXHIBIT 2.31. Spinning Tops

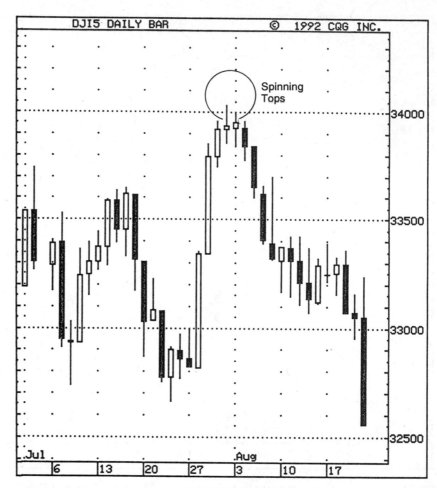

EXHIBIT 2.32.   Spinning Tops, Dow Jones—Daily

that the bulls were unable to maintain the momentum of their advance. The arrival of the spinning tops showed that the market was losing its vitality. The black candles after the spinning top added more reason to suspect a turn.

Accumulation and Distribution

One of the most powerful and important aspects of candle charts is their ability to meld themselves with any other form of technical analysis. Let us, for example, uncover how one candle (the spinning top), combined with volume, can provide critical information about the inner workings of the market.

Two key concepts relating volume to price action are those of accumulation and distribution. Accumulation occurs when, at a low price level, there is a high volume session with stagnant prices. The high volume relays that the bears are attacking full force, throwing all their resources and ammunition into the fray. But the stagnant prices during the session show that the bears are unable to drag down prices. All that the bears have tried to sell has been accumulated by the bulls. After such a scenario, the bears may either run out of ammunition or just give up. The consequence of either of these is a rally.

Distribution is the opposite of accumulation. Distribution occurs when, at a high price level, there is heavy volume but virtually frozen prices. What is happening in such an environment is that the ''smart'' money is thought to be distributing their supply to meet all the buying that is entering the market. With distribution, the sellers are offering enough supply to meet all the buyer's demand, thus keeping prices in check. Distribution should therefore be viewed as a topping scenario.

Note that as part of the definition for either accumulation or distribution, there must be little price movement. A spinning top reflects a session in which there is little price action (as defined by the difference between the open and the close). So, by combining volume with spinning tops, we can determine when there is accumulation or distribution.

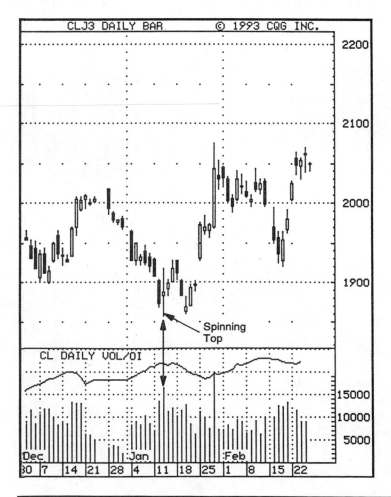

EXHIBIT 2.33. Spinning Tops and Accumulation, April 1993 Crude Oil—Daily

Exhibit 2.33 shows that a spinning top candlestick emerged on January 12. Note also the heavy volume of that session. As describe above, stagnant prices and high volume at a low price level are classic signs of accumulation. The high-volume spinning top in this example shows that the selling pressure was easily absorbed. This positive sign was further reinforced by the fact that this spinning top session made a new low for the move, yet the bears were unable to maintain these new lows.

In Exhibit 2.34, June's tall white candle session was also a high-volume session. This was a very bullish development insofar as the market moved up sharply with strong buying interest (as gauged by the high volume). However, what occurred in the next session was cause for concern. In that session, a small real body (i.e., a spinning top) emerged. The volume on the spinning top session (circled on the chart) was not as extreme as it was the prior day. Yet, looking back at the volume at the bottom of the chart, we see that it was nonetheless a very high-volume session compared to the prior periods. Consequently, there was a high-volume spinning top session. What does that tell us? The high volume reflects a market in which the bulls came out in force, but the small real body—the spinning top—means that the bears were aggressive enough to almost stalemate the bull's advance. This action was a classic sign of distribution. The small real bodies over the next few sessions

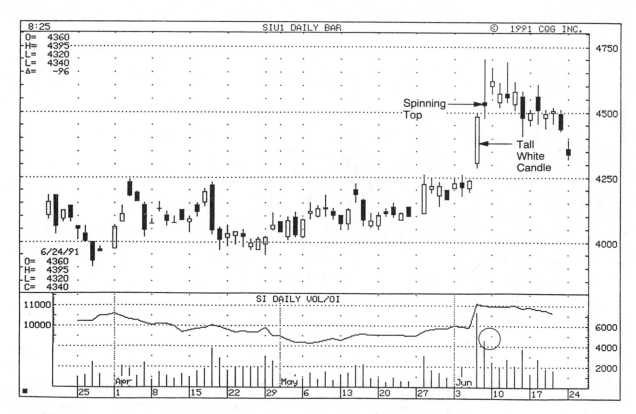

EXHIBIT 2.34.   Spinning Top and Distribution September 1991 Silver—Daily

continued to echo the inability of the bulls to propel this market. Note how the longest real bodies following the spinning top were black. This showed that the bears had gained a foothold on the market.

Doji

One of the more important individual candlestick lines is the doji. As shown in Exhibit 2.35, a doji session has a horizontal line instead of a real body. This is because a doji is formed when the session's open and close are the same (or almost the same). If the market is trading laterally, a doji is neutral. In essence the doji is echoing, on a micro scale, the indecision reflected on a more macro scale by the market's sideways action. However, a doji that emerges after the mature part of an uptrend or sell-off has a greater chance of a market turn. At such a time, the Japanese say that a doji provides ''a hint of tops and bottoms.''

One should be especially cautious about a doji that arises after a tall white candle which in turn appears after a significant uptrend. This is true whether the doji is within the prior long white real body or above it. Such action represents a disparity about the state of the market. Specifically, the rally and tall white candles during such a rally tell us that the bulls are still in charge. But a doji means that the bulls are failing to sustain the upside drive. This is shown in Exhibit 2.36.

How do you decide whether a near doji day (i.e., where the open and close are very close, but not exact) should be considered a doji? One method is to look at a near doji day and compare it to recent action. If there is a series of very small real bodies, I would not view the near doji day as significant since so many other recent periods had small real bodies or doji. (Other methods are covered in my first book).

As mentioned before, a doji is meaningful when it arises after a tall white candle during an uptrend. In this scenario, the market is consid-

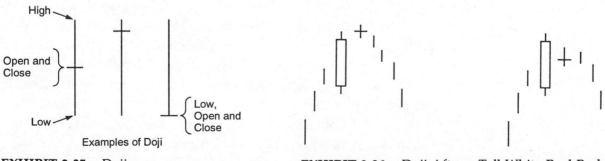

EXHIBIT 2.35. Doji

EXHIBIT 2.36. Doji After a Tall White Real Body

EXHIBIT 2.37.   Doji as Resistance

ered by the Japanese to be "tired." Also, as shown in Exhibit 2.37, the top of a doji session (that is, the top of the upper shadow) often represents resistance. However, if the highs of the doji session are exceeded, then the market's uptrend should continue. This is discussed in more detail below.

A common mistake among those who use candles is to use a doji as an outright buy or sell signal. This is not correct. The doji indicates, as the Japanese say, "a crossroads between the bulls and the bears." While the doji can mean the market may reverse its prior trend, traders should view the doji as echoing a market in transition rather than being an outright reversal pattern. Based on this, traders should wait until the next session or two after the doji to show them which way the market will move.

If there is a doji during a rally, and if the market continues strong after this doji, it is a bullish indication since the market has resolved itself from the state of transition (as shown by the doji) to its new trend—up. Thus, while a doji that appears after a rally could be an indication of a reversal (since the market is at a crossroads), it is best to wait for bearish confirmation over the next day or two to get a top reversal confirmation. For those who sell on a doji, the doji should act as resistance (see Exhibit 2.37). If the market closes above the high of the doji, the Japanese say the market has become "refreshed." Based on this, a buy stop should be placed above the high of the doji. The opposite would be true with a doji in a downtrend. To wit, a doji in a downtrend shows that the market is at a point of indecision, and a white candle after such a doji shows that the market has resolved itself to the bull side. A buy based on the doji after a downtrend should have a sell stop under the doji's low (including the lower shadow). This is because such a scenario is viewed as a bearish continuation signal.

One of the most fascinating aspects about candle charts is that, in spite of their underlying simplicity, they provide so much valuable information about the state of the market. For example, what is more il-

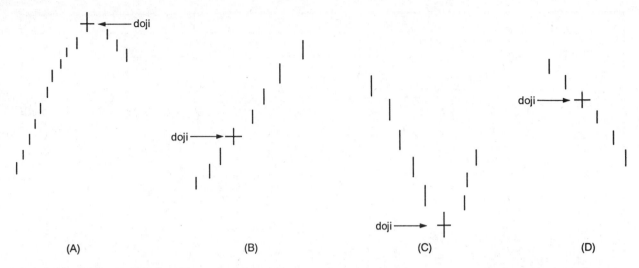

EXHIBIT 2.38. Doji After Extended Move

lustrative of a market in balance than a doji? That simple, individual candle line relays how a market is in a state of balance between the bulls and bears. As a result, the market may be at a transition point. All this information in one candle line!

An important aspect about doji (the plural of doji is also doji) is that traders should look at where the doji appears in a trend. Exhibit 2.38 shows a doji in relation to the trend. As in Exhibit 2.38(A), the appearance of a doji after a steep advance or in an overbought market could be a top. However, as shown in Exhibit 2.38(B), if the market just started to rise, it indicates there is less of a chance that the market is at a top. In Exhibit 2.38(C) we see how the emergence of a doji after a precipitous decline could mean a bottom. Exhibit 2.38(D) displays a market that has just begun to fall. In this scenario, prices may continue their descent even after a doji. The main concept behind Exhibit 2.38 is that doji become more important as a reversal signal the more overbought or oversold the market.

In Exhibit 2.39, we notice a rally that started in early November stalled after two doji following a tall white candle. The appearance of these doji told of a market in which the bulls and bears were in equilibrium. This was very different from the prior session when the tall white candle displayed a vibrant and healthy market in which the bulls were in control. These doji were showing, as the Japanese would phrase it, that "the market is separating from its trend."

As discussed before, doji become resistance. In this chart, there is also a long black real body candle (at the arrow) a few days after the doji. This black real body should also be resistance. With this in mind, the doji sessions and the long black real body provided a resistance zone in

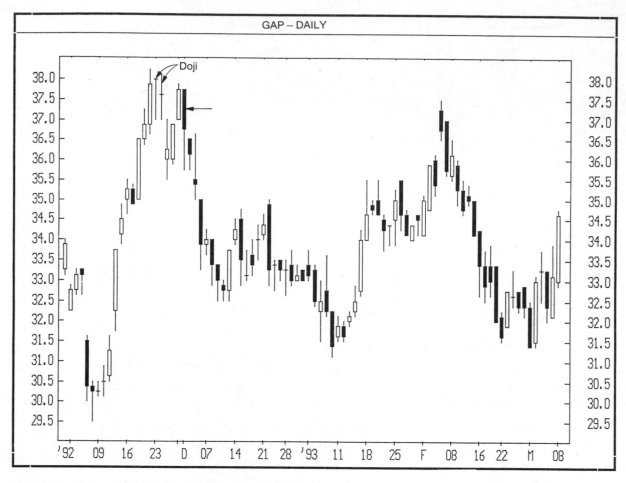

EXHIBIT 2.39.   Doji After a Tall White Candle, Gap—Daily

the $37 to $38 area. It was within here that the market failed during the early 1993 rally.

The arrow in Exhibit 2.40 points to a doji session in which the open, low, and close are at the bottom end of the session's range. This doji is known as a gravestone doji. A gravestone doji looks like a wooden memorial used in Buddhist funerals that is placed at a gravestone. It is said that those who buy at a high price level after this doji will die and become ghosts. (Those familiar with candle patterns will note how this doji was part of a classic evening doji star pattern [this pattern is discussed in Chapter 3]).

Exhibit 2.41 shows how the small real bodies at 1 and the doji at 2 warned that the market was losing its upside drive. After trading in a lateral range for a few weeks, prices ascended to new highs in late January. However, there were two clues that the rally might not be sustainable. The first was the doji at 3. This showed that, although the market had reached new highs, the upside drive had stalled. Another clue was

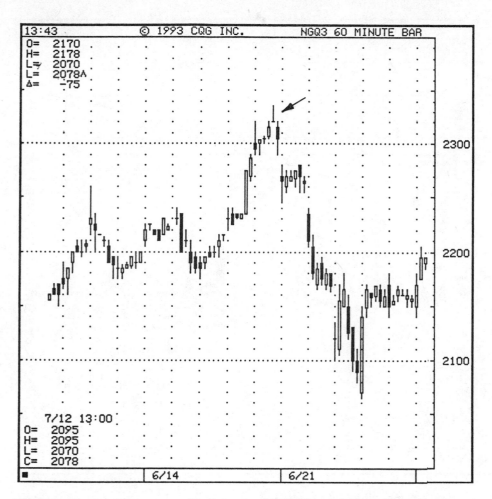

```
13:43           © 1993 CQG INC.        NGQ3 60 MINUTE BAR
O=  2170
H=  2178
L=  2070
L=  2078^
Δ=   -75
```

EXHIBIT 2.40.   Gravestone Doji August 1993 Natural Gas—Intra-Day

provided by the rate of change (ROC) oscillator. This oscillator compares today's closing price to that of ten sessions ago.

For this example, I show the ten day ROC. This compares today's close to that of ten days ago. With a healthy market, traders would like to see an increasing ROC oscillator. This reflects that the market's upside momentum is growing as prices are ascending. However, note how at doji 2, Dell touched a new high, yet the ROC oscillator was at a lower reading than it was at the prior highs in December. This underscores a slackening of the upside drive.

Thus, the ROC oscillator helped reinforce the bearish implication of doji 2. As further confirmation of a top, there was the long black candle on the day after doji 3. A few days after this black candle, the ROC oscillator fell under 0 (some technicians view that as a time to sell). This chart is an example of how easy it is to combine the candles with Western technical tools.

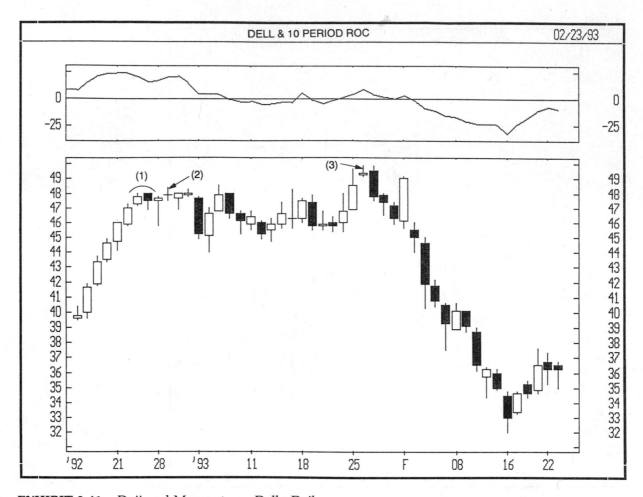

EXHIBIT 2.41. Doji and Momentum, Dell—Daily

SHADOWS

While the real body is often considered the most important segment of the candle, there is also substantial information to be gleaned from the length and position of the shadows. Thus, the location and the size of the shadow should also be considered when analyzing the psychology behind the market.

A tall upper shadow is especially important when it appears at a high price level, at a resistance area, or when the market is overbought. This is because such a candle line would hint that there is either heavy supply entering at higher prices or an evaporation of buying. In either case (see Exhibit 2.42), a long upper shadow could be a bearish development. A long lower shadow candle that bounces from a support area, or appears in an oversold market, could be an important clue that the bears are losing control.

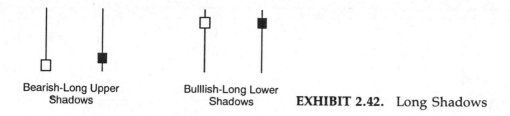

Bearish-Long Upper
Shadows

Bulllish-Long Lower
Shadows

EXHIBIT 2.42. Long Shadows

In Exhibit 2.43, in early 1992 there was a hint of trouble with the doji following the tall white candle. Remembering the concept that the doji session should be resistance, the market stalled at the doji's high over the next two weeks. The two candles after the doji had long upper shadows. These shadows displayed that there was either very aggressive selling near the 109 level, or that buying quickly evaporated near these highs. In either case, these long lower shadows showed a dampening of the rallying strength. Further evidence of the importance of this resistance was the failure there in mid-1992.

Exhibit 2.44 displays that candles 1, 2, and 3 rebounded from near 59¢ via long lower shadows. These long lower shadows reflected the solidity of the support and the eagerness of the buying. Also important was the length of the base that had been built. For almost two months,

EXHIBIT 2.43. Long Upper Shadows Confirm Resistance, Notionnel Bond—Weekly

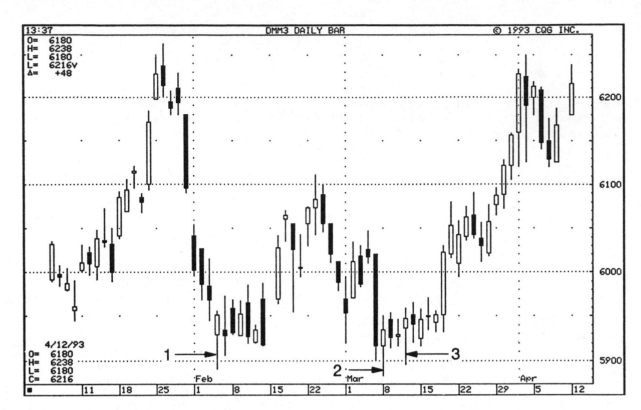

EXHIBIT 2.44.   Long Lower Shadows Confirm Support, June 1993 Deutsche Mark—
Daily

the bears tried to break prices under 59¢ and they failed. In general, the
longer the base, the more solid the scaffolding on which a rally can be
built.

A popular moving average among futures traders is the 65-day moving average. This line often swerves as support or resistance. For example, note how in Exhibit 2.45 that it was support in early November
and again in early January. The test of this support in early January via
long lower shadows, shows how strongly and quickly the market sprang
from there. For those who are familiar with candles, the first long lower
shadow candle is a hammer. Hammers will be explained in the next
chapter.

High-Wave Candles

A candle with a long upper and lower shadows is called a *high-wave candle*
(shown in Exhibit 2.46). It shows that the market is in a standoff between
the bulls and bears. When a high-wave emerges after a downtrend or
uptrend, the Japanese say that the market has lost its sense of direction.
This lack of market orientation means that the prior trend is in jeopardy.

EXHIBIT 2.45. Long Lower Shadows Confirm Support, March 1993 S & P Futures—Daily

A doji that has long upper and lower shadows is either called a high-wave doji or a long-legged doji.

In Exhibit 2.47, a series of high-wave candles are displayed at 1, 2, and 3. The high-wave candle at 1 hinted that the bulls and bears were at a standoff. The action that preceded candle 1 had a bearish bias. Thus, with the appearance of high-wave candle 1, the market had sent out a clue that the trend was probably in the process of change. This outlook was reinforced by the dual white candles after high-wave candle 1. The market ascended from candle 1 until it got to another high-wave candle (at 2). From there, prices declined sharply in the next session via a long black real body. However, at the session after this long black real body, a candle with an extended lower shadow (at X) showed that the lows

EXHIBIT 2.46. High-Wave Candles

EXHIBIT 2.47.   High-Wave Candles, December 1993 Crude Oil

from the prior week had become an attractive buying area. As prices ascended from candle X, a whisper of trouble emerged via the high-wave candle at 3. Two days later the long black candle showed that the bears had entered the market in force, and as a result, increased the likelihood that the high-wave candle at 3 was a top reversal.

CHAPTER 3

THE PATTERNS

···

意思あるところに道あり

"He Whose Ranks are United in Purpose Will Be Victorious"

Since the publication of my first book, I have had new Japanese material translated, have met new Japanese traders, and have continued my dialogues with those Japanese traders who have previously helped me. In addition, I have also had another three years of hands-on experience. As a result, I have gleaned new insights and concepts that will be conveyed to you in this chapter.

This chapter will not be a reference to all the patterns that are in my first book. Instead, my aim here is twofold. For those new to candles, this chapter will reveal how some of the more common and important candle patterns can provide powerful insights into your market analysis. For those already knowledgeable about the candles, you will discover new refinements and trading techniques. It is especially important to read the detailed descriptions of the charts. It is in these that you will most easily see some of the new refinements of candle theory, as well as some new concepts.

As one of the Japanese books I had translated stated, "the psychology of the market participant, the supply and demand equation, and the relative strengths of the buyers and sellers are all reflected in the one candlestick or in a combination of candlesticks."[1] In this chapter, I will describe the many uses and trading insights provided by individual candle lines and candle patterns based on two or more candle lines. The organization of this chapter is based on the number of lines that form the pattern. Consequently, this chapter's first section will focus on individual candle lines, such as the hammer and shooting star. The next section will delve into candle patterns comprised of two candle lines.

These include the dark cloud cover and two gapping black candles. The final section in this chapter will address those candle patterns, such as the evening star and record sessions, which have three or more candle lines.

SINGLE CANDLE LINES

In Chapter 2, I detailed how the length of the shadows can relay information about the resiliency of the bulls or the bears. For example, a long upper shadow echoes the ability of the bears to regain control of the market during a rally. A long lower shadow pictorially reflects the bulls' ability to rally the market after the market's new session lows have been made.

In this section, the single candle lines I will be describing (the hammer, hanging man line, and the shooting star) either have a long upper or lower shadow. But, because they also possess the important aspect of having a small real body near the top or bottom of the trading range, these candles lines take on increased importance when using candle charts.

The Hammer

As shown by Exhibit 3.1, the hammer, with its long lower shadow and a close near or at the high, is easily understood to be a bullish signal. The term ''hammer'' derives from the fact that the market is ''hammering out a base,'' or that a bottom is so solid that it does not break, even when a hammer knocks away at it.

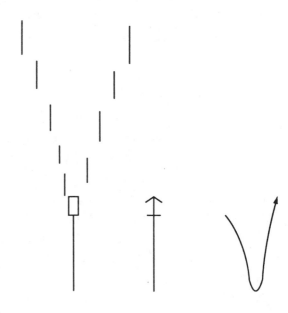

EXHIBIT 3.1.   The Hammer

An aspect of the hammer is that it must appear after a significant downturn or in an oversold market to have significance. The hammer is a reversal indicator, and as such, should have a downtrend to reverse. A hammer that appears after a fall of, say, two or three days is usually not important. Since the hammer is most useful after a significant downturn, it should be noted that there may be selling on a rally from the hammer. As such, the first bounce from the hammer may fail and the market may return to test the hammer's support.

Consequently, trading with the appearance of a hammer depends on a trader's aggressiveness and risk adversity. Some traders may decide to buy immediately after the hammer appears in case the market does not pull back to retest the hammer. Some traders may decide to wait to see if the market returns to the hammer, and if so, will buy on that return move. If the market successfully tests the hammer's support area, there is then a more solid support area and a better chance for a rally. A method that I sometimes recommend to our clients is to lightly test the waters from the long side after a hammer, and then add the remainder of the long position after (and if) there is a successful test of the hammer. Whichever methodology is used, a stop (based on the close) could be placed under the lows of the hammer.

Exhibit 3.2 displays a classic hammer in that the extreme length of the lower shadow reflects how aggressively the bulls were able to propel prices off the lows of the session. The bounce from this hammer stalled during the next few sessions. But the pullback held the hammer's support. This action helped enlarge the base upon which to build a more substantial rally.

A trading tool that I find useful with candles is a Western technique called a *spring*. As shown in Exhibit 3.3, a spring occurs when the bears are unable to hold prices under a broken support area. Because such action proves that the bears were unable to grab control of the market when they had their chance, it should be viewed as a bullish development. The opposite of a spring is an *upthrust*. An upthrust occurs when the market makes a new high, but then fails to hold that high. Upthrusts will be addressed in the section titled "The Shooting Star" later in this chapter. (Springs and upthrusts are described in detail in my first book.)

An ancient oriental book on military tactics referred to gaining an advantage over the enemy by acting as a "moving shadow." This term, as used by the warrior who wrote that book, means that when you cannot see the state of your opponent, you pretend to make a powerful attack to uncover the intention of the enemy. This concept, as related to trading, is one of the reasons a spring is so important.

Probes of support or resistance areas are attempted throughout the markets by large-scale traders. They want to discover how the market

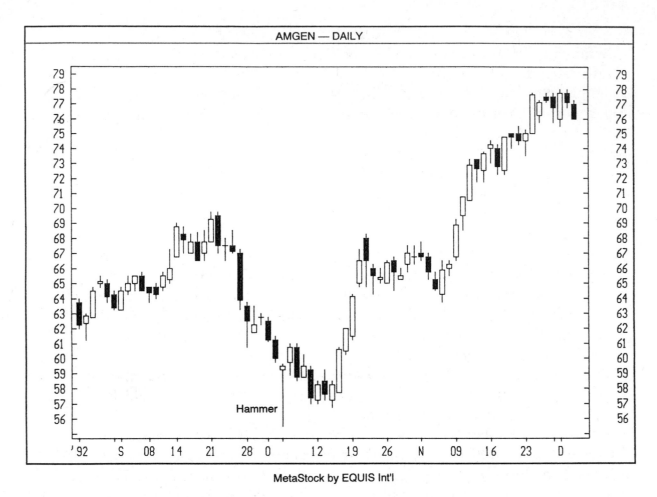

EXHIBIT 3.2.   Hammer as Support, Amgen—Daily

will react once a support or resistance area is pierced. In effect, these traders act like the aforementioned "moving shadow," testing the battlefield by entering a large order to try and break support (or resistance). For example, if a large-scale trader places a sell order as the market gets near support, their sell order may be enough to drag prices under the support area. Now, this trader, as a "moving shadow," will now learn about the underlying strength of the market. If the market fails to hold under a broken support area and forms a spring, these "moving shadows," (i.e., the sellers who were attempting to probe the market), now have learned about the tenacity of the bulls and as a result may decide to cover their shorts.

EXHIBIT 3.3.   Spring

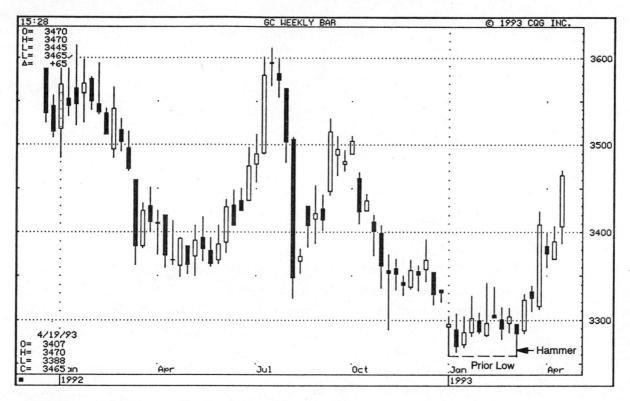

EXHIBIT 3.4. Hammer and a Spring, Gold—Weekly

In Exhibit 3.4, we see one of the more powerful combinations of Eastern and Western technicals—a hammer and a spring. The 1993 low was formed by a hammer. This hammer was also a spring since the low of the hammer's lower shadow slightly punctured a support zone, but sprang back above this broken support line. Also of interest in this chart is that the high made near $360 in mid-1992 was formed by a doji following a tall white candle.

The Hanging Man

As shown in Exhibit 3.5, a hanging man has a very long lower shadow, a small real body (white or black) near the upper end of the trading range and little or no upper shadow. This is the same shape as the hammer line. However, as expressed in the Japanese literature, "If it appears from below, buy, and if appears from above, sell."

This phrase means that the same shape line can be bullish or bearish, depending on where it appears in a trend. If this line appears "from below," that is, during a decline, it is a bullish hammer. However, if this same shape line appears "from above," that is, during an uptrend, it is a sell signal and is referred to as a hanging man line.

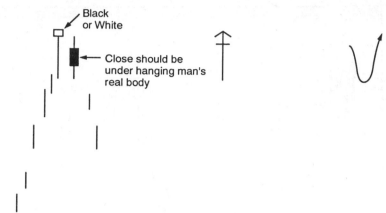

EXHIBIT 3.5.   The Hanging Man

Thus, the hanging man line is a top reversal signal that must arrive during a rally, while the hammer is a bottom reversal line that must appear during a decline; the same line can be bullish or bearish, depending on the trend preceding it. In this context, it is interesting that the Japanese have two words for rice. They call it either "raisu" or "gohan." Raisu is the Japanese term for rice when it is prepared Western style. The term "raisu" even sounds like the Western word "rice." Gohan also means rice, but it is rice prepared Japanese style. In other words, the Japanese refer to the exact same product—rice—by different names. What surrounds the rice determines whether the rice is referred to as raisu or gohan. So it is with the hammer and hanging man. Whether the candle line is a bullish pattern (the hammer) or a bearish pattern (the hanging man) is dependent on what precedes the line.

With the hanging man's long lower shadow reflecting buying interest, it may seem that the hanging man is a bullish signal. However, the hangman's action shows that once the market has fallen, it has become very fragile. The small real body of the hanging man also shows that the prior uptrend may be in the process of changing. Because of the bullish action of the hanging man session (during the session the market sells off and then rallies by the close), an important aspect of the hanging man lines is that there should be bearish confirmation. A common method of bearish confirmation of a hangman is to wait to see if the next session's close is under the hanging man's real body. This is shown in Exhibit 3.5.

The reason for the importance of this confirmation has to do with the fact that the hanging man's long lower shadow shows that there is still rising power left in the market. However, if prices fall under the hanging man's real body, it translates into the fact that everyone who bought at the open or close of the hanging man session is now losing money. In such a scenario, these longs may decide to liquidate, and by doing so, may engender a further weakening of prices.

Since my seminar on the candles at the World Bank in Washington,

NYC 27Oct93 22:02   Technical Analysis 3.01
GERMAN BUND CANDLE STICK (DAILY)

Hanging Man

Confirmed

Amount
88.8
88.6
88.4
88.2
88
87.8
87.6
87.4
87.2
87

06Mar92   13Mar   20Mar   27Mar   03Apr   10Apr   17Apr   24Apr

Reuters Graphics

EXHIBIT 3.6. Confirmation of a Hanging Man, German Bund—Daily

DC, some of their traders have asked my opinion on candle patterns on various markets. One of their traders asked what I thought about the chart of the German Bund shown in Exhibit 3.6. She asked my opinion on April 10 after the hanging man was formed. I explained to her that if the hanging man were confirmed by a weaker session the next day, the outlook would be bearish. In this case, the market confirmed the bearish hanging man during the next session.

Exhibit 3.7 shows how important it is to wait for confirmation of a hanging man session. In that chart, we see a hanging man. However, note how the following week the bulls pushed prices above the high of the hanging man. This means that those who bought during the hanging man session now have a profit. Consequently, there is little reason for them to liquidate their longs. The result is that a higher close than the hanging man session voids any of the bearish potential of the hanging man. That is what happened here as the market exceeded the hanging man session. Also of interest in this chart is that in April 1992, there was a hammer that was also a bullish spring, since the hammer made a new low which failed to hold.

An article about my work with candles in *The Wall Street Journal* displayed the chart shown in Exhibit 3.8. In this article, I discussed how the hanging man at $40 helped confirm a top. I explained that before the 1990 Mid-east crisis, the highest crude oil futures reached was around $32 (crude oil futures began trading in 1983). Once the market exceeded that level, I had a target at around $40. That was a resistance area in the cash market back in 1979. Note that at the $40 area, there was a bearish candle signal via the hanging man line. The market retreated from this $40 level and tested a support line. It then rallied and, with sort of a last

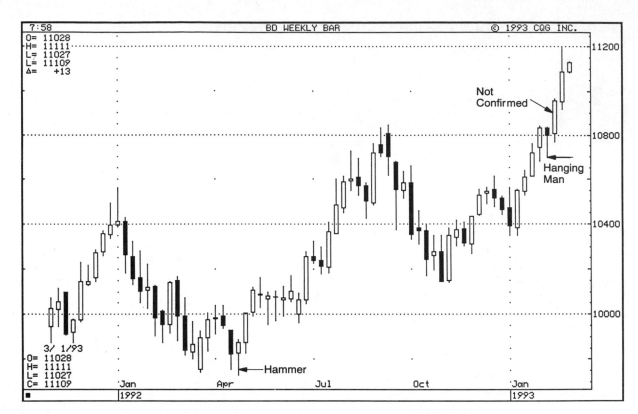

EXHIBIT 3.7. Waiting for Confirmation of a Hanging Man, Bonds—Weekly

EXHIBIT 3.8. Hanging Man Confirms Resistance, November 1990 Crude Oil—Daily

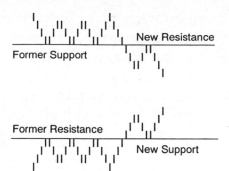

EXHIBIT 3.9. Change of Polarity Principle

gasp, the bulls temporarily nudged the market above $40 before the floor fell out of the market.

There is a basic Western technical concept that states that a penetrated resistance area should then be converted to support and a broken support area should be resistance. I call this concept the *change of polarity principle* (it is discussed in detail in my first book). This concept is shown in Exhibit 3.9. I find the change of polarity a very useful tool, especially when joined with candles. You should find that the more often a support or resistance area is tested before prices break them, the better the change of polarity principle should work.

In Exhibit 3.10 we see that an evident support area from mid- to late

EXHIBIT 3.10. Hanging Man and the Change of Polarity Principle, March 1993 Crude Oil

November was slightly above $20. Once this important support was broken, the change of polarity rule implied that this $20 support should then become resistance. This is what unfolded as this $20 resistance area was confirmed with the mid-December hanging man session. The long black real body, also near $20, on December 28, showed that the bears had taken control.

The Shooting Star

A session with a long upper shadow and a small real body near the bottom end of the trading range is called a *shooting star* (see Exhibit 3.11). Just as the long lower shadow of a hammer is bullish, so the long upper shadow of the shooting star is bearish. The long upper shadow means that the bears have been able to sharply drag prices back from their highs.

In Exhibit 3.12, we see how the mid-August shooting star's long upper shadow reflected the aggressiveness of the bears. Following this shooting star, another symptom of market uncertainty came with the high-wave candle. The fact that the shooting star and the high-wave candle both appeared near the psychologically important 100 area reinforced the importance of those signals.

In Exhibit 3.13, I show how a support area from late August (marked S) changed to resistance through September and into October. The October failure of this resistance area was via a shooting star. The long upper shadow of this line reflected the heaviness of supply towards the 1.66 level. Another attempt to breach 1.66 failed in early October with a long black real body.

In the section on hammers, I discussed the concept of springs (when the price springs back above a broken support area) and that the opposite of a spring is an upthrust. As shown in Exhibit 3.14, an upthrust is created when prices break above a resistance area, but then retreat back under the previously broken resistance. This scenario has bearish impli-

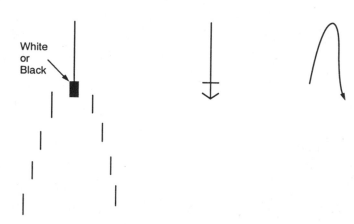

EXHIBIT 3.11. The Shooting Star

EXHIBIT 3.12. Shooting Star with a High-Wave Candle, September 1993 Japanese Yen

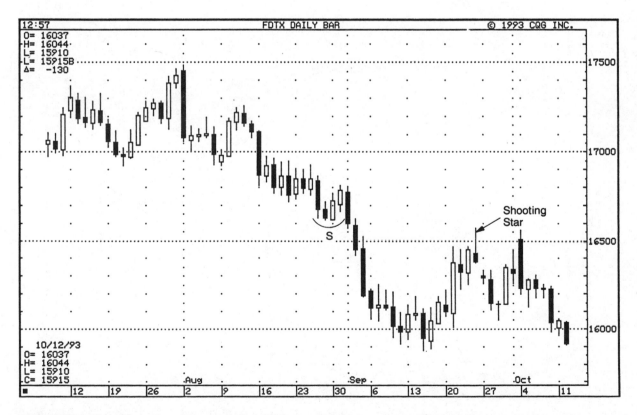

EXHIBIT 3.13. Shooting Star and the Change of Polarity, Cash Deutsche Mark

EXHIBIT 3.14.   An Upthrust

cations. At times, the upper shadow of a shooting star can also be part of an upthrust.

In Exhibit 3.15, there is a shooting star that pierced the January 7 and 8 resistance area with its long upper shadow. The failure of the bulls to keep prices in the new territory created a bearish upthrust.

To help clarify the difference between the hammer, hanging man, and shooting star lines, I have annotated Exhibit 3.16 with an example of each candle line. Note that for each signal the market must be in a clearly defined trend.

1. Shooting star—We can see how the shooting star must appear after an uptrend. The shooting star's long upper shadow reflects market rejection of higher prices.

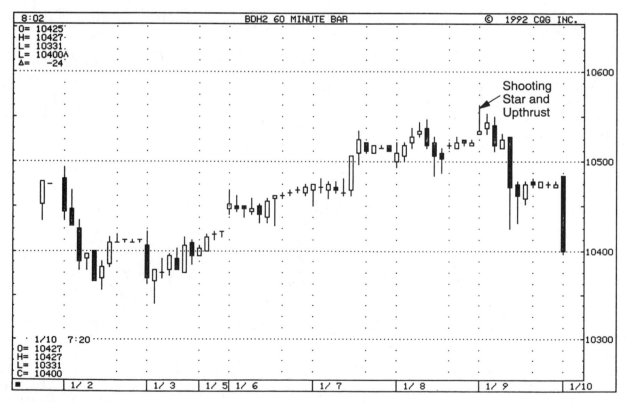

EXHIBIT 3.15.   Shooting Star and Upthrust, March 1992 Bonds—Intra-Day

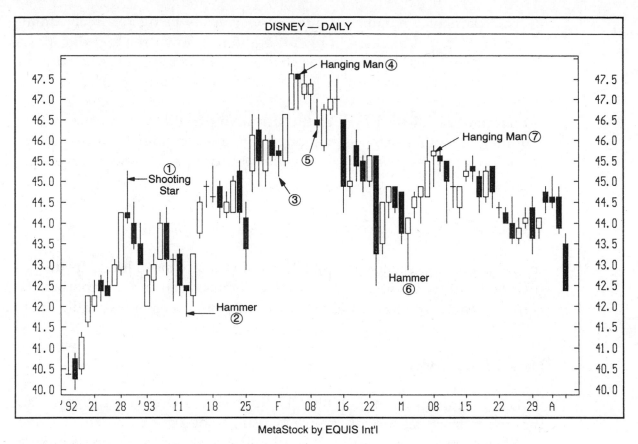

DISNEY — DAILY

MetaStock by EQUIS Int'l

EXHIBIT 3.16. Hammer, Hanging Man, and Shooting Star Lines, Disney—Daily

2. Hammer—A long lower shadow candle that must appear during a downtrend.

3. Although this has the correct shape of a hammer or hanging man line (a long lower shadow with a small real body near the highs of the session), candle 3 is neither a hammer nor a hanging man. This is because this line did not appear during an uptrend or a downtrend, but was in the middle of a trading range. Thus, line 3 is not a hammer (although the long, lower shadow could be viewed as a positive signal).

4., 7. Rallies preceded these hanging man lines, which were confirmed during the next session by a close under the hanging man's real body. In line 7, we can see a small upper shadow. If the upper shadow is relatively small, it is still considered a hanging man. (A small upper shadow is also allowable with a hammer.) Note how the real body of the hanging man can be white or black.

5. This line has the correct shape of a shooting star (a tall upper shadow and a small real body at the lower end of the session's range). However, since it does not appear after an uptread, it does not have the bearish implications as would a traditional shooting star.

6. This particular hammer should be viewed as being relatively unimportant since it appeared only after a minor downtrend. It did, however, show, via its long lower shadow, a successful test of a support area near $43 from the late January and early February lows.

To summerize, always look at the preceding trend to determine if the hammer, shooting star, or hanging man lines should be acted upon. Remember that as reversal signals; they need a prior trend to reverse.

DUAL CANDLE LINES

In the preceding section, I looked at individual candle lines. In the remainder of this chapter, I will review some of the more important or common candle patterns that are comprised of two or more candle lines.

Dark Cloud Cover

A dark cloud (shown in Exhibit 3.17) shows, as the Japanese express it, that the market has a poor chance of rising. The dark cloud cover's first candle is a strong white session. During the next session, there is buying pressure left over and the market opens higher, but later in that session, prices decline as the market closes under the center of the previous session. This pattern reflects a period in the market when the upward power of the tall white candle has been dissipated by next session's weak black candle. Note how the blended candle line in Exhibit 3.17 has a longer

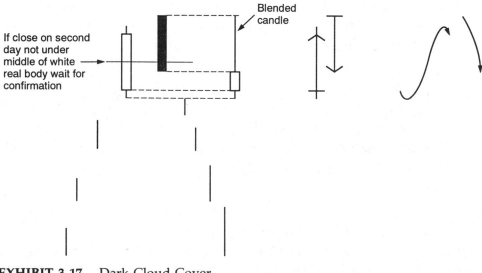

EXHIBIT 3.17. Dark Cloud Cover

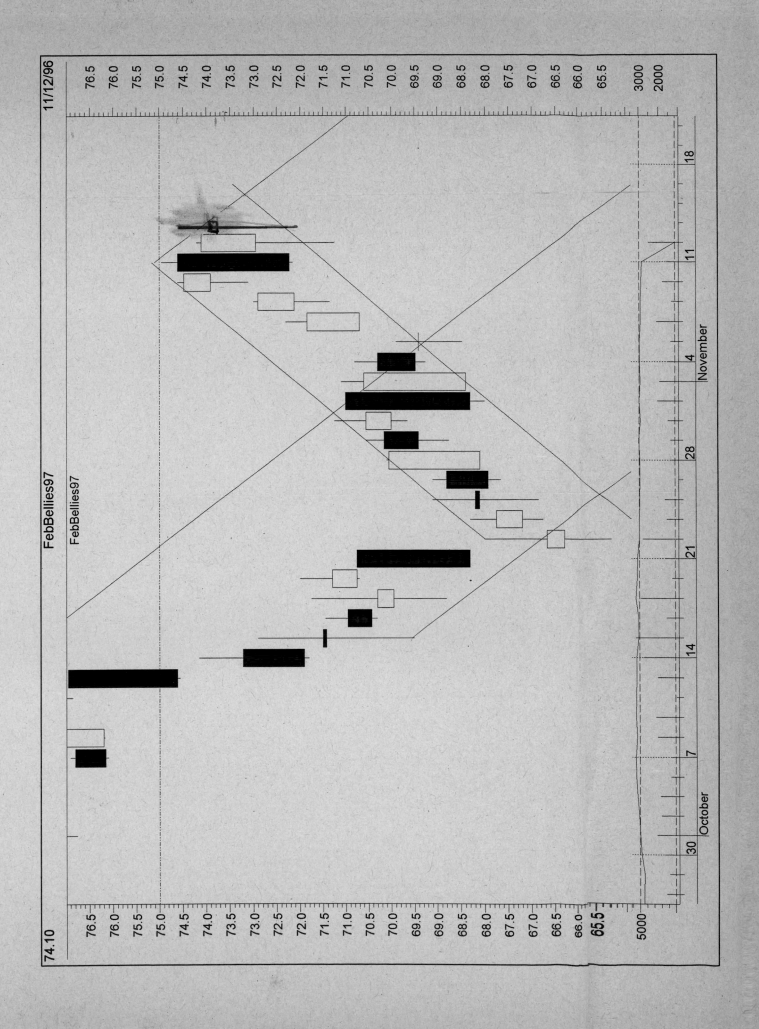

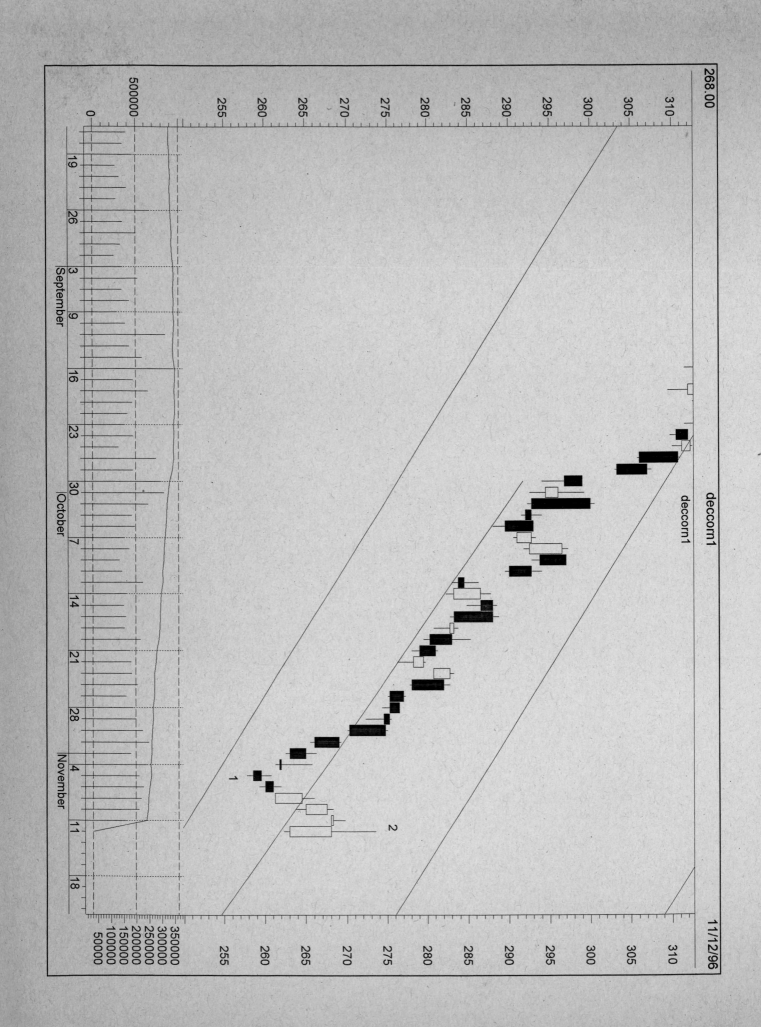

upper shadow. In other words, the dark cloud cover displays pictorially a time in the market in which selling pressure is exceeding the buying pressure.

An ideal dark cloud cover's second session should close under the midpoint of the prior white candle. If the black candle does not close below the halfway point, it is considered by some Japanese traders to be an incomplete dark cloud cover. In such cases, it is best to wait for confirmation during the next session in the form of a weaker close. As a general rule, the deeper the close of the dark cloud cover's second session pushes into the white candle, the more bearish the signal.

A dark cloud that fails to move under the center of the prior candle is shown in Exhibit 3.18. Looking at the blended candle in Exhibit 3.18, we see how there is less of an upper shadow than in the case of the more classic dark cloud cover's blended candle shown in Exhibit 3.17. This means the dark cloud cover in Exhibit 3.18 may be less bearish than a standard dark cloud cover. This is why there should be confirmation by further weakness after the type of dark cloud cover shown in Exhibit 3.18.

There is a difference in how I would view the dark cloud cover in stocks and futures. The ideal dark cloud cover has the second session's open above the high of the prior session. Since there is generally higher price volatility in the futures market as compared to stocks, it means that I am more flexible about the definition of a dark cloud cover with stocks than with futures. Specifically, with stocks I still view it as a dark cloud cover if the second session opens above the prior session's *close*, rather than its high. This is shown in Exhibit 3.19.

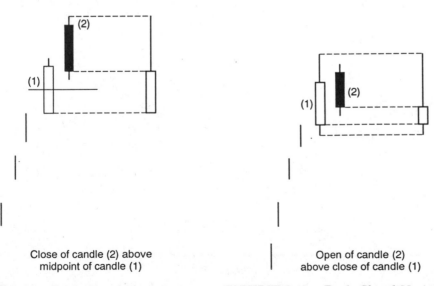

Close of candle (2) above
midpoint of candle (1)

Open of candle (2)
above close of candle (1)

EXHIBIT 3.18. Dark Cloud Variation 1   **EXHIBIT 3.19.** Dark Cloud Variation 2

However, if the second session of the dark cover of a stock does open above the prior session's high (instead of its close), it would be more of a potential reversal signal. This is because it is more bearish if the market reverses after failing from a new high than it is if the market fails from an area that was not a new high.

A dark cloud cover often becomes resistance. In Exhibit 3.20, we see a dark cloud cover in late January near $75.50. The market retreated from there until a hammer (that was also a spring) formed near $69 in February. The rally from this hammer stalled in March at the resistance set by the dark cloud. However, as with any form of technical analysis, there should be a price at which you should reconsider your original outlook. For a pattern like the dark cloud cover, if the market closes above the high of the dark cloud cover, the chances are that the market will continue its upward path. In this example, observe how the market not only closed above the high of the dark cloud cover in late March, but did so via a bullish rising gap. Another interesting aspect of this gap is that the ses-

MetaStock by EQUIS Int'l

EXHIBIT 3.20.   Dark Cloud Cover as Resistance, Southwest Bell—Daily

sion after the gap created a shooting star. Yet the bearish implications of the shooting star was not confirmed since the market failed to close under the rising gap (this will be discussed in detail later in this chapter under the section on "windows"). Thus, when selling short based on a dark cloud cover, consider a stop on a close above the highs of that pattern. For those who are looking to buy, you should consider it when on the close, prices pierce the high of the dark cloud cover.

Exhibit 3.21 is an example of two less than ideal dark cloud covers at 1 and 2. Dark cloud cover 1 was not ideal since the second session (the black candle) failed to close under the mid-point of the prior session. Dark cloud cover 2 lost some of its bearish importance because the second session of the pattern opened just above the prior close instead of the prior high. Yet, since both of these non-classic dark cloud covers emerged so close to one another, they served to reinforce each other. In other words, both dark cloud covers reflected the fact that as prices made new highs near $45, the bears were able to drag prices back down under the

EXHIBIT 3.21.   Dark Cloud Covers in Close Proximity, Eastman Kodak—Daily

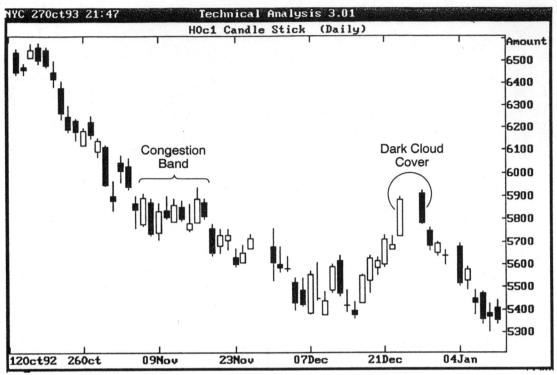

NYC 27oct93 21:47   Technical Analysis 3.01
                    HOc1 Candle Stick (Daily)

Congestion
Band

Dark Cloud
Cover

Amount
6500
6400
6300
6200
6100
6000
5900
5800
5700
5600
5500
5400
5300

12oct92 26oct   09Nov   23Nov   07Dec   21Dec   04Jan

Reuters Graphics

EXHIBIT 3.22. Dark Cloud Cover Confirms Resistance, February 1993 Heating Oil

prior closes. This is not a healthy scenario. The gap lower was final proof of a break to the downside.

Exhibit 3.22 shows a congestion band between 59 and 60¢ during the first half of November. When the market trends laterally for an extended period, the congestion zone often becomes a resistance or support area once prices break out of that range. This is because the longer the market trades sideways, the more traders get involved in the market as either buyers or sellers. In this example, once prices broke under the bottom end of the early November congestion band, those who went short while the market was within the lateral band were making a profit on the downside breakout. However, those who went long while the market was within that early November trading band were in a losing trade when prices broke under the bottom end of the congestion band. This means that if the market rallies back up to the congestion band, those longs may use that rally to try to get out of their losing trade. In other words, the existing longs should be new sellers on rebounds to the congestion band. In Exhibit 3.22, once the early November congestion area was broken, it then became resistance. The December failure at that resistance area came with the dark cloud cover (the empty area between the two candles of the pattern was due to a holiday).

The Piercing Pattern

As shown in Exhibit 3.23, the piercing pattern is the opposite of the dark cloud cover. The dark cloud cover appears after an uptrend, and is comprised of a black real body that closes well into the prior white body. The piercing pattern is a white real body that closes within the prior black real body. This pattern shows that there is fierce buying at lower levels.

The following is an interesting and graphic explanation used in a Japanese book to describe what happens during the formation of the piercing pattern

> the last of the bulls that were backed into a corner and came out fighting in a heroic fight. Kamikaze fights are always frightening, so the bears seeing this take to the sidelines for the moment. In this quiet period, the bulls may get reinforcements, or after all the selling that has occurred, the supply road for the bears may be already broken."[1]

In other words, the downward energy of the market has been dissipated.

There are various names for the two candle patterns that have the second white candle close less than halfway into the prior black candle. These are discussed in detail in my other book. For the purposes of the discussion here, these names are unimportant. What is important is the general concept that the more the white candle pierces the black candle, the more constructive the signal. If the white candle fails to move deeply into the black candle, it reflects a weak counterattack by the bulls and

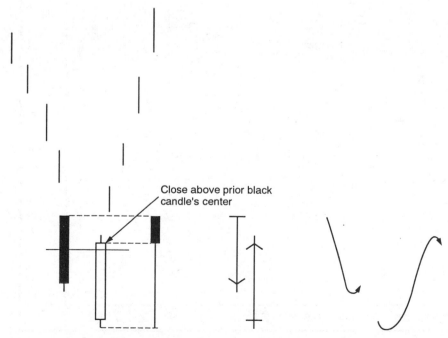

Close above prior black candle's center

EXHIBIT 3.23. The Piercing Pattern

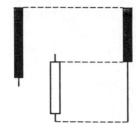

EXHIBIT 3.24. White Candle Under Center of Prior Black Candle

selling could resume. As illustrated in Exhibit 3.24, you can see that a pattern that has the second session below the midpoint of the prior black candle creates a blended candle with a short lower shadow. Note, by comparison, the long lower shadow of the blended candle in Exhibit 3.23. This shows the bulls successfully mounted a strong counterattack. Also consider that the lower the second candle's opening, the longer the lower shadow of the blended candle will be. This means that a piercing pattern that has a low opening second session and then closes well into the prior candle would be an optimum example of that pattern.

EXHIBIT 3.25. Piercing Pattern and Retracement, Disney—Weekly

It has been my experience that dark cloud covers are more prevalent than are piercing patterns. Part of the reason may have to do with an old Wall Street saying, ''In on greed, out on fear.'' Although both greed and fear are strong emotions, I think many would agree that of the two, fear is the one that could cause the most volatile markets. During market bottoms, traders or investors usually have the opportunity to wait for an opportunity to enter the market. They may bide their time and wait for a pullback or for the market to build a base, or to see how the market reacts to news. Fear is more prevalent at tops. Fear is saying, ''I want out—now!''

In Exhibit 3.25 we see that an advance that started in late 1991 stalled at the doji following the tall white candle. The extended upper shadow in May echoed the importance of the resistance area set by this doji. The market then retreated until August's piercing pattern. The piercing pattern was also at a support area based on a 50% retracement of the rally from the December low to the May high. The 50% retracement area should be closely monitored by traders because such retracements are widely watched by technicians. This pattern became support that was held in October with a high-wave candle. The rally from this base near $33 stalled at another doji following a tall white candle in early 1993.

Exhibit 3.26 displays that April's piercing pattern confirmed a support

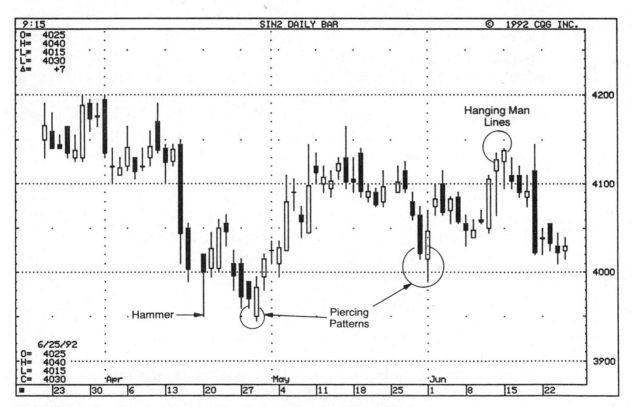

EXHIBIT 3.26.   Piercing Pattern Confirms Support, Silver—July 1992

area provided by the prior week's hammer. Another piercing pattern in late May and early June signaled a temporary base for another assault at May's resistance area near $4.15. A series of two hanging man lines appeared at that resistance. Note how the first hanging man was not confirmed (since the next session did not have a lower case). Only on the day after the second hanging man session, with its close under the second hanging man's real body, was the hanging man line confirmed.

The Engulfing Patterns

An engulfing pattern is a two candle pattern. A bullish engulfing pattern (shown in Exhibit 3.27A) is formed when, during a downtrend, a white real body wraps around a black real body. A bearish engulfing pattern (Exhibit 3.27B) is completed when, during a rally, a black real body envelops a white real body.

The engulfing pattern visually shows how the opposing forces had gained control of the market. For example, a bullish engulfing pattern reflects how the bulls have wrested control of the market from the bears. A bearish engulfing pattern shows how a superior force of supply has overwhelmed the bulls. The Japanese say that with a bearish engulfing pattern, "the bulls are immobilized." We previously saw how with the dark cloud cover, the bears were able to move prices into the prior white real body, but with the bearish engulfing patterns, the power of the bears was such that they were able to pull the close under the entire prior white real body. The same concept can be used to compare a piercing pattern to a bullish engulfing pattern. With the piercing pattern, the bulls counterattack strongly enough to push the close of the second white real body well into the prior black real body. However, with the bullish engulfing pattern, the bulls' strength is that much greater since the close of the white candle session is above the top of the prior black real body. Although this generally means that the bearish engulfing pattern is more bearish than a dark cloud cover, and a bullish engulfing pattern more bullish than a piercing pattern, it is equally important to see where these patterns emerge before deciding which is more important. For instance, a piercing pattern that confirms a major support area should be viewed more likely as a bottom reversal signal than a bullish engulfing pattern that does not confirm support. This vital aspect of viewing the candle patterns in conjunction with the overall technical picture will be discussed in depth in the next chapter.

The basic definition of an engulfing pattern is that the second real body must engulf an opposite color real body. However, not all engulfing patterns are equally important. The importance of the engulfing pattern

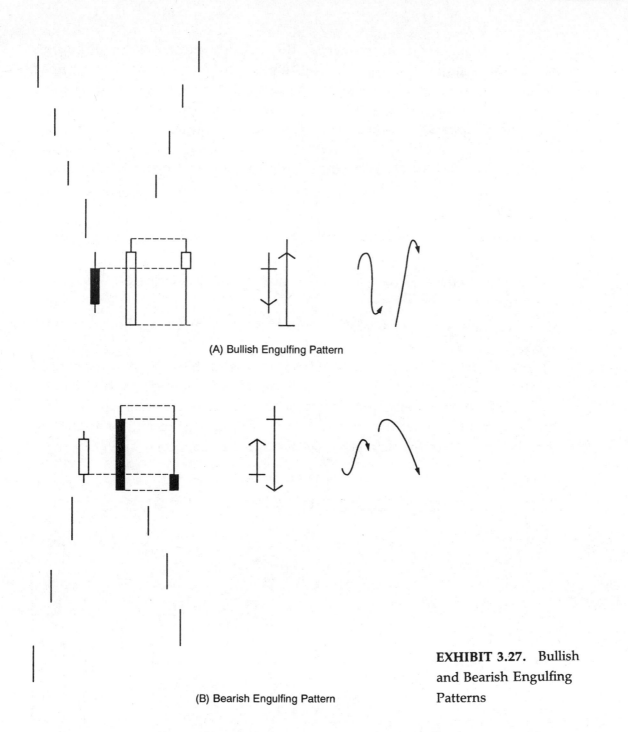

(A) Bullish Engulfing Pattern

(B) Bearish Engulfing Pattern

EXHIBIT 3.27. Bullish and Bearish Engulfing Patterns

is dependent on the relative size of the real bodies, the relationship of the shadows to one another, and other factors. For example, the strictest definition of an engulfing pattern would be if the first candle is small and the second candle very large, and the second real body wraps around the entire first candle—including its shadows. The next strictest definition would be if the shadows of the second candle exceeded the shadows of the first candle (in other words, on the second day of the engulfing pattern, the market made a higher high and a lower low).

As with a dark cloud cover, if the market surpasses an engulfing pattern, it is said to go opposite to the pattern. This means that if prices close above the top of the bearish engulfing pattern (including the upper shadows), the outlook turns from bearish to bullish.

Aspects addressed in this section's charts include:

1. how engulfing patterns become support and resistance;
2. how an engulfing pattern can be combined with Western technical tools;
3. why traders should be more flexible in defining an engulfing pattern with stocks compared to futures;
4. the importance of comparing the size of the two real bodies of the engulfing pattern;
5. the danger signal of a bearish engulfing pattern after a doji.

In Exhibit 3.28, the first sign of trouble was with the high-wave candle in late August. During the first two sessions of September, more trouble arose with a bearish engulfing pattern. The market backed off from there, and found support at the mid-August rising gap. (We will look at how gaps become support or resistance later in this chapter.) The rally from

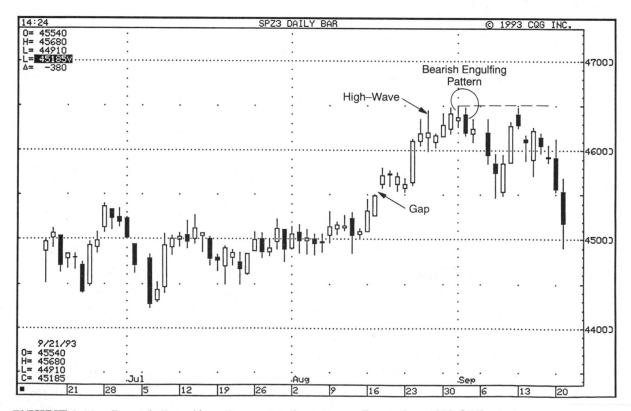

EXHIBIT 3.28.   Bearish Engulfing Pattern as Resistance, December 1993 S&P

this gap stalled at the resistance area set up by the bearish engulfing pattern.

Exhibit 3.28 also displays how the candles can offer reversal signals not available to those using Western technical tools. With Western technicals, there is a reversal signal called a top outside reversal session, sometimes also known as a key reversal. This occurs when prices make a new high for the move and then close lower than the previous session's close. Note how in the bearish engulfing pattern highlighted in the S & P was not a reversal session since the second session of this bearish engulfing pattern (i.e., the black candle) failed to make a new high for the move. Yet, because the black candle enveloped the white candle, it was a bearish engulfing pattern. Consequently, while no reversal pattern was revealed with western technicals, there was a reversal with candle charts.

In Exhibit 3.29, we see how a selloff in December commenced with the doji following the tall white candle. This area's resistance was con-

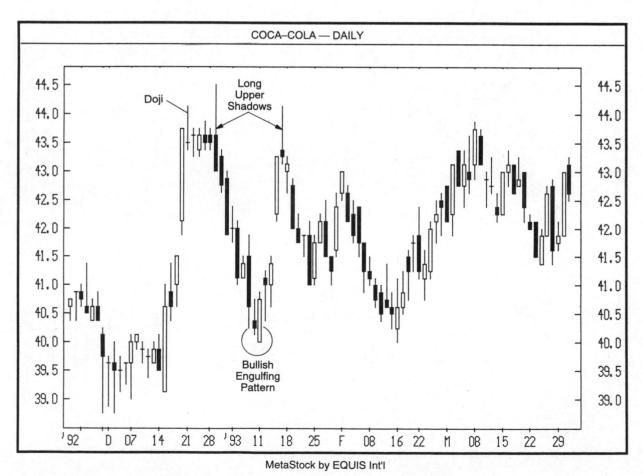

EXHIBIT 3.29.   Bullish Engulfing Pattern as Support, Coca Cola—Daily

firmed by the long upper shadow candle near $44 a few sessions later. The selloff found a base in January 1993 near $40 via a bullish engulfing pattern. From there, the market rallied, and again stalled via a long upper shadow candle near the previously discussed resistance area of $44.

Based on the action described thus far, we know that $44 is resistance and the bullish engulfing pattern near $40 is support. Thus, for traders looking for a buying zone, it could be done on corrections to the bullish engulfing pattern (near $40) with a target towards $44 and a stop on a close under the lows of the bullish engulfing pattern. This scenario unfolded in February. The concept of risk–reward is very important. Before placing a trade with candles or any other form of technical analysis, risk–reward must always be considered (in Chapter 4, I will discuss this critical subject in more depth).

Exhibit 3.30 displays a classic bearish engulfing pattern near $50. It was classic since a very tall black real body enveloped a very short white real body. In March, there was another bearish engulfing pattern. This

EXHIBIT 3.30.   Engulfing Pattern Confirms Retracement, Dell—Daily

one confirmed a resistance area defined by a 50% retracement of the selloff from A to B.

Because stocks often open relatively unchanged from the prior close (as compared to the futures market), there should be more flexibility in defining an engulfing pattern with stocks than with the more volatile futures markets. Specifically, I still view it as an engulfing pattern if the open of the second session of the candle pattern is the same as the close of the first candle. This is shown in Exhibit 3.31.

Exhibit 3.32 shows an example of a bullish engulfing pattern in which the open and the close were about the same. The importance of this pattern was reinforced by the fact that it became support during the April 1993 pullback.

When looking at an engulfing pattern, you should consider the relative sizes of the real bodies that form the pattern. An ideal bearish engulfing pattern has a very large real body enveloping a small white real body. The diminutive size of the first small body of a bearish engulfing pattern shows that the momentum of the prior rally is slackening. The large black real body after this small candle then proves that the bears have overwhelmed the bulls.

However, if there are two almost equal size candles that comprise the engulfing pattern, the market may move into a lateral band, rather than reverse (this concept may be useful for options traders who are looking to sell volatility). I will use Exhibit 3.33 to illustrate this important concept. In this deutsche mark chart, there was a bearish engulfing pattern in July 1992 (1 on the chart). Note how the white and black candles were about equal in height. The fact that they are about equal means that the bears and the bulls are about equally strong. With no clear-cut victory of the bears over the bulls, it should not have been unexpected to see prices move sideways for a few weeks. On a breakout from this engulfing pat-

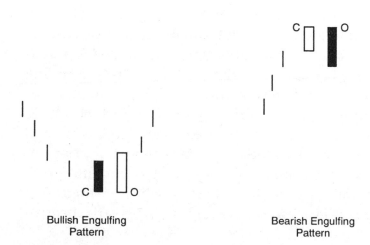

Bullish Engulfing
Pattern

Bearish Engulfing
Pattern

EXHIBIT 3.31. Engulfing Patterns Where Open and Close are the Same

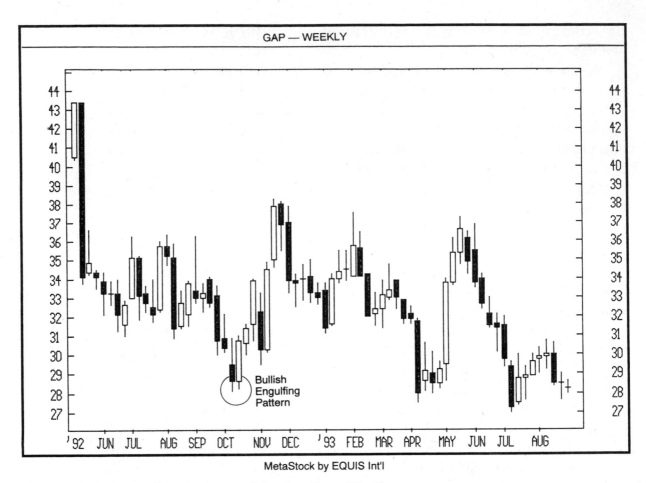

EXHIBIT 3.32.   Engulfing Pattern and Stocks, Gap—Weekly

tern's resistance band, the market stalled at another bearish engulfing pattern at 2.

The bearish engulfing pattern at 2 was more significant with its small white real body and massive black real body. It was thus more likely to presage a price turn rather than a move into a lateral environment. This engulfing pattern then became a resistance area.

Exhibit 3.34 displays a bearish engulfing pattern in early 1991. Note how the white and black candles were about equal. As just discussed, this could mean a period of consolidation; this is what unfolded as prices moved into a lateral trading band. The highs of this bearish engulfing pattern set up a resistance area that was confirmed by a long upper shadow. Another bearish engulfing pattern appeared in October 1992. Because the October bearish engulfing pattern had a very large black real body and a small white one, it was more important than the prior engulfing pattern. Even more portentous with the October engulfing pattern was that it followed a doji. Specifically, if there is a bearish engulfing pattern that follows a doji, it is viewed as being a particularly bearish combination.

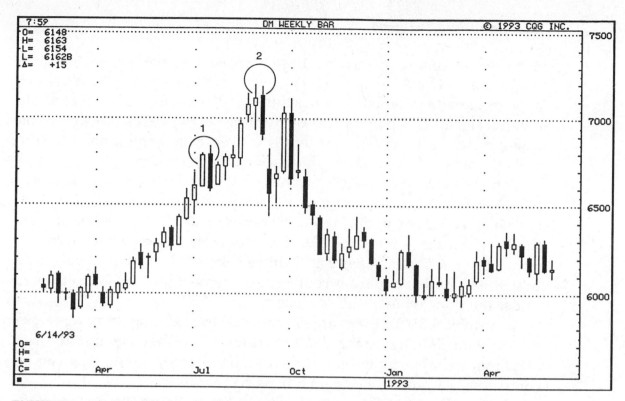

EXHIBIT 3.33. Engulfing Patterns and Size of the Real Bodies, Deutsche Mark—Weekly

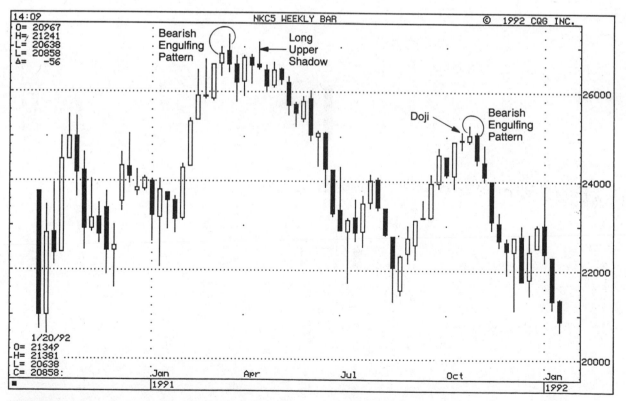

EXHIBIT 3.34. Bearish Engulfing Pattern Following a Doji, Nikkei—Weekly

Last Engulfing Patterns

A bearish engulfing pattern is a large black candle that envelops a small white real body *after an uptrend*. However, if a bearish engulfing pattern appears *during a price decline*, it has the potential of being a bullish bottom reversal signal. This pattern is known as a *last engulfing bottom* (see Exhibit 3.35(A)). The last engulfing pattern is viewed as a turning point for the bulls if prices can close above the black candle's close.

A bullish engulfing pattern is a two-candlestick pattern in which, *during a downtrend*, a large white candle wraps around a prior small black real body. However, if, during a *rising market*, a large white candle engulfs the previous day's black candle, it is a potentially bearish pattern, referred to as a *last engulfing top* (Exhibit 3.35(B)). In candle theory, the bearishness of this pattern is confirmed if the next day the market closes under the prior white candle's close.

In Exhibit 3.35(B), the merged candle of the last engulfing top looks bullish with its long upper shadow. However, remember that the last engulfing top appears in an uptrend, so the merged candle line can be compared to a potentially bearish hanging man line.

The Japanese colorfully compare the last engulfing pattern top to dou-

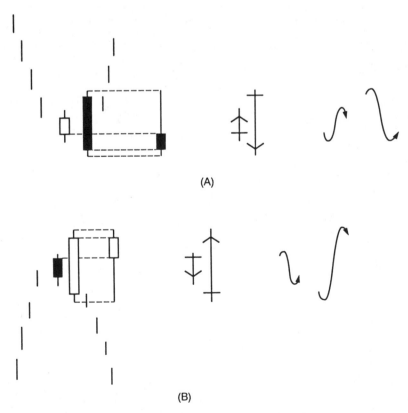

(A)

(B)

EXHIBIT 3.35. Last Engulfing Bottom and Top

ble lovers' suicide. This is because you fall in love with the market (be-cause of the last engulfing pattern's long white candle), but both you and the market perish together. These words might be a little strong, but they convey the cautionary approach traders should take after the emer-gence of a last engulfing pattern.

In April 1992, in Exhibit 3.36, there was a bullish engulfing pattern (note how, because this was a stock, I still viewed it as a bullish engulfing pattern although the second session's open was the same as the prior close). The rally from that pattern stalled at the last engulfing top. Note how both of these patterns just discussed had a white candle enveloping a black real body. But what was the difference? In the regular bullish engulfing pattern in April 1992, the combination of the white enveloping the black candles surfaced during a downtrend. In August 1992, the same combination of candles appeared after an uptrend, thus becoming a last engulfing pattern top. The fact that the next day's session closed under the long white real body's close was confirmation of the last engulfing top.

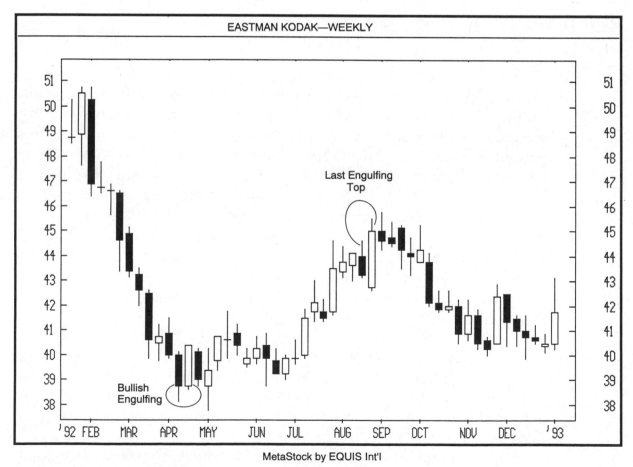

EASTMAN KODAK—WEEKLY

Last Engulfing
Top

Bullish
Engulfing

MetaStock by EQUIS Int'l

EXHIBIT 3.36. Last Engulfing Top, Eastman Kodak—Weekly

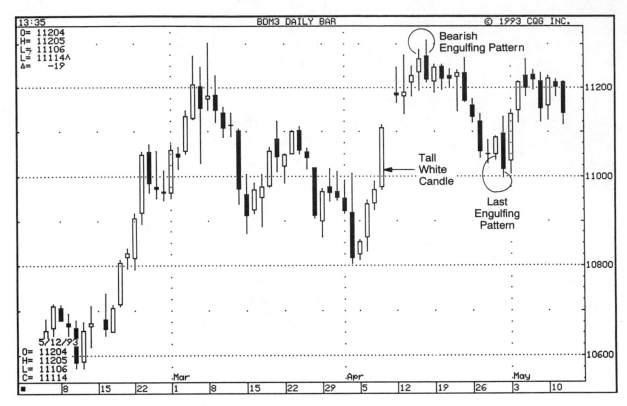

EXHIBIT 3.37.   Last Engulfing Bottom, June 1993 Bonds—Daily

In Exhibit 3.37, a bearish engulfing pattern arose at April's price peak. Prices then descended, finding support at the bottom of the tall white candle. This support was tested in late April with a black candle wrapping around a white real body. This had the shape of a bearish engulfing pattern, but it appeared during a downtrend. As such, it became a bullish last engulfing bottom.

In Exhibit 3.38, at the September lows, there was a last engulfing bottom. One of the more interesting aspects of this chart is that the volume on the long black candle session was unusually high. This could be viewed as a selling climax. This increased the chance that the last engulfing pattern was a bottom reversal.

Harami

The harami is comprised of a long real body and a small real body within its range. The harami is the reverse of an engulfing line. Whereas in an engulfing pattern there is a long candle engulfing the previous real body, a harami is an unusually long real body followed by a very small real body.

After a downtrend, the emergence of a harami shows, as expressed in Japan, that "the decline is exhausting itself." A harami, after an ad-

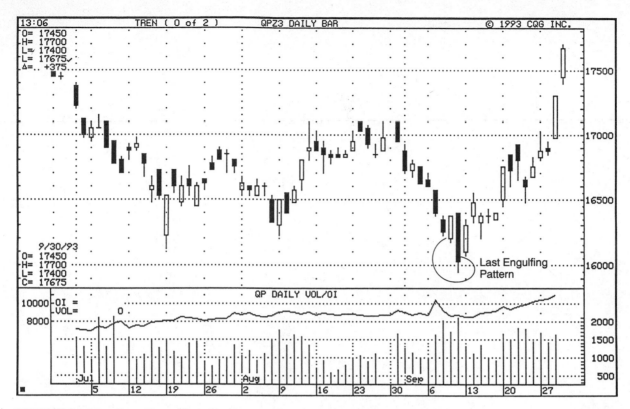

EXHIBIT 3.38. Last Engulfing Pattern and Volume, December 1993 Gas Oil

vance, shows that the market must have failed to maintain higher prices.

As shown in Exhibit 3.39(A), either candle of the harami can be white or black; all combinations are called harami. However, after a downtrend, a white–black (meaning the first candle is white and the second is black) or a white–white harami is viewed more bullishly than a black–white or a black–black harami. This is because a long white candle is by itself viewed as bullish, so its appearance in a harami increases the chance that the falling power of the market will come to an end.

The same rationale applies to a harami after an uptrend. As displayed in Exhibit 3.39(B), a harami with a long black real body can be viewed as more bearish than a harami in an uptrend that has a long white real body. This is because a long black real body after a rally is construed as bearish, so when it is the first part of the harami pattern, the degree of pessimism is increased.

Other aspects that will increase the importance of a harami include the following.

1. If the second real body is in the middle of the trading range of the first real body. If, after a rally, the second real body of the harami is near the upper end of the first real body, the odds increase that the

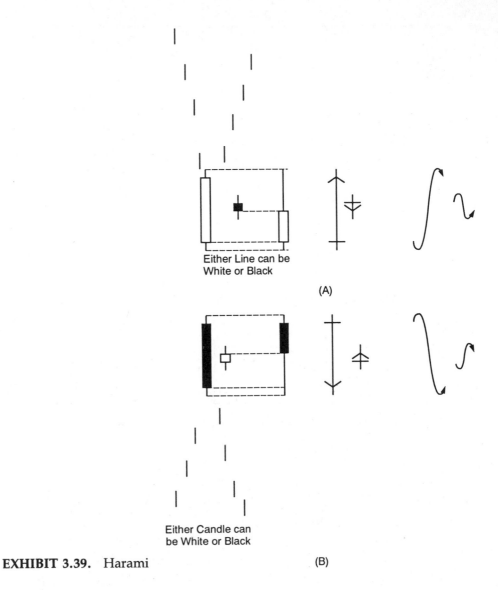

Either Line can be
White or Black

(A)

Either Candle can
be White or Black

EXHIBIT 3.39.   Harami   (B)

market will consolidate rather than reverse. I refer to such a harami
as a *high-price harami* since the second session's price is in the upper
end of the prior range. In a downtrend, if there is a harami with the
second small real body near the bottom end of the trading range of
the prior long real body, then the outlook is more likely for a market
lull rather than for a price reversal. I call this type of harami pattern
a *low-price harami*.

2. If the entire range, that is, the open, high, low, and close, are within
   the prior real body, the chances increase for a price reversal.

3. The smaller the shadows and the shorter the real body of the second
   candle, the better the signal. If the second candle is a doji instead of
   a small real body, it increases the probability of a reversal. This combination of a long candle followed by a doji in the first candle's real
   body is called a *harami cross*.

Some Japanese literature refers to harami as transition periods in the market. This means that if a harami in an uptrend is exceeded, it is viewed as a bullish continuation signal. If the price closes under the low of the harami session in a downtrend, then expect more selling pressure.

Exhibit 3.40 illustrates how a rally that started with November's bullish engulfing pattern hesitated at a harami in December. This harami had two aspects that increased its reliability: the second day's small real body was almost in the middle of the first real body, and the entire range of the second session (including the shadows) was within the real body of the first session. It is interesting how the same scenario unfolded in February. Again, a rally began from a bullish engulfing pattern, and then again stalled with a classic harami. With the harami, as the Japanese would say, ''a crack has entered the market.'' A shooting star a few sessions after the February harami was also a bearish upthrust in which the market made a new high, but the bulls failed to hold these highs. (Although the shooting star session had a real body within the prior long

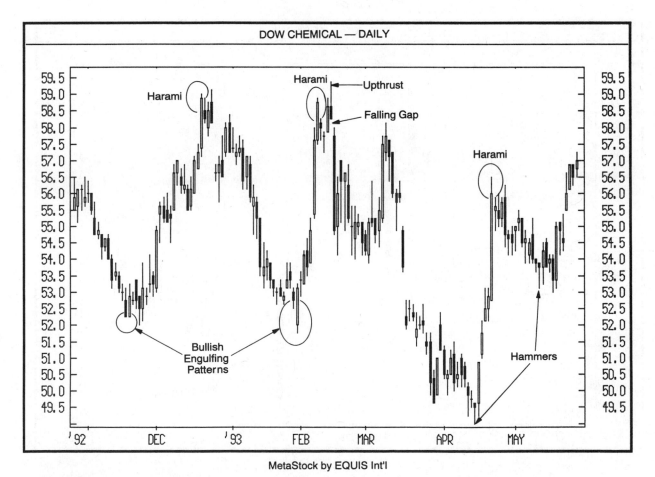

MetaStock by EQUIS Int'l

EXHIBIT 3.40. Harami, Dow Chemical—Daily

white candle, these two candles did not form a harami because the upper shadow of the shooting star was too far outside the prior session's range.)

If there was any doubt about the serious trouble this market was in, the falling gap at the arrow should have been the final proof. Note how the harami sessions in December and February became a ceiling. The low in this market was made via a hammer in April. Later that month, a violently long white real body was immediately followed by a diminutive real body. This formed a harami that precipitated a decline until the emergence of another hammer.

In the chart shown by Exhibit 3.41, the selloff from a bearish engulfing pattern found a foundation with May's harami. This second candle of the harami hovered near the bottom of the prior long black real body. As a result, there was more likelihood that prices would move sideways near the lower end of the tall black candle's real body. Note that the long lower shadows after this harami reflected healthy buying interest as prices

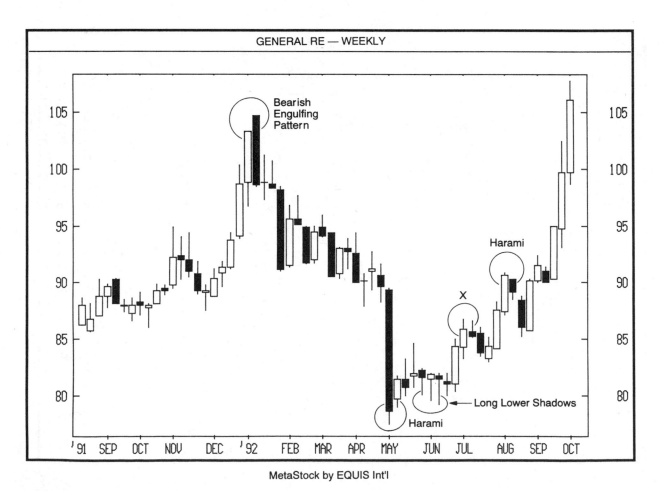

EXHIBIT 3.41. Harami, General Re—Weekly

EXHIBIT 3.42.   Harami and the Size of the Second Real Body, November 1992 Heating Oil

got near $80. The pattern marked X was not a harami because the white real body was not unusually long. For a harami, the first real body has to be very long relative to the preceding bodies. Another harami appeared in early August, but after an initial setback, prices exceeded the harami so the trend resumed higher.

Exhibit 3.42 shows two examples of harami in which the open, high, low, and close of the second real body are within the first real body. The October harami pattern was more important because of the extremely short real body. Its small size made it like a doji session. Thus, October's harami could be viewed as a harami cross. The series of three long black real bodies (labeled 1, 2, and 3) following October's harami underscored the inherent weakness of the market.

In Exhibit 3.43, in February 1992, we see how a support area (which included a hammer) formed within a $19.00–$19.50 area. Based on the axiom that old support becomes resistance (the change of polarity principle), we would expect $19.00–$19.50 to become resistance. That is what developed as this resistance was first confirmed by a shooting star. From there, the market descended until the piercing pattern occurred. Another assault at the $19.00–$19.50 resistance area materialized in May. At that time, a harami pattern was followed by a dark cloud cover. Another failed

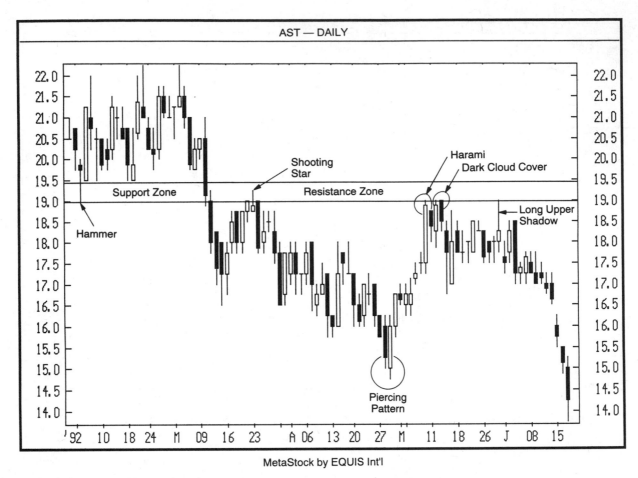

EXHIBIT 3.43.   Harami Confirming a Resistance Zone, AST—Daily

attack at the resistance in late May occurred via a long upper shadow candle (this candle was not a shooting star because it did not appear after a rally).

As discussed before, the ideal harami pattern has the second session's real body in the middle part of the first candle. However, if during an uptrend the second candle hovers near the top of the prior candle (i.e., a high-price harami), the chances increase for a consolidation rather than a price reversal. In Exhibit 3.44, we see how several high-price harami (marked 1 through 3) developed from early June through late July. After each of these, the market consolidated for at least a week before moving out of the trading range. This chart brings out another use of a high-price harami (or a low-price harami in a downtrend)—option traders can consider selling volatility. This is because after a high-price harami in an uptrend or a low-price harami in a downtrend, a trader could expect that the market posture may temporarily settle into a lateral band from a previously strong trend. This could mean a decline in volatility.

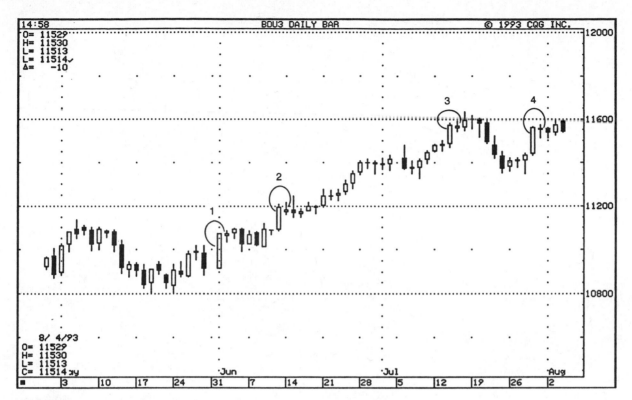

EXHIBIT 3.44.   Harami with Second Candle Near Top of Prior Candle, September 1993 Bonds

THE WINDOW

The window, also known as disjointed candles, is one of the more powerful candlestick patterns. As shown in Exhibit 3.45(A) and (B), a window is the same as a gap in the West. That is, for a rising window, the top of yesterday's upper shadow should be under the low of the today's lower shadow. A falling window means that the low of yesterday's session (i.e., the bottom of the lower shadow) is above the top of today's upper shadow. Windows are a good visual clue because they clearly display that the action and market sentiment is so one-sided.

In a talk I gave before a group of traders, I mentioned how, based on my experiences, the window was a candle tool that I have found to work well. After I mentioned this, a trader in the audience told me that he used to work at a Japanese bank. After my explanation of the importance of windows, he said that he then understood why the Japanese traders at the bank would routinely go to the charts looking for gaps—sometimes even going back years to find one. This comment reinforced what I have found to be true about the windows—it is a candle technique not to be ignored.

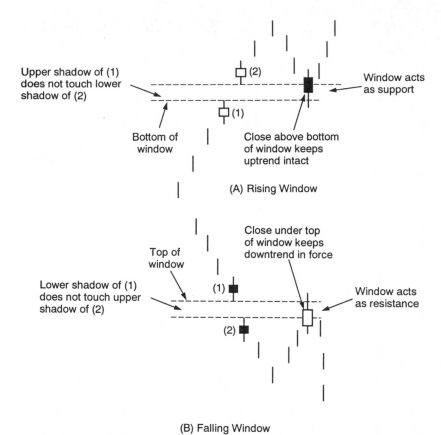

Upper shadow of (1)
does not touch lower
shadow of (2)

Window acts
as support

Bottom of
window

Close above bottom
of window keeps
uptrend intact

(A) Rising Window

Top of
window

Close under top
of window keeps
downtrend in force

Lower shadow of (1)
does not touch upper
shadow of (2)

Window acts
as resistance

(B) Falling Window

EXHIBIT 3.45.   Rising and Falling Windows

Windows are continuation patterns in which the market resumes the trend taken before the continuation pattern emerged. Thus, after a rising window, which is a bullish continuation pattern, the prior uptrend should continue. A falling window has bearish implications since it means the prior trend, in that case down, should resume.

There is a saying used in Japan about windows, "The reaction will go until the window." In other words, the window should be the limit on a reaction. Thus, for a rising window, reactions (i.e., selloffs) should stop within the window. For a falling window, rebounds (i.e., rallies) should stop within the window.

When using windows as support and resistance, it should be noted that the price may fall below the bottom of a rising window or above the top of a falling window temporarily before prices move back in the direction of the window. This is illustrated in Exhibit 3.45(A) and (B).

A general rule that I have found useful based on my experience is that if the price *closes* through the window, I then view the prior trend as being voided. For example, if there is a rising window between $83 and $85 and then the market closes under the bottom of the window (i.e., under $83), the uptrend can be considered as over. Conversely, if there is a falling window between $62 and $60, once the bulls close the market above the top of this window (at $62), then the bulls have broken the back of the bear market.

Based on the discussion above, an intra-session move under a rising window (or above a falling window) is not proof of a break. The consequence of this is that you should wait for the market to close under the bottom of a rising window (or above the top of a falling window) to confirm that the uptrend is over (or that the downtrend has been voided). On a weekly chart, you should wait for a weekly (that is, a Friday) close under the bottom of the window to say that a window's support had been broken. The risk in waiting for a close to confirm the break of a window is that, by the time this happens, the market may be sharply higher or lower than you may have wanted to risk.

In this section, I will discuss:

1. waiting for a closing price to confirm the break of a window's support or resistance area;
2. how volume can influence the importance of a window;
3. using windows to confirm a trend reversal;
4. how windows can provide a quick clue to the market's health;
5. waiting for three sessions for confirmation of a window;

EXHIBIT 3.46. Intra-Session Break of a Window, December 1993 S&P

6. three windows and confirmation of a trend reversal;

7. two black gapping candles;

8. gapping doji.

Exhibit 3.46 shows that a selloff from a bearish engulfing pattern held August's rising window as support. The long lower shadow of candle 1 and the tall white real body of candle 2 echoed the importance of this support area. Candle 1 pulled under the window on an intra-day basis, but by the close, the bulls had managed to push prices above the bottom of the window. This left the uptrend intact.

Exhibit 3.47 shows that there was a rally that started with the October 5 hammer. The force behind the bulls' move was echoed later that month by the rising window and its accompanying high volume (see the arrow). When a window opens via a tall white real body, it has the nickname of a *running* window (based on the fact that the market is "running" in the direction of the window). The rally from this window hesitated via a doji

EXHIBIT 3.47.   Windows and Volume, Apple—Daily

after the tall white candle. The fact that the pullback from this doji held support at 50% of the white body (see the dashed line) showed the power of the bulls to support the market. Note how, as the market ascended, the midpoint of the tall white candles became support.

Exhibit 3.48 illustrates how June's dark cloud cover short-circuited the prior rally. The sell-off from this pattern found a floor at April's window. Other aspects of this chart are interesting. The low of June's price decline was a harami. This harami appeared within the support band, as predicted by the window. This same combination of a harami within the window also emerged in May. Notice how the June rebound from the window stalled at the resistance area set up by the dark cloud cover.

A shooting star is potentially bearish, but what if the shooting star session also forms a rising window—which is bullish? In Exhibit 3.49, we see that such a scenario unfolded as in mid-January. After the shooting star line appeared, I was asked by a client whether this was a sell signal (the client knew that a shooting star was normally a bearish signal). I pointed out that while this was indeed a bearish shooting star, there was another aspect that was perhaps even more important—the rising window. I suggested to this client that if he wanted to sell short, he should wait for the market to close under the bottom of the window to confirm that the uptrend was over. Since the bears could not pull prices under

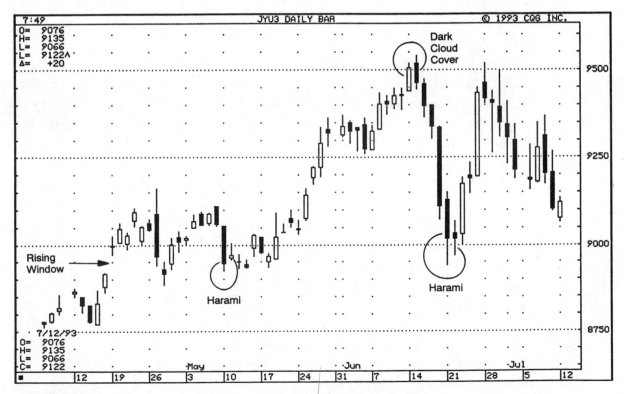

EXHIBIT 3.48.   Window as Support, September 1993 Japanese Yen

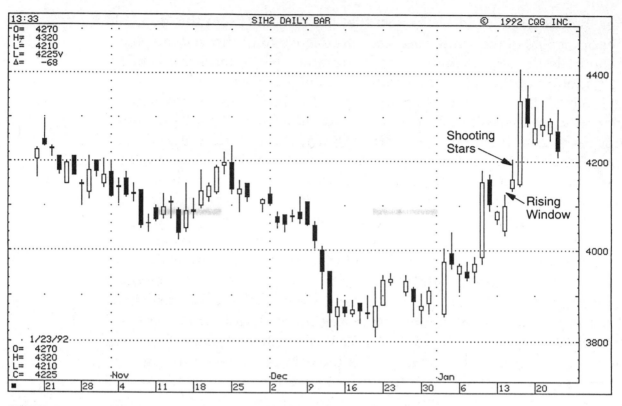

EXHIBIT 3.49.   Shooting Star and a Rising Window, March 1992 Silver

the window, a short sale was unwarranted. After the next session's rally, the client, who did not go short, ordered ten copies of my first book to give to his friends!

Exhibit 3.49 demonstrates a critical concept sometimes forgotten, even by practitioners of the candle charts. Namely, that an individual candle pattern should be viewed in the context of the surrounding technical picture. In this example, a shooting star viewed in isolation (that is, by not looking at the window preceding it) could have caused a poorly positioned trade.

When I show Exhibit 3.50 at my seminar, I title it, "Saved by the Light of the Candles!." This is because the chart is an example of how candles can help avoid a bad trade. In mid-March, the market closed above a major resistance line that went back to December 1991 (only the last part of this resistance line is shown on the chart). This breakout action could have been viewed as potentially bullish. However, there was still a lack of confirmation based on the candles. Specifically, there was an open window in early March that was yet unclosed. Based on candle principles, until the market closes above the top of the window (in this case at $1088), the trend was still down. Observe that, in spite of the breakout from the resistance line, the bulls could not push the market high enough to close above the top of the window. So although a resis-

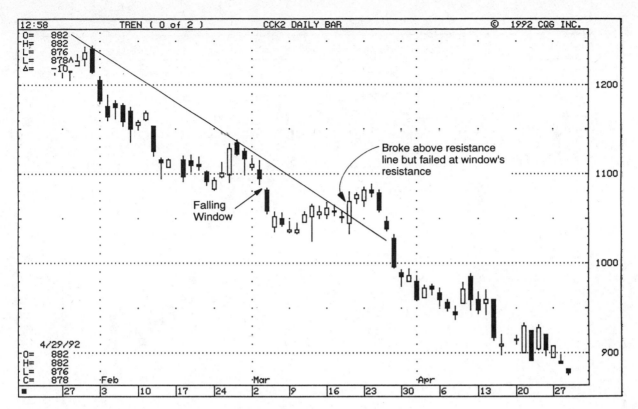

EXHIBIT 3.50.   Window as Extra Confirmation, May 1992 Cocoa

tance line was pierced, those who knew about the candles were kept
from going prematurely long.

The window can be used as a potent confirmatory mechanism. If there
is a reversal signal followed by a window in the same direction, traders
should be more confident of a price reversal. Exhibit 3.51 is an example
of this aspect. There was a bearish engulfing pattern in May. Prices descended slightly, and then moved up to reach new highs in early July.
As this time, another bearish engulfing pattern appeared. However, unlike May's bearish engulfing pattern, July's was followed by a falling
window. This window served to reinforce that a top had been put in
place.

Exhibit 3.52 shows how candles can help give a quick understanding
of the market's health (or illness). In this case, there was a stock that one
of my friends had bought. Some very bullish news came out, and immediately after this news, the stock soared to a new high (see the arrow).
There were a few ominous signs that appeared in spite of this bullish
news. First was the fact that the day the market moved to a new high,
it finished the session by closing under the prior day's close. This formed
a dark cloud cover.

The other problem was more significant. As I explained to my friend,
a market that fails to hold new highs on supposedly bullish news is a

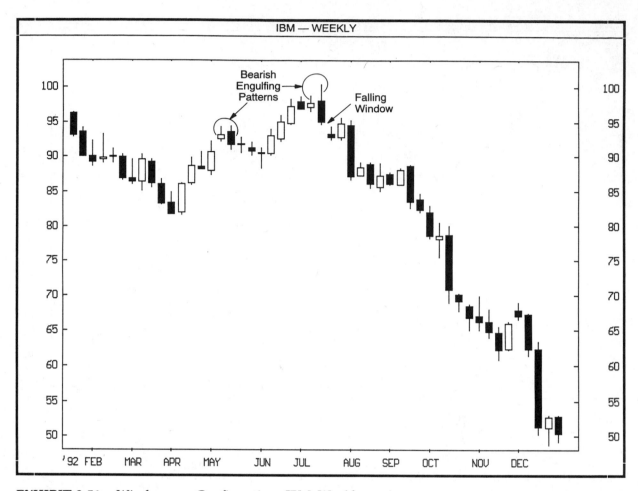

EXHIBIT 3.51.   Windows as Confirmation, IBM–Weekly

dangerous market to be long. A stock's price is composed of the total of all information, whether the information is known by the general public or by a select few. Many shares of this stock were held by relatively few people. The failure to hold the new highs probably meant that they knew something the general public did not. They may have taken the opportunity to sell into the rally. Of course, there was always a chance for recovery to the new highs. But, after I saw the falling window, I mentioned to my friend that until the market closed above the top of the window, the market was in a downtrend. This window became resistance as shown by the dual shooting stars. Notice that in August, another falling window opened.

Some Japanese traders believe that if a window is not filled within three sessions, it is confirmation that the market should move in the direction of the window. That is, if there is a falling window that is not filled within three sessions, the market action is viewed as confirming that prices should move lower. In one of the books I had translated, it said that if a window is not filled within three sessions, then there is

DAXRO — DAILY

EXHIBIT 3.52. Windows as a Mechanism for Quickly Analyzing the Market, Daxro—Daily

power to go thirteen more sessions in the direction of the gap. I do not agree with the preciseness of the last part of that statement, but this technique of waiting three sessions for confirmation may provide a method to confirm a window's support or resistance.

In Exhibit 3.53, there was a falling window that opened in early March. Based on the above discussion, a method to trade with this window could be to wait three sessions and see if within that time the market can close above the top of the window. If the bulls cannot push prices (on a close) above the top of the window, candle theory states that this should increase the chance that the downtrend will continue. After all, the bulls had three sessions to move prices through the window and failed to do so. In this example, we see how the falling window acted as resistance as the bulls tried in the third session to unsuccessfully push prices above the window. Attempts in May at this window's resistance level at 62¢ stalled via a dark cloud cover and then a long upper shadow candle (at the arrow) a few sessions later.

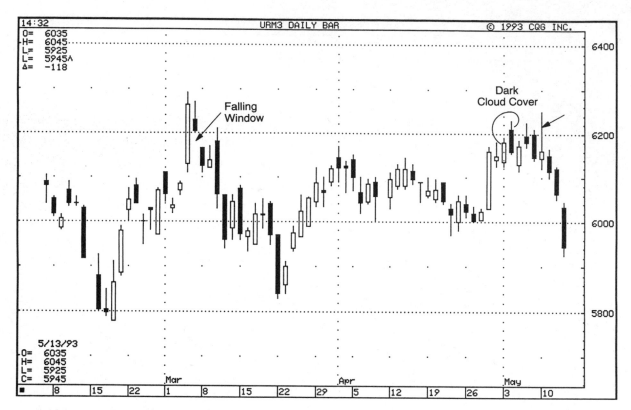

EXHIBIT 3.53.   Windows and Waiting Three Sessions, June 1993 Unleaded Gas

I would be careful about putting too much emphasis on three sessions. The Japanese place much importance on the number three in their culture, and this has spilled into their technical analysis. Thus, look closely at what happens when you get a window in your market. You may find that if the window is not filled in within two, four, or even five sessions, rather than the more traditional three sessions, it could be proof of continuation of the trend predicted by the window.

Three Windows

As discussed above, the Japanese emphasize the number three. In this context, the Japanese view a market that has had three rising or falling windows in a row as a market that has reached maturity. The market in such a scenario is viewed as being overextended and correction is likely. Three windows are shown in Exhibit 3.54.

Besides the windows, Exhibit 3.55 is of interest because it shows examples of many candle patterns. After a series of bottoming patterns in January that included a high-wave candle and the morning star, the market gave final bullish confirmation with a rising window. The market ascended strongly from there until a harami pattern was formed. The

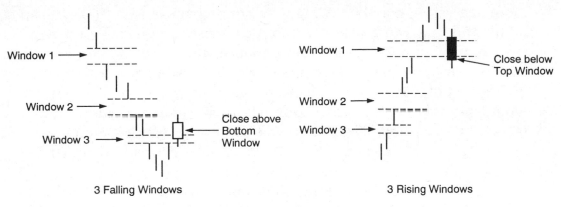

EXHIBIT 3.54.   Three Windows

correction from this harami stopped in mid-February with a successful test of January's window. From the February lows until the dark cloud cover in early March, there were three rising windows (numbered 1, 2, and 3). The market then broke lower via a falling window. Note how that falling window became resistance over the next few days.

As shown in the example above, if there is a bearish candle signal after three windows, one should offset long positions. However, the

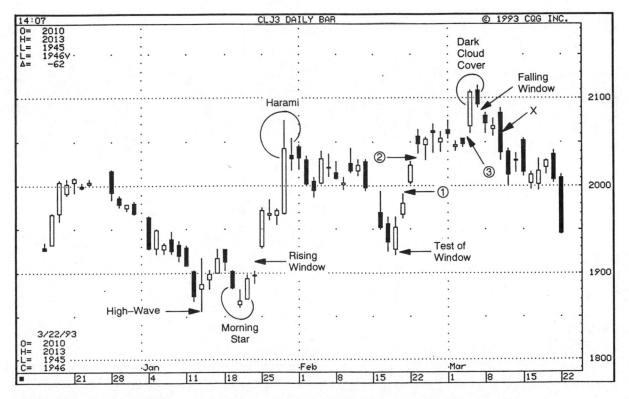

EXHIBIT 3.55.   A Dark Cloud Cover After Three Windows, June 1993 Crude Oil

more aggressive may be willing to, as the Japanese say, "take a leap of faith" and they can go short without a bearish candle clue of a turn.

It is my opinion, based on experience, that even if there are three windows in the same direction, I would not trade against the direction of these windows until I see more proof of a trend reversal. To me, this would require that the market moves through the last window on a close (as shown in Exhibit 3.54). Based on this, bearish confirmation in Exhibit 3.55 came with the candle at x (in March), which closed under rising window 3.

Exhibit 3.56 highlights how important it can be to wait for the top window to be filled in before going short after three rising windows. This gold chart shows a rising window in April that is labeled "window 2." This is because prior to this date, and not shown here, there was another rising window. This made April's window the second rising window. Another window followed this, forming the third rising window. A few sessions after window 3, there was a dark cloud cover that was completed on May 3. This pattern signaled a change in the trend as the market went from vertical to sideways. However, although the trend did change, there was not yet confirmation that prices would descend because the bears had yet to close the market under the top window (window 3). This

EXHIBIT 3.56. Waiting for Confirmation of a Trend Reversal After Three Rising Windows, December 1993 Gold—Daily

window stayed open, and the market then continued on its upward course. Interestingly, the same scenario as just discussed unfolded as another dark cloud cover (dark cloud cover 2) formed after window 4. After dark cloud cover 2, prices again went from an uptrend into a lateral band. But the widow (number 4) remained unfilled on a close as it was successfully defended by the bulls via a hammer. Note how the window was filled on an intra-day basis, but prices did not close under the bottom of window 4. This meant that the major uptrend was still in effect. Consequently, I usually recommend our clients to use three or more rising (or falling windows) at a time to offset or protect existing positions, but not to go countertrend until the last window is filled in on a close.

Two Black Gapping Candles

While a falling window is bearish, it is even more portentous if the two candles immediately following the window have black real bodies. Such a combination is called *two black gapping candles* (Exhibit 3.57). The dual black candles reinforce the fact that the trend has turned from up to down. This pattern is a sign, as the Japanese express it, of the "rout of the bulls."

The chart of Delta in Exhibit 3.58 gave a plethora of signals that it was experiencing trouble as it got in the $50 to $60 area. The topping signals included:

1. a bearish engulfing pattern;
2. a harami pattern;
3. an evening star;
4. a bearish engulfing pattern;
5. a bearish engulfing pattern;
6. long upper shadows, with the black candle following the white candle, forming a dark cloud cover, and for those knowledgeable about the

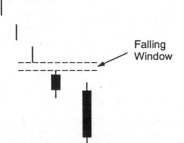

Falling
Window

EXHIBIT 3.57.   Two Black Gapping Candles

EXHIBIT 3.58.   Two Gapping Black Candles Confirm Resistance, Delta—Daily

candle patterns, the three black candles following the white candle, forming a three-crow pattern.

The coup de grâce came with two black gapping candles in mid-November.

In Exhibit 3.59, December's harami followed by a long black real body was an important warning. Also note how those three candles (that is, the two candles of the harami and the next candle) all had long upper shadows. After this group of bearish signals, there was a falling window with two black candles. This completed the two black gapping candles.

Gapping Doji

Exhibit 3.60 shows a joji session that gaps lower during a decline. It is said this is a time where selling meets more selling and thus is a bearish

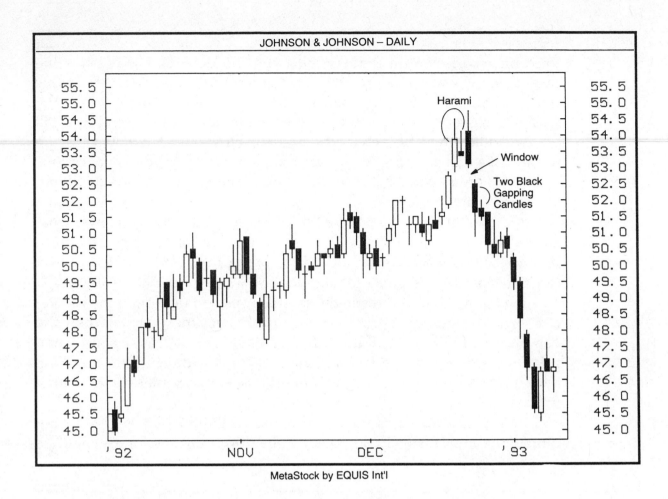

EXHIBIT 3.59. Two Black Gapping Candles, Johnson and Johnson—Daily

signal. I would recommend waiting for confirmation for this pattern on the session after the doji. The reason for waiting is that if the session after the doji is a long white candle that trades higher, it would turn out to be bullish morning star pattern.

In my studies, I have seen reference to this gapping doji only in a falling market, not to a gapping doji in a rising market. However, I see no reason not to view such a pattern as being bullish since it has the

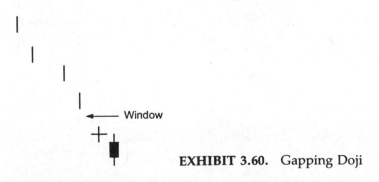

EXHIBIT 3.60. Gapping Doji

requisite rising window. In such a scenario, I would also prefer to wait for a higher session on the day following the doji. This is because the doji could be a sign of a tired market and if a white candle followed this doji it would show that the market would then be refreshed.

As discussed in the section on doji, a doji after an uptrend or a tall white candle could be potentially bearish. However, I would view the fact that if a doji gaps higher, some of the potentially bearish implications of the doji are negated because the rising window shows the underlying strength of the market.

As shown in Exhibit 3.61, the doji at session 1 did not gap lower (that is, the high of doji session 1 was above the low of the prior session). Because of this, doji 1 is not a classic gapping doji, although the market came so close to opening a falling window with doji 1 that I still viewed it as a gapping doji. Interestingly, the next session (at doji 2) the market did form a gapping doji. A sign of further weakness arose when the hammer and bullish engulfing pattern at 3 failed to hold as support when prices closed under the support area set up by the bullish engulfing pattern. At 4 the market gave an important bearish signal via the falling window.

The gapping doji is a rare pattern, but in Exhibit 3.62 there is a falling candle line with a small real body. While not a doji session, it could be

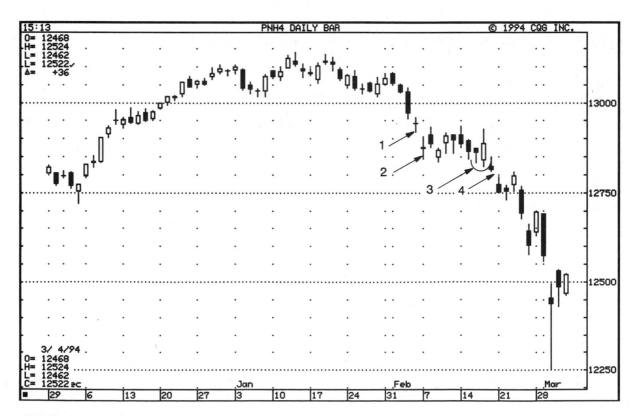

EXHIBIT 3.61.   Gapping Doji, March 1994 Notionnel Bond

EXHIBIT 3.62.   Gapping Doji, IBM—Daily

viewed as similar to a gapping doji in that the small real body is almost a doji and it gapped under the prior lows. (Even if a trader did not view this as a gapping doji, it could also be viewed as two black gapping candles.) This chart has some interesting candle signals that illustrate how IBM was basing out near $40. These include the long lower shadow at candle 1 and a tall white real body at candle 2. A shooting star in late August created problems on the rally from candle 2. The market broke under the lows of the mid-September hammer, but it is interesting how easily we can see the selling pressure evaporating during this sell off (at X) by a series of gradually shrinking black real bodies. The long white candle at Y showed that the bulls had taken control.

THREE OR MORE CANDLE LINES

The Evening Star

As shown in Exhibit 3.63, the evening star is a three-candlestick pattern. The criteria for this pattern include an uptrending market in which a long

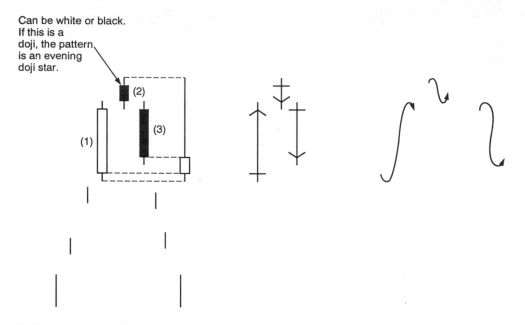

EXHIBIT 3.63.   The Evening Star

white candle (candle 1 in the Exhibit) is followed by a small real body (candle 2). The small real body of the second candle line can be black or white and should not touch the real body of candle 1. The third candle of this pattern is a black real body that does not usually touch real body 2, and then closes well into the white candle line that make up the first candle of this pattern. If the second candle of the evening star is a doji instead of a small real body, then the pattern is an *evening doji star*.

In the Introduction to this book, I referred to the book written in the mid-1700s entitled, *The Fountain of Gold—The Three Monkey Record of Money*. In that book, reference is made to Yin and Yang markets. Yang is another term for bullish (for example, a white candle is sometimes referred to as a yang line). A Yin move is a downturn. For instance, a black candle line can be called a yin line. The *Fountain of Gold* has a section that reads, ''When movement reaches an extreme, there is stillness. This stillness gives rise to Yin.'' This is a verbal description of the evening star. To wit!

1. ''When yang movement reaches an extreme''—the appearance of the long white candle of the evening star pattern
2. ''There is stillness''—describes the small real body. The small real body reflects a market at a transition phase in which the trend goes from up to a period of ''stillness.''
3. ''This stillness gives rise to Yin''—aptly describes how the Yin (the black candle) follows the stillness of the second candle line.

It is important to wait for the third line to get the bearish confirmation of this pattern. This is because, after the second candle line, all we known about the market is that it went from an uptrend to period in which the bulls and bears were in a stalemate as gauged by the small real body of this second candle. It is only after the long black candle moves into the first session's white body that we get the proof that the bears have taken control of the market.

Exhibit 3.64 is an example of how an evening star confirmed a resistance area set up by a bearish engulfing pattern. Because this bearish engulfing pattern and evening star arose near the same area, both patterns formed a potential double top near $45. In Western technicals, a double top is confirmed by a move under the low between the two price peaks that make up the double top. In this chart, this low was made in February at $40½. A double top gives a measure derived on the range from the highs to the low of the pattern. In this case, there was about a $5 range that is subtracted from the February low of $40½. This gave a target to about $35½. Thus, for those wanting to buy on price dips, a

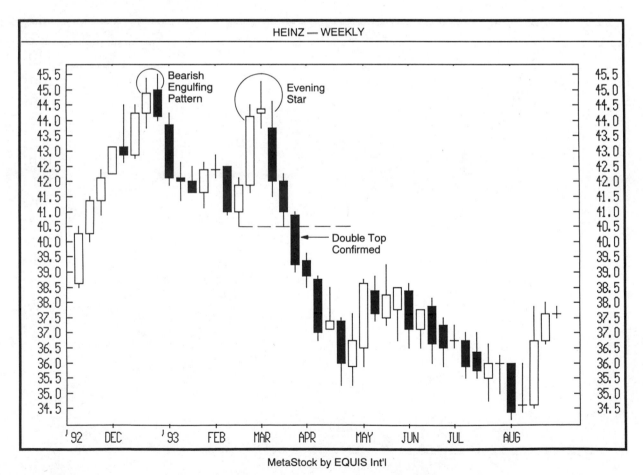

EXHIBIT 3.64. Evening Star Confirms Resistance, Heinz—Weekly

measured move target towards $35\frac{1}{2}$ should be the area. We can see from this example how smoothly candle charts can be merged with classic Western charting methods (e.g., the double top).

In Exhibit 3.65, I illustrate that the evening star can become resistance. As shown on this chart, November's evening star stopped the December rally. I use the highest point of the three candles, that form the evening star—that is, the top of the highest upper shadows, as my resistance. If you can withstand the risk, I would recommend using a close (rather than an intra-session move) above the evening star's high as a buy stop. In this case, it would require a weekly (that is, a Friday close) above the dashed line to confirm a breakout from the evening star's resistance area.

As previously discussed, there should be more flexibility in using candles in the stock market than in some of the other markets, such as futures. As shown in Exhibit 3.63, the classic evening star's three real bodies should not be touching. However, because in the stock market the open price is usually near the prior session's close, the real bodies may touch. In Exhibit 3.66, we see how the opening of the middle candle

MetaStock by EQUIS Int'l

EXHIBIT 3.65. Evening Star as Resistance, Pfizer—Weekly

EXHIBIT 3.66. Evening Star and Flexibility, Waste Management—Daily

of the pattern was about the same price as the prior session's close. While some flexibility may be allowed with stocks in regard to the relation of the real bodies, it should be remembered that the more ideal the pattern, the greater the likelihood of a top.

The evening star from late August illustrated in Exhibit 3.67 is different from the more traditional evening star in that the third real body of this one is a small black real body rather than a long black one. However, I viewed this as an evening star variation with all the bearish implications of the more traditional evening star for a few reasons, which I will now address:

1. The third candle of this evening star, although not a tall black candle, nonetheless reflected the potency of the bears by the fact that they were able to drag prices well into the white real body of this pattern.
2. This evening star variation verified a resistance area. In mid-August, there was a group of bearish candle signals that included a shooting

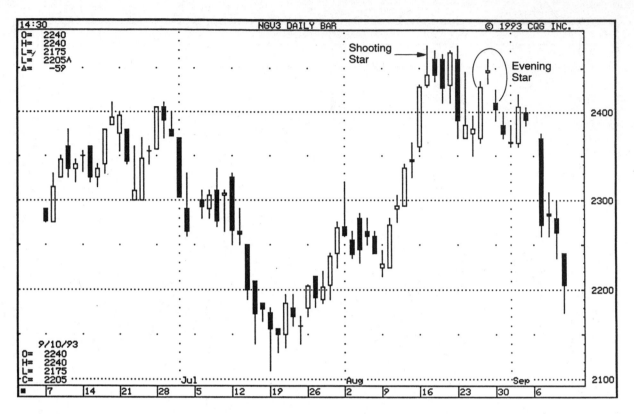

EXHIBIT 3.67. Evening Star and Flexibility, Natural Gas—September 1993

star, then three tall black real bodies after this shooting star, and then a long upper shadow of the candle of August 24. Note how all these bearish candles emerged near $2.50 This is the level where the variation of the evening star appeared.

Exhibit 3.68 shows a collapsing doji star. At a high-price level, the market moves higher. After this, the market gaps lower via a falling doji. This is a point where selling overwhelms buying. If the next session is a

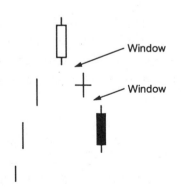

EXHIBIT 3.68. The Collapsing Doji Star

black candle that gaps lower, it is called a *collapsing doji star*. The three candles that make up this pattern are the same three as those needed for the evening doji star. The difference is that the evening doji star has the doji above the tall white real body, while the collapsing doji star has the doji gapping under, instead of above, the first white candle. This pattern is said to be an "omen of a large decline."

While not an ideal version, candle lines A, B, and C in Exhibit 3.69 could be viewed as the collapsing doji star pattern. This chart shows the three main conditions needed for the collapsing doji star pattern: 1) an uptrend to reverse (at the white candle at A), 2) a doji session that gaps under the prior session (at B), and 3) another black candle that moves under the doji session (at C).

Candle lines D and E show a gapping doji pattern (discussed in the section on windows). While similar in appearance to the collapsing doji star, the gapping doji is a bearish continuation pattern. This means that it occurs during a downtrend, while the collapsing doji star is a top reversal pattern that occurs after an uptrend.

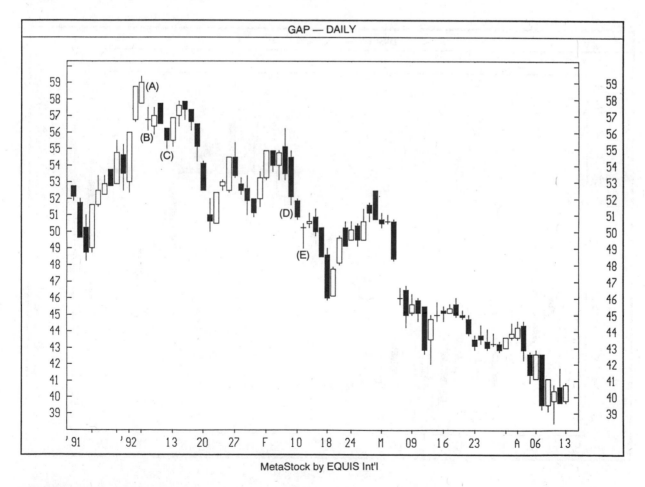

GAP — DAILY

MetaStock by EQUIS Int'l

EXHIBIT 3.69. Collapsing Doji Star, Gap—Daily

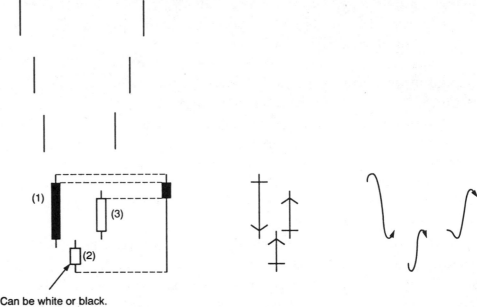

EXHIBIT 3.70. The
Morning Star

Can be white or black.
If this is a doji, the pattern
is a morning doji star.

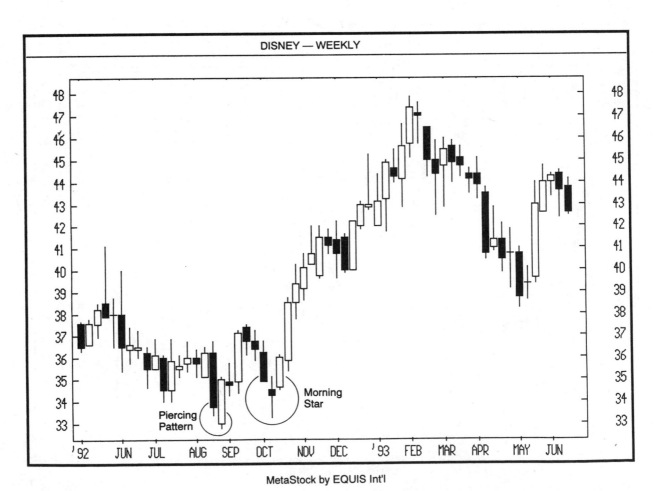

MetaStock by EQUIS Int'l

EXHIBIT 3.71. Morning Star Confirms Support, Disney—Weekly

The Morning Star

Exhibit 3.70 shows that the classic morning star has none of the three real bodies that make up the pattern touching. We can see from the blended candle in Exhibit 3.70 that the more that real body 3 pushes into real body 1, the longer the blended candle's lower shadow, and hence the more bullish the pattern.

As shown in Exhibit 3.71, the area in which August's piercing pattern appeared became support again in October via a classic morning star. Also, the middle candle of this morning star was a high-wave candle.

The three candles highlighted in Exhibit 3.72 at the August lows created a morning star. When, as in this case, the star portion of this pattern is a doji, the pattern is referred to as a morning doji star. There is another interesting aspect about this morning star. If there is a doji session that has a gap before and after it, is called an *abandoned baby*. In this chart of Penney, note how there was a gap between sessions 2 and 3 of the morning star and almost a gap between the first two sessions. Thus, this

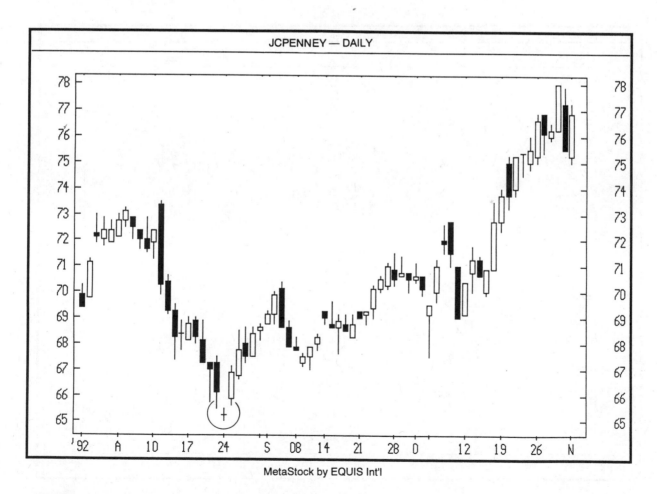

JCPENNEY — DAILY

MetaStock by EQUIS Int'l

EXHIBIT 3.72.   Morning Star, JCPenney—Daily

was almost a very rare abandoned baby pattern. The abandoned baby bottom is, in terms of a bar chart, an island bottom that is also a doji. You can image how rare this combination is.

In the next chapter, I will focus on weighing the overall technical picture in relation to an individual candle pattern. In Exhibit 3.73, I will briefly address this issue.   The hammer is September (at hammer 1) was a potentially bullish signal. However, this bullishness was mitigated by the fact that on the day of the hammer, the market opened a falling window. Note how this window then became a resistance area. A few sessions later, another hammer formed (shown at hammer 2). The session after hammer 2 completed the third line needed for the morning star pattern. So, although there were two hammers in this chart, the overall technical picture for hammer 2 was more consecutive than it was for hammer 1 because of hammer 2's longer lower shadow and because hammer 2 was part of a morning star pattern. As a result, for those looking to buy, the area to have considered would be after the completion of the morning star. Traders who needed more bullish confirmation could

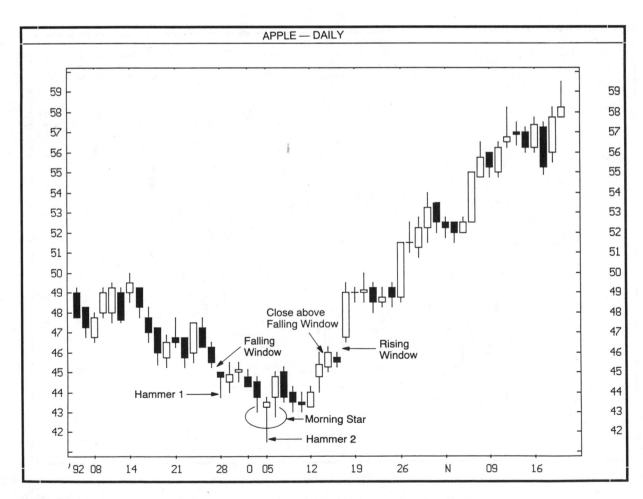

EXHIBIT 3.73. Morning Star and Overall Technical Picture, Apple—Daily

have waited until a close above the falling window's resistance area from mid-October. The rising window in mid-October gave even more bullish proof.

In Exhibit 3.74, there was a hint of a bottom near $12 based on the June 1992 bullish engulfing pattern. In late July, the support area of this pattern (i.e., the lows of the bullish engulfing pattern at $12) was successfully defended. However, in August, these lows were breached, but only temporarily as the bulls were able to regain control of the market by pulling prices back up over $12 again. In doing so, the market formed a morning star pattern and a spring.

As shown in Exhibit 3.75, the first candle of a classic morning star has a large black real body. The third candle of the pattern is a tall white real body that pushes well into the first candle of the pattern. In the morning star pattern M1, the first candle had a small white real body instead of a long lack real body. At patterns M2, the third candle (at the arrow) was a small white real body instead of the more traditional long white real body.

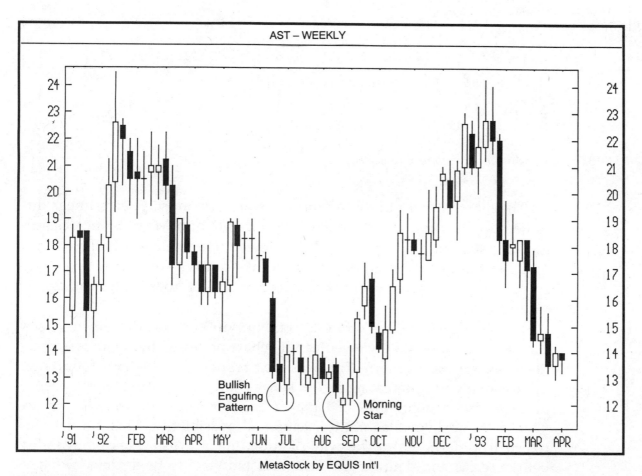

MetaStock by EQUIS Int'l

EXHIBIT 3.74. Morning Star and a Spring, AST—Weekly

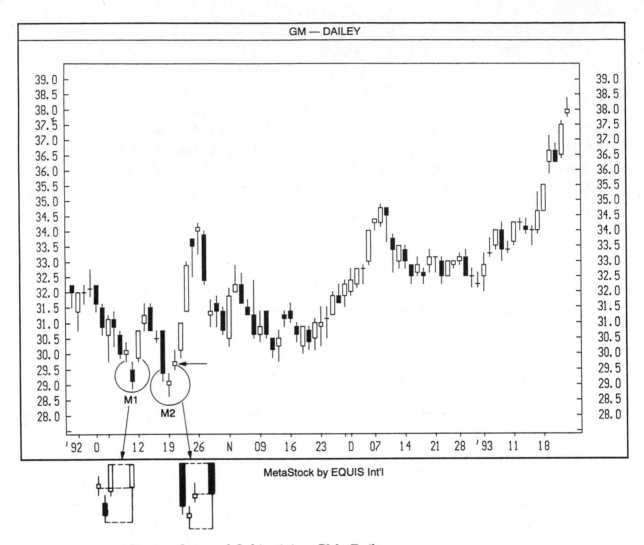

EXHIBIT 3.75.   Morning Star and Subjectivity, GM—Daily

The fact that both of these morning star variations appeared near the same support area meant that while both M1 and M2 were not classic morning star patterns, they should be viewed nonetheless as bullish clues. This chart underscores an important point—candles are a form of pattern analysis, and as such, there is a subjectivity that goes with candlestick analysis.

In this regard, I once wrote to the Nippon Technical Analysts Association to see how they viewed candle chart patterns that were less than ideal versions of a pattern. This was their response: "We have found our discussions very interesting in the sense that you try to be very specific in determining definitions of Japanese exhibit readings while we try to keep them flexible so as not to exclude all possibilities. This . . . may be traced to differences in the way of thinking of Westerners who prefer being precise and definite and Orientals who like to be flexible."

This highlights an important point in that the exhibits I have illustrated are mostly ideal versions of the patterns, but in the real world, one should not exclude the possibility that a less than ideal version of that pattern is valid. How do you determine if you should trade from a less than ideal pattern? Based on the Japanese literature, may conversations with Japanese candle traders, and my experience, here are a few suggestions:

1. Wait for more confirmation of that pattern's prediction. For example, an ideal dark cloud cover should have the second session's close more than halfway into the first candle's white real body. If the close is less than halfway into the white real body, then wait until the next session to see if the market remains weak.

2. If the less than ideal pattern confirms a support or resistance area, or if it appears in a very oversold or overbought market, the greater the odds that the pattern will be a reversal. For example, if there is a hammer in which the lower shadow is not very long, but if this "hammer-like" line confirmed a 50% retracement area, I would view such action as having all the bullish import as would a more traditional hammer.

3. A method you may find useful in helping to determine the significance of a less than ideal pattern is to make a blended candle from that pattern. Then see if the blended candle confirms the pattern's forecast. For example, look at Exhibit 3.75 (GM) previously discussed. I used this chart to draw the blended candles from morning star variations M_1 and M_2. Notice how each of these blended candles had long lower shadows. The long lower shadows of both of the blended candles and the fact that both M_1 and M_2 emerged near the same support with the long white candle following M_2 gave clues that the bears were losing control of this market.

RECORD SESSIONS

Most candle patterns are composed of one, two, or three candles. This aspect shows one of the major advantages of the candle charts—they can often send a reversal signal in only a few sessions, whereas bar charts can take much longer. Although some candle patterns do take longer to unfold, they are nonetheless extremely valuable. One of these longer term pattern techniques is the *eight to ten record sessions*.

When a candle session makes a higher high, the Japanese call it a record session high. A lower low is called a record session low. In candle theory, when there are eight to ten record sessions (that is, eight to ten almost consecutive higher highs or lower), it increases the possibility that the preceding trend will change. Exhibit 3.76(A) shows ten record highs and ten records lows.

Eight to ten record sessions are so important in Japan that they have been described as being ''the bones of Sakata's body.'' The meaning of this expression is that just as the bones, or skeleton, of a person's body are its foundation, so are record sessions the foundation or essence of the Sakata charts. (Sakata charts are another name for candle charts. Sakata was the port city in which Homma traded. In recognition of this, there are many references throughout the Japanese literature to candle charts being called Sakata charts.)

I will now discuss how to count record session highs, but the theory will be the same for record session lows. First, confirm that a low price for the move has occurred. The top of Exhibit 3.76(A) displays how, after a new low, the next session made a higher high. This session became record session 1. Record session 2 occurs when another new high is made (this includes the upper shadow). Note how the session after record session high 1 was not a record session. This was because a new high

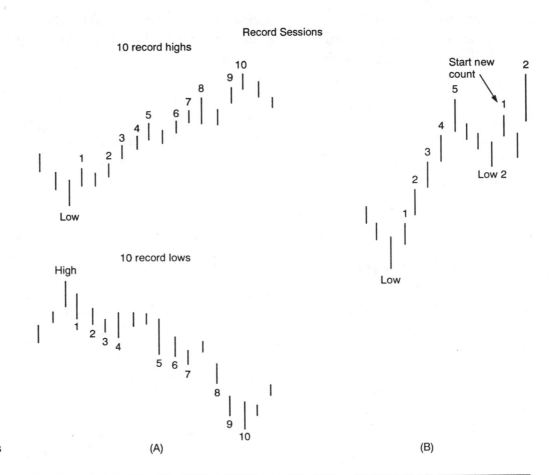

EXHIBIT 3.76.

Record Sessions   (A)   (B)

was not created. Only when a new high was touched was it counted as record session 2.

To count record sessions in a downturn, first confirm that a new high has been set. The session that makes a lower low then becomes record session 1. The next lower low then becomes record session 2.

The theory of record high sessions is that during a rally, a trader should stop buying after eight to ten record session highs (or liquidate longs, or sell short with the appearance of a bearish candle signal after these record session highs). The same philosophy, but in reverse, should be considered after a decline with eight to ten record session lows. To wit, a trader should stop selling after about eight record session lows (or cover shorts, or buy looking for a bounce with a bullish candle signal after eight or more record session lows).

The record session count need not be consecutive. A few sessions of consolidation can be ignored when counting the new highs or lows. Generally, there should not be more than two or three sessions of sideways action between the record sessions, nor should there be a sharp move counter to the record session trend.

The reason that record sessions should be almost consecutive has to do with the underlying concept of record sessions. In the case of eight–ten record session highs (lows), the market becomes overbought (oversold). In an overbought (oversold) situation, the market becomes vulnerable to a price dip (rally) as those who are currently long (short) may decide to take their profits.

The market can relieve an overbought or oversold situation in one of two ways—by trading laterally or by experiencing a sharp price correction. If the market corrects the overbought or oversold situation by either of these methods, the record session count is no longer valid since the market is no longer overextended, and thus is less vulnerable to a correction. For example, in Exhibit 3.76(B), observe how the market got to record session high 5, then quickly sold off for three sessions. Because of the extent of the selloff during these three sessions, the market relieved its overbought condition. As shown, a new count is then started after low 2.

Do not be too concerned with the specific number of record sessions. The eight to ten record session rule is a guidepost. Each market has its own personality. Just as those who follow cycles may find that different markets have different cycles, so some markets may correct after six or twelve record session instead of the more normal eight-ten sessions.

In Exhibit 3.77, from the low at X, we start the record session high count at the next candle since it made a higher high. After record session 8, the market formed two doji. These doji reflected a market that is tiring. For those who were looking for a reason to exit longs, these doji and the

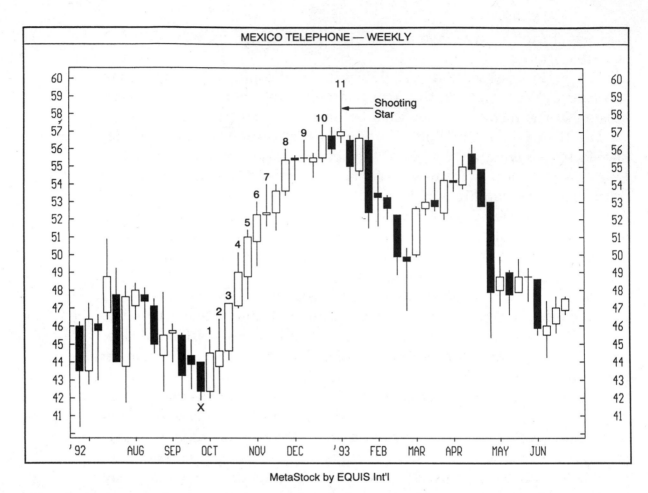

MetaStock by EQUIS Int'l

EXHIBIT 3.77.   Record Session Highs, Mexico Telephone—Weekly

high number of record sessions were valid reasons. A final push occurred in late 1992 as the extended upper shadow candle—the shooting star—in record session 11 denoted a last gasp for the bulls.

Exhibit 3.78 illustrates how a steep price decline that started with a bearish engulfing pattern dragged the market down over 50% from its highs within a few months. After nine record session lows, the market started to stabilize. Exhibit 3.78 is an example of how the candles not only show the trend of the market, but also can give more insight into the market's health by the color of the candles. The Japanese have a saying, ''as different as snow from coal.'' The short term rally from October (from the bullish engulfing pattern) showed that the bulls were in charge based on the series of white real bodies (the ''snow''). The post November selloff pictorially displays the market's weakness with an almost consecutive series of black real bodies (the ''coal'').

In Exhibit 3.79, a gravestone doji appeared in early September. Inter-

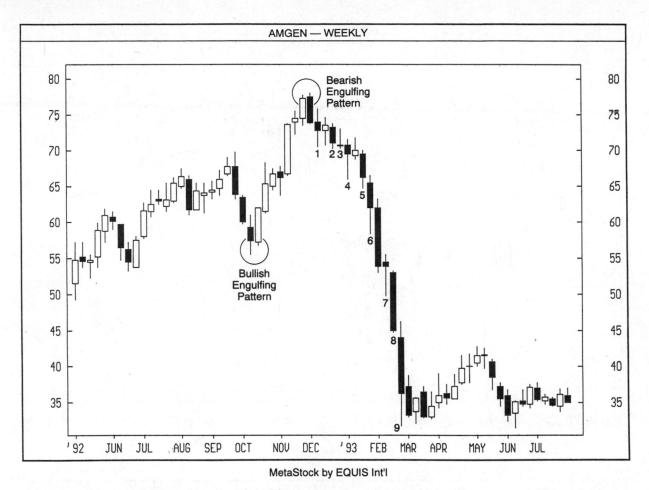

EXHIBIT 3.78. Record Session Lows, Amgen—Weekly

estingly, this gravestone also confirmed that there was a potential top based on the record session concept. After making a new low at L, the market on the next day made a higher high. This was record session 1. After record session 3, the market took a breather for a few days before going on to a fresh new high, and then formed record session 4. As we can see, between record sessions 3 and 4, the market can trade laterally for a few sessions without interrupting the count for record sessions. (However, if these sessions after record session 5 were sharp selloffs, then the record session count would have to start again). By the time the Nikkei gets to record sessions 7 and 8 (which are shooting stars), the market is already in trouble, with the gravestone doji at record session 9 becoming a top.

In Exhibit 3.80, a piercing pattern emerged after a nine-count record session. As a result, a rebound could be expected. From the 1993 high near $21 to the low of the piercing pattern, we get a 50% retracement

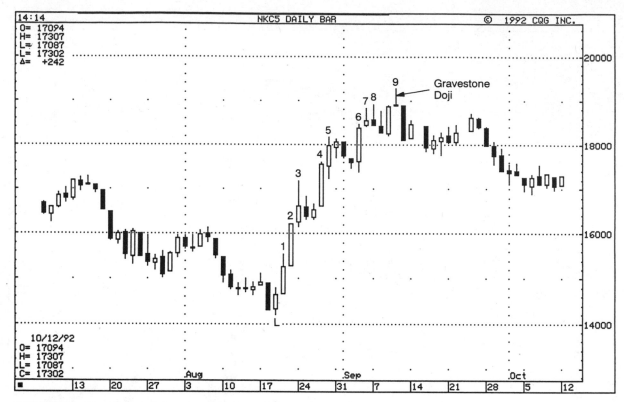

EXHIBIT 3.79.   Record Session High and Bearish Confirmation, Nikkei—Daily

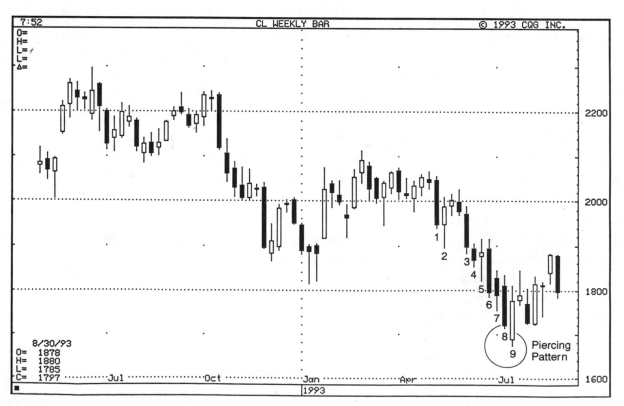

EXHIBIT 3.80.   Record Session Lows and Retracement Levels, Crude Oil—Weekly

level near $19. This is where the market stalled after the rebound from the piercing pattern.

Note

[1]Sakata, Goho, p. 92.

CHAPTER 4

CANDLES AND THE OVERALL TECHNICAL PICTURE

....

井の中の蛙大海を知らず

"He Who Sits in a Well to Look at the Sky Can See But Little"

A Japanese book that I had translated states that, "Action that ignores the condition of the market is only asking for a loss and an ambush encounter."[1] This picturesque saying (using the typical military analogy so common in Japanese technical analysis) means that you must consider the overall market condition before trading with the candles. Otherwise, you may be in for a "loss and ambush encounter."

A member of the Nippon Technical Analysts Association wrote to me that he views the overall technical picture as more important than an individual candle pattern. I certainly agree with that sentiment. Effective candle charting techniques require not only an understanding of the candle patterns, but a policy of using sound, coherent trading strategies and tactics. It is unfortunate that some traders who know about the candle patterns often ignore such tactics. The candles are a tool that must be incorporated with other trading guidelines. In this sense, I have always viewed the candles as being another color, albeit an important one, on my technical palette.

A disciple of Confucius once asked him who would he take to war with him. Confucius answered that he would not want someone who did not care whether he lived or died. He would take someone who approached difficulties with appropriate caution and who preferred to succeed by strategy. And strategy is the focus of this chapter; here I show the importance of such strategic principles as using stops, determining the risk and reward aspects of a trade, observing where a candle pattern is in relation to the overall trend, and monitoring the market's action after a trade is placed. By understanding and using these trading principles, you will be in a position to most fully enhance the power of the candles. By the end of this chapter, you should understand that what emerges before and after a candle pattern is a critical element of trading.

STOPS

"Even Monkeys Fall from Trees"

There should always be a price at which you say your outlook is wrong. The protective stop out level is that price. No matter how reliable the technical tool, there will be times when the signal obtained from that tool is wrong. By using stops, you are defining the risk of a trade. In effect, the use of stops provides one of the most powerful aspects of technical analysis; it offers a risk management approach to the market.

Many of the candlestick patterns can become a support or resistance area. For example, a dark cloud cover often acts as resistance. As such, for those who are short, a protective buy stop can be placed on a close above the high of the dark cloud cover. In Exhibit 4.1, we see that an uptrend that started in early January stopped via a dark cloud cover as the market went from an uptrend preceding this pattern into a lateral band after the dark cloud. The dark cloud cover acted as resistance for the next 7 sessions. But the rising window and then the close above the high of the dark cloud cover were signs that the market was ready to once again advance.

It is human nature that when price action turns against you, wishful thinking enters the picture. For instance, after the market pushed above the stop out level in Exhibit 4.1 (the high of the dark cloud cover), some traders who were short may have hoped that the market would then turn around and decline. But in the market, there is no room for hope. Staying in a market that moves through a stop out level in the hope that prices will then turn is, as a picturesque Japanese proverb states: "To lean a ladder against the clouds."

In Exhibit 4.2, we see that a rising window emerged in April 1993. Based on candle theory, this window should be support, as it was during the September 1993 pullback. Whether a trader bought on a pullback into the window, or whether he or she was previously long, a protective sell

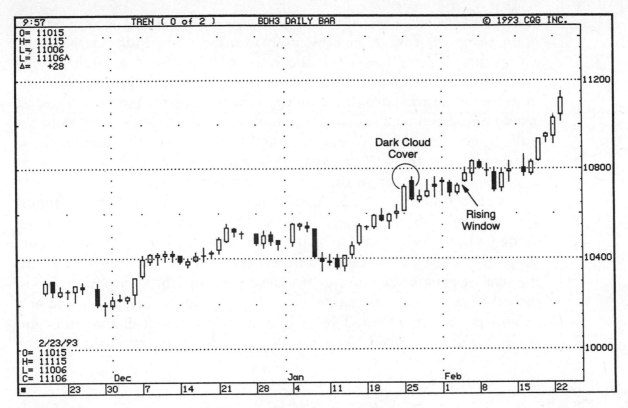

EXHIBIT 4.1. Exceeding a Dark Cloud Cover, Bonds—March 1993

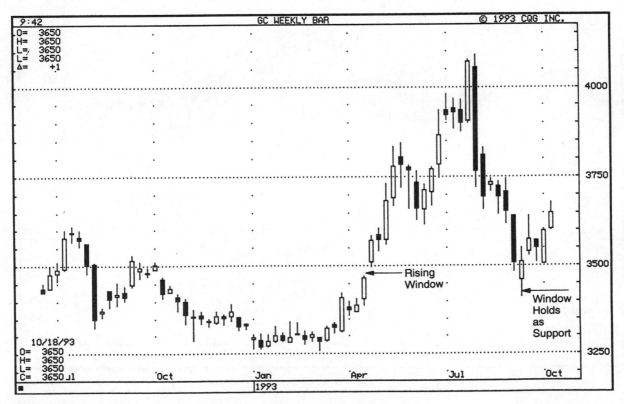

EXHIBIT 4.2. Stops and Risk Tolerance, Gold—Weekly

stop should be on a weekly close (i.e., a Friday close) under the bottom of the rising window. Note how, in this market, the window was pierced on an intra-weekly basis, but the bears did not have enough staying power to maintain prices under the bottom of the window by the close of the week. In this case, the window held as support, but not all traders would have been able to stand the emotional ride in this market as prices pulled under the window and then sprang back above the bottom of the window before the Friday close. This example illustrates how trading depends to a large extent on a trader's temperament.

As shown in Exhibit 4.3, Amgen held the rising window as support when it pulled back to there in November. The successful test of the rising window confirmed the health of the market. The rebound from the successful test of the window pushed prices above $75. At that point, the market gave some clues of trouble based on a harami pattern. Over the next few weeks, the market started to top out via a classic head and shoulders pattern denoted by S–H–S (the Japanese call the head and shoulders a *Three-Buddha Pattern*). When prices penetrated the neckline

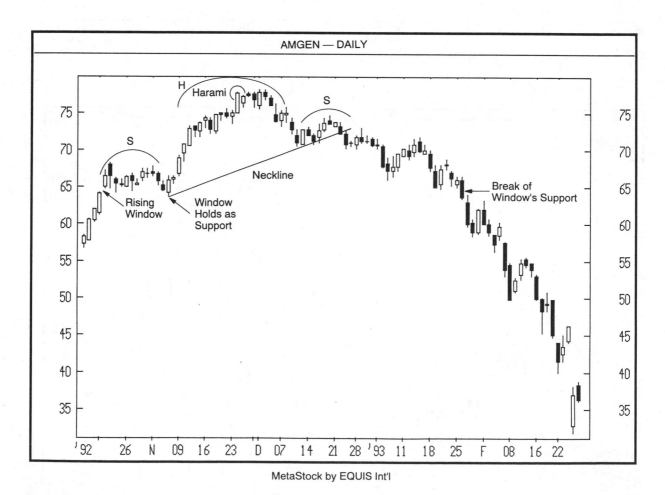

EXHIBIT 4.3.   Stops, Amgen—Daily

of this head and shoulders top, it should have been a sign for longs to exit. A final warning about the weak state of the market was given when, in early 1993, the bears finally managed to drag prices under the rising window, which heretofore had been support. This break of the window could have been another protective sell stop signal for existing longs.

RISK/REWARD

"The Side that Knows When to Fight and When Not to Will Take the Victory"

I often find that, after my seminars, people in the audience are so excited about the new "light" offered by the candles that they cannot wait to get back to their offices or homes to place a trade based on a candle pattern. However, as one of the books that I had translated stated (a trader must) "wait for time to ripen, waiting for just the right moment is virtuous, a patient mind or spirit is essential."[2] In other words, just because there is a candle pattern, it does not mean that the "time is ripe" for a trade. I try to warn my audiences that one of the most important aspects in determining the "right moment" for a trade is to inspect the risk/reward aspect of the market at the time the candle pattern is formed. In this context, a trader who was in an institutional trading group for whom I gave a special seminar wrote to me that, "You were certainly correct—a little knowledge can be dangerous. We're all running around the office shouting 'Doji, Doji.'"

A stop, by defining the risk of a trade, is one of the components of the risk and reward picture. The other component is the price target of the trade, or the potential "reward." There are many ways to determine price targets, from Elliott Wave to previous support or resistance areas. Because candle charting techniques usually do not provide a price target, I often recommend the joining of Western technicals with candles. The candles are excellent for sending a reversal or a continuation signal, while the Western tools, such as retracements or trend lines, can help provide a price target. You probably already have your own methodology to obtain price targets.

A key point to remember is that unless there is an attractive risk/reward ratio at the time the candle pattern is completed, stay away from the trade. As a Japanese proverb says, "His potential is that of the fully drawn bow—his timing the release of the trigger." The timing of the "release of the trigger" depends on the risk/reward aspect of the trade.

There will be times when you should not release the trigger. For example, without an attractive risk/reward ratio at the time that a bullish or bearish candle signal emerges, the trade should be ignored (unless a trader is using the candle signal to offset a position). Another time to step away from the market is when there is an exchange of big black candles and big white candles: "Just like it was an earthquake of magnitude 8,"[3] as one of the Japanese technical analysis books states. As this same Japanese book graphically states about trying to enter such a market, "Dying in vain is not fun."[4]

As shown in Exhibit 4.4, there was a bearish engulfing pattern in early September. Based on the concept that the high of the bearish engulfing pattern should be resistance, a trader wanting to sell short could place a protective buy stop above the high of this bearish engulfing pattern at 465. This defines the risk. To obtain a target, the trader could, for instance, look for the mid-August rising window as a support area on any price retreats. With this window as a target, the appearance of the bearish engulfing pattern made for an attractive short sale because of the relatively low risk stop as compared to the target.

In Exhibit 4.5, we see that a rally that started with a bullish engulfing pattern in January formed a rising window later that month. Two sessions after this window, the market formed a bearish engulfing pattern. A question that a trader who is looking to sell short on that signal must ask

EXHIBIT 4.4.   Candles and the Aspects of Risk/Reward, S & P—December 1993

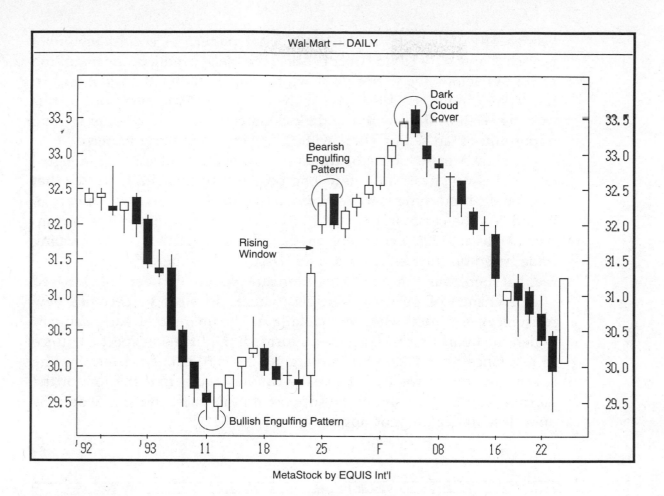

EXHIBIT 4.5. Candles and the Importance of Risk/Reward, Wal-Mart—Daily

is: "Does a short sale based on this bearish engulfing pattern offer an attractive risk/reward?." (Selling short is relatively rare in the stock market. Nonetheless, this chart can be used as a guidepost for other markets, such as futures, where short selling is more common.) Looking at the overall technical picture and considering the risk/reward aspect, such a trade would not be warranted. This is because of the rising window that preceded the bearish engulfing pattern. A short sale from this bearish engulfing pattern should mean a stop above the high of the bearish engulfing pattern. With the support at the rising window, this is not an attractive risk/reward trade since, in this case, the risk and reward are about equal. A few weeks later, a dark cloud cover arose. Now, with the high of the dark cloud cover as a stop and the window as a target, this becomes a more attractive trading opportunity from the short side.

Exhibit 4.5 underscores the difficulty of trying to determine which of the candlestick patterns is more important. In this chart, there was a bearish engulfing pattern. Normally, that pattern is considered more bearish than a dark cloud cover because the black candle of the engulfing pattern envelops the entire prior white candle, rather than just part of the white candle, as is the case with the dark cloud cover. But in this example, selling short with the dark cloud cover offered a better trading opportunity than selling short with the bearish engulfing pattern.

As shown in Exhibit 4.6, the appearance of a bullish candle signal does not always warrant a new long position. In this chart, we see that that a bullish morning star was formed by the price action on January 8, 9, and 10. The close on January 10 (the day the morning star was completed) was at $1205. Let us look at whether a buy at $1205 is an appealing trade based on the risk/reward ratio. First, to determine the reward, we see that there was a support area from late November near $1220. Based on the change of polarity principle (where old support becomes new resistance), a trader who was looking at the market in early January (when the bullish morning star was formed) might then expect a bounce to resistance near $1220. So the target is near $1220. To determine the risk in this trade, we would use the candle theory that the low of the morning star pattern should be support. In this case, the stop would be on a close under the morning star pattern at $1169.

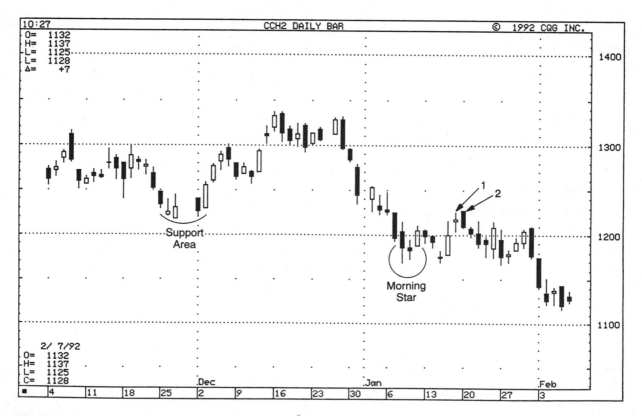

EXHIBIT 4.6.   Risk/Reward, Cocoa—March 1992

Consequently, the parameters of this trade are: buying at $1205 (at the completion of the morning star pattern), a stop at $1169, and a target near $1220. This means a $36 risk and a $15 target. Not an attractive risk/ reward trade by any stretch of the imagination! The morale of the story: do not place a trade just because a candle pattern emerges. Note how the bottom of the morning star became support a week later. The rally from there stalled at the expected $1220 resistance area via a high-wave candle at 1 and the long black real body at 2. These two candles formed a bearish engulfing pattern. Normally, a bearish engulfing pattern after such a small preceding uptrend is not too important. But in this specific case, it took an extra significance since it confirmed the $1220 resistance area.

TREND

"It is Easier to Run Down a Hill Than Up One"

There is a beautiful Japanese phrase, "as clouds to the wind and winds to the blossom." In the context of trading, I would compare the trend to the wind and the price to the clouds or blossoms, whose movements are controlled by the wind. Thus, determining where the most current price is in relation to the trend is of vital importance. This means that a candle pattern should be viewed in the context of the prevailing trend before deciding if a new position should be initiated.

The method I usually recommend for incorporating the candle patterns into the trend is to place a new trade in the direction of the prevailing trend and to offset a position when there is a reversal signal against the prevailing trend. For instance, bearish candle signals in bull trends should be used to offset longs (or to take other protective measures such as selling calls or moving up sell stop levels). But a bullish candle signal in a bull trend could be used to place a new long position. The opposite would be true in markets with major downtrends. To wit, initiating a short sale on a bearish candle signal should be the main goal in a bear market. A bullish signal in a bear market could be used to cover shorts.

There are many ways to determine trend. (In Part 2 of this book, I will reveal some popular methods of trend determination used by Japanese traders and investors.) The goal of this section is not to help you find the best way to determine trend, but to get you to think about some ways to incorporate trend into your candle analysis. In this section, I will discuss some of the more common Western methods of trend determination such as trendlines and moving averages.

For those who would like to learn more about the practical applications of some of the most popular Western technical tools, including those techniques to help determine trend, I highly recommend the book, *Technical Traders Guide to Computer Analysis of the Futures Market*, by Charles LeBeau and David Lucas (Island View Financial Group, Torrance, CA). Do not let the title of the book dissuade you if you do not use computers to trade. This book is a must for any trader who uses Western technical techniques.

One of the most basic methods of determining trend is to use a trendline. In Exhibit 4.7, we see how a resistance line from late June to early August kept the trend bearish. The candles gave some early warnings of a market that was bottoming. Specifically, the hammer in July, the morning star in early August, and a small rising window in late August (which also completed an island bottom). Yet, all these bullish signals were in the context of a bear market (as defined by the downward sloping resistance line). It was not until the break above the trendline that a new bullish trend was confirmed. Note how the rally from this breakout stalled at September's dark cloud cover. That dark cloud cover then became a resistance level.

Exhibit 4.8 shows how in early July, there was a bearish engulfing

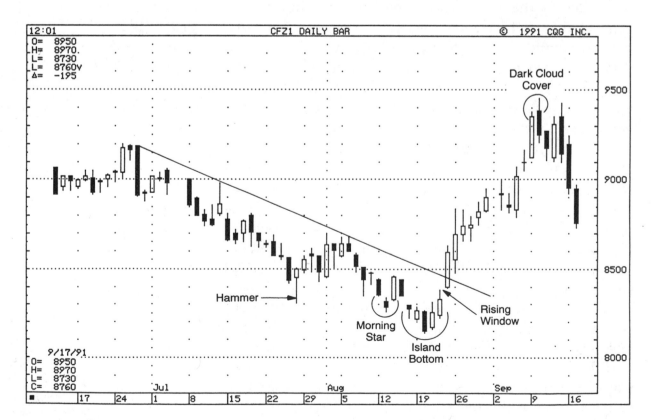

EXHIBIT 4.7.   Confirming a Trend Reversal, Coffee—December 1991

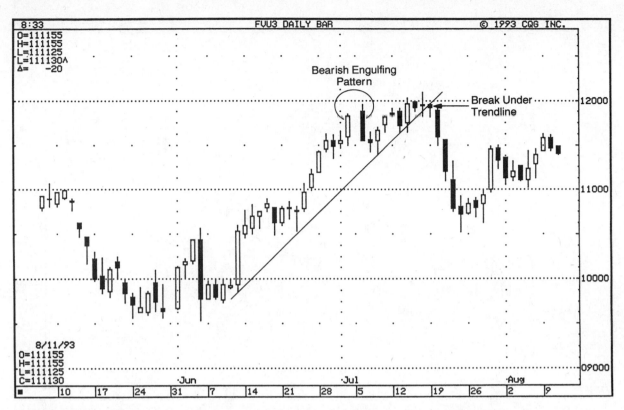

EXHIBIT 4.8.   Candle Signals and Trendlines, Five-Year Note—September 1993

pattern (the empty space was due to a holiday). But looking at the overall technical picture, including the trendline, it is obvious that a short sale based on the bearish engulfing pattern would not offer an attractive trade based on risk/reward levels. This is because the target should be the support defined by the trendline, and a stop should be above the high of the bearish engulfing pattern. The uptrend was confirmed as broken when the market closed under the trendline on July 19.

Using Exhibits 4.9(A) and (B), I show an example of how a bullish candle signal could be used as a buying opportunity on a pullback in bull trend. Exhibit 4.9(A) is a chart that shows a nicely defined uptrend support line (the more often a trendline is tested, the more important it should be). Candle 1 is shown as it looked on the morning of September 15, 1993. Since the session was not yet over, candle 1 is not yet formed for the day (remember that a completed candle needs a closing price). As shown in Exhibit 4.9(A), at the time the chart was drawn (the morning of September 15), the market had just tested a long-term uptrend support line. Shifting over to the intra-day 30-minute candle chart in Exhibit 4.9(B), note how a bullish engulfing pattern unfolded during the morning of September 15. The dashed line in Exhibit 4.9(B) represents the same trendline on the daily chart. We see how a bullish candle signal appeared during a selloff to an uptrend support line. This showed the concept that,

EXHIBIT 4.9(A).   Candles and Trendlines, Bonds—December 1993, Daily

EXHIBIT 4.9(B).   Candles and Trendlines, Bonds—December 1993, Intra-Day

in a bull trend, we look for corrections on which to buy with a bullish candle signal.

For those who use moving average to help define the trend, I illustrate in Exhibit 4.10 how to use candle signals to trade within the trend. Based on the fact that the market is under the moving average, the trend is down. In such an environment, bearish candle signals can be used to sell short and bullish candle signals should be used to cover shorts. For traders who are more risk oriented and may want to buy in a bear market, use a short-term resistance area as a target. In this example, a rally started with a harami in June. However, as the market got to the 52-week moving average resistance area, the candles reflected increased selling pressure as shown by the long upper shadow candle at 1 and the long black real body candle at 2. For traders who bought at the harami, the resistance area defined by the moving average should be an area to liquidate. For those who were looking to go in the same direction as the overall trend (in this case, sell on bounces), then the aforementioned bearish candle

EXHIBIT 4.10. Trading with the Trend, International Paper—Daily

signals could be used to sell short. The falling window showed that the bears gave the market an extra pull lower. The long white candles in mid-July was a hint of strength. The rally from these candles stopped via a doji that stalled at the moving average resistance area. This was an extremely attractive short sale since that doji area was not only at the 52-week moving average, but it was also at the falling window's resistance area. Note how after this sell-off the market bounced back after 9 record session lows.

BECOMING A MARKET CHAMELEON

"An Army Manages its Victory in Accordance with the Situation of the Enemy"

When first placing a trade, you have expectations about how the market should act. However, the market is fluid, ever flowing, and ever changing. As a result, you must continually monitor the market's path to see if price action performs according to your expectations. If not, you will have to take appropriate action. Adapting to changing market conditions is what I call being a *market chameleon*. Being a market chameleon, that is, quickly and effectively adapting to a new market environment, is a vital element to successful trading. There is an appropriate quote that I heard years ago. It compares trading to fencing. It said that in trading, as in fencing, there are the quick and the dead. Being a market chameleon means that you are quick enough to adapt to the market so as to "live" to trade another day.

When a trader has a market opinion, there should be a price that tells him or her that their market forecast is wrong. I will look at this aspect in Exhibit 4.11. In that chart, there was a dark cloud cover in the latter part of October. At that point, I turned bearish on this market because a confluence of technical factors hinted that prices would not close above $36. There were four reasons to expect any rallies to stall in the $35.50–$36.00 area. These were:

1. The high of the dark cloud cover at $35.50 should become a resistance area.
2. A small falling window provides resistance near $36.
3. The lows of the three session prior to the falling window were near $36. Based on the concept that old support becomes resistance, this $36 support should be converted to resistance.
4. A Fibonacci 62% retracement of the decline from A to B was near $35.50.

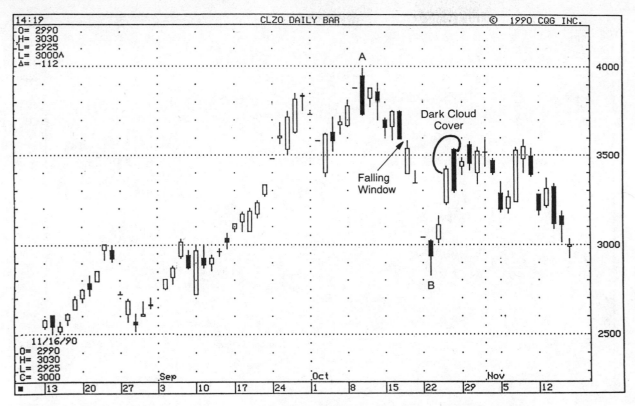

EXHIBIT 4.11. Looking for a Price to Adjust a Market Opinion, Crude Oil—
December 1990

In this case, if the bulls had enough force to close prices above the top end of my $35.50–$36.00 resistance area, I would then have had to change my bearish stance. In other words, I would have had to adapt to new market conditions. We can see that although the bulls tried for a few weeks after the dark cloud cover to push the market above the top end of the $35.50–$36.00 resistance area, they failed.

Exhibit 4.12 displays a resistance area in late December near $20 that was verified by a hanging man and bearish engulfing pattern (the space between these two candles was due to a holiday). The price slide that began near this $20 area tried to stabilize in early January near the $19 support area from the month before. The long black real body of January 12 broke this $19 support. Thus, up until that time, all the signals coming from the market were negative. However, candle clues that the market was changing its complexion came with the high-wave candle after the long black real body. Another warning about having to adjust from a bearish view to a more constructive view about the market came the following week with the morning star pattern. Final proof of a turn-around came with a rising window.

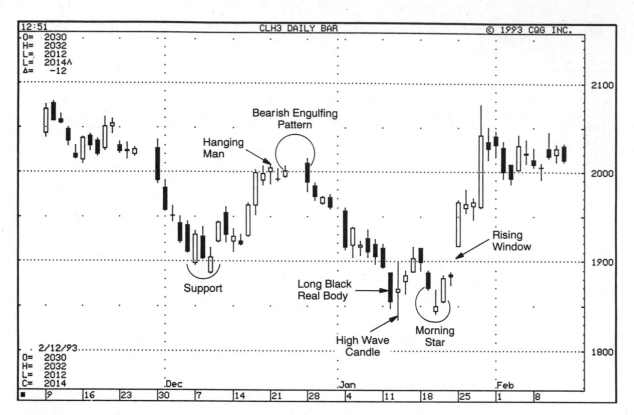

EXHIBIT 4.12.   Being a Chameleon by Adapting to the Market, Crude Oil—March 1993

COMPUTERS AND CANDLES

"Even Beautiful Things Have Disadvantages and Must be Used with Caution"

Many technical analysts base their trading strategies on computer testing. With the widespread use of computers and the popularity of candles, there may be traders who may want to use computers to find the most important or reliable candle patterns. For those who may decide to do such testing, I think it is important that other aspects, besides just having the computer pick out the candle patterns, must be taken into account with such testing. That is the focus of this section.

The Importance of Where a Candle Pattern Appears

As discussed previously, one should never view a candle signal without seeing the pattern in the context of what happened before the pattern appeared. This aspect is related to a question frequently asked of me—which are the most important candle patterns? In answering this, I first suggest thinking about what the pattern is relaying about the market's action. For example, in comparing a dark cloud cover with a bearish engulfing pattern, I would normally consider the bearish engulfing pattern as more important. This is based on the fact that the second session of the bearish engulfing pattern has a close under the prior white real body. The dark cloud cover's second session, however, has a close within the prior white real body. As such, the bearish engulfing pattern shows that the bears had more control of the market as compared to the dark cloud cover (see Exhibit 4.13).

But candle patterns can never be viewed in isolation. A trader always has to consider the surrounding technical picture. For example, a dark cloud cover that arises at a major resistance area should be construed as being more likely a reversal than would a bearish engulfing pattern that is not at resistance. An instance of the danger of looking at a pattern in isolation is shown in Exhibit 4.5 on page 135 where, because of risk/reward considerations, a dark cloud cover offered a more attractive trade than did a bearish engulfing pattern. Thus, looking at a candle pattern in isolation can be a dangerous procedure. As was nicely expressed to me by a Japanese trader, "where you stand is more important than an individual pattern." As a result, if you decide to test out the reliability of the candle patterns, remember not to just use a buy or sell signal based solely on the candle pattern. You must first factor into your analysis just where the pattern emerged.

The Question of Determining Specific Criteria for the Pattern

The candle patterns are based on sound psychological reasoning. (Think about what happens with a dark cloud cover. After a strong white session, the market opens higher and then closes well under the white session's close. Doesn't that clearly illustrate how the bears have managed to wrest control from the bulls?) But candles, unlike mathematically

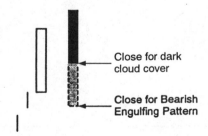

Close for dark
cloud cover

Close for Bearish
Engulfing Pattern

EXHIBIT 4.13. Comparing a
Dark Cloud Cover With a Bearish
Engulfing Pattern

concrete numbers, such as moving averages or oscillators, may not be easily adaptable to computer testing. A moving average either is, or isn't, above yesterday's close. This is a yes–no choice for the computer. But candle signals are not this clear-cut, and subjectivity is required in determining what is or is not a candle pattern.

A classic dark cloud cover should have the close of the black candle session more than halfway into the prior white's real body. That is a rule that can be quantified. But what if there were a less than ideal dark cloud cover in which the close of the black candlestick session did not get more than halfway into the prior white session's real body? That, based on the standard definition of a dark cloud cover, would not be a dark cloud cover pattern and the computer might not pick up such a pattern. The question then becomes: What happens when a less than ideal dark cloud cover shows up near a resistance area? Does a computer read that as a dark cloud cover or does it ignore the pattern? In such a scenario, I would say that the less than ideal dark cloud cover should be viewed as being just as bearish as a more traditional dark cloud cover. This is the scenario that unfolded in Exhibit 4.14. Note the annotation that has a question

EXHIBIT 4.14. Candles and Subjectivity, Bank America—Daily

mark after the term "dark cloud cover." This was not an ideal dark cloud cover because the close did not move under the center of the prior white candle. However, although this was not an ideal dark cloud cover, I still viewed it as a dark cloud cover for a few reasons. First was the extremely long upper shadow of the black candle of the pattern. This showed how quickly prices retreated from the new highs. In addition, by the close of this black candle, the market was technically damaged because the bears were able to drag prices back under a prior high (marked H on the chart). This formed a bearish upthrust. Finally, the lower close after the dark cloud cover helped confirm the market's inherent weakness.

Thus, even the most basic step of having the computer find the candle pattern may cause problems. So, for those using a computer to pick out the candle patterns, remember that the candle patterns should be used as guideposts. While the ideal patterns may be relatively easy to quantify, the less than ideal patterns are often useful trading signals that should also be accounted for. In this context, there is a large degree of subjectivity required. This is no different from standard bar chart pattern recognition.

Placing the Trade

If a candle pattern emerges, does that mean that a buy or sell signal is automatically given? Of course not. As I previously discussed, you should not base a trade on a candle pattern in isolation. You must first determine the overall technical picture at the time the pattern forms.

As an example of this aspect, let us consider a shooting star. A computer program that bases a sell signal on the shooting star alone would have given an improper sell signal if that shooting star also formed a rising window (this scenario unfolded in Exhibit 3.49 on page 98). Thus, having a computer signal a trade just because a candle pattern emerges, and ignoring the overall technical picture (i.e., the major trend, the price action preceding the candle pattern, etc.), could be a mistake.

Another aspect is the concept of risk/reward discussed early in this chapter. Just because a pattern appears does not mean that one should place a trade on the candle signal. For example, what if there is a morning star in gold, but the risk for the trade is $15 and your objective is also $15? Would a long position on that pattern be warranted? In this case, the answer is no. Whether a trade is warranted or not is dependent on the risk/reward parameters of the market at the time the pattern is formed.

As an example of this, in Exhibit 4.15, I show two hammers. Hammers are potentially bullish signals, but the risk/reward aspect of each of these

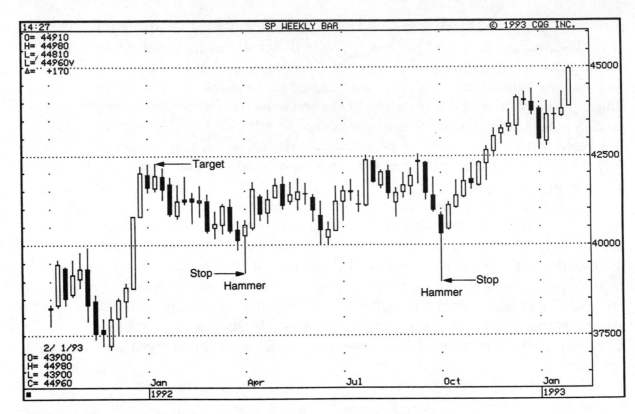

EXHIBIT 4.15.   Risk/Reward Aspects of a Trade, S & P—Weekly

hammers would not justify a long trade. In both cases, there would have been a 15–20 point risk (based on a stop under the hammer's lows) for a possible 20–25 point target (based on the resistance area near 425). Thus, an automatic buy based on a computer trading program would have worked in this example because the market rallied from both hammers. Nonetheless, these buy signals would not have been a trade based on sound money management principles since the risk would have been too large for the potential reward.

When to Offset a Trade

Placing a stop may be relatively easy with a computer (some testing is even done without stops—a very dangerous procedure and one that defeats the concept of a risk management approach to trading), but how is an objective picked? One time, a trader's objective may be last week's lows, but maybe on the next trade, the objective will be a support line, or maybe a 50% retracement. Every trader has his or her own style, so be sure to take this into account when merging candles and computers.

Exhibit 4.16 shows an evening star pattern and a bullish engulfing

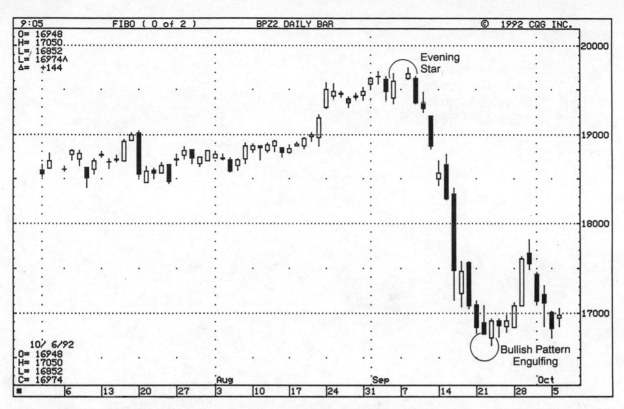

EXHIBIT 4.16. Candles and Price Targets, British Pound—December 1992

pattern. After the bullish engulfing pattern, an up leg could be expected. However, the price target of such a rally would be based on other technical tools besides candles since candles do not usually give targets.

Based on the concept that old support becomes resistance, a trader might have been looking for a move to the July–August support area near $1.85. For that trader, this trade would not have been successful. However, another trader who uses Fibonacci retracements may have been more successful since the market made a Fibonacci 38% bounce of the entire move from the September highs to the September lows. Since the first trader's $1.85 target was not met, he would say that the bullish candle signal was not reliable. Yet, for the second trader, whose target (the 38% bounce) was reached, the bullish candle signal was successful. Thus, each trader's style must be taken into account when looking at testing the candles' reliability.

How you trade with candlesticks will depend on your trading philosophy, your risk adversity, and temperament. These are very individual aspects. If you decide to test the candle patterns or use computers to help you trade with candles, it should be based on trading criteria and rules chosen by you. Only by applying the candles to your markets, with your own trading style, can you discover whether the candles will give you that extra edge.

Notes

[1]Sakata, Goho, p. 46.
[2]Sakata, Goho, p. 46.
[3]Sakata, Goho, p. 70.
[4]Sakata, Goho, p. 70.

PART 2

THE DISPARITY INDEX AND NEW PRICE CHARTS

故きを温ねて新しきを知る

''Consider the Past and You Will Know the Future''

INTRODUCTION

....

$\mathbf{A}$ Japanese book on technical analysis insightfully stated that, "The market is a tug of war where the strategy is to overrun the enemy territory. In a tug of war, once the balance of power is lost, one side is pulled and the result is decided. The market often acts this way, and one should pay attention to the balance of powers."[1] The new (at least in the West) techniques addressed in Part 2 of this book will help you determine whether it is the bulls or bears who have the "balance of power."

A widely used Japanese tool is the disparity index. It is similar to Western dual moving averages, but this technique allows for better market timing than do the traditional Western moving average techniques. The disparity index is addressed in Chapter 5.

The charts detailed in Chapters 6, 7, and 8 are called three-line break charts, renko charts, and kagi charts. Of the three, the kagi is probably the most popular, followed by the three-line break and then the renko chart. These charts are most closely comparable to the Western point and figure charts. However, it is not necessary to understand point and figure charts to understand any of these Japanese charts.

Just as candle charts predate bar charts, the three-line break, renko, and kagi charts predate point and figure charts. These charts are based on generations of use in the Far East. A member of the Nippon Technical Analysts Association told me that he had seen a kagi chart of the rice market dated 1876. However, my research shows that unlike candlestick charting, which has a rich history, there is very little historical reference material for the three-line, renko, and kagi charting techniques. This is probably because candles are more colorful, offer more flexibility and are more widely used. In contrast, the three-line, renko, and kagi charts are more rigid, offering less room for subjective interpretation, and their use has mostly been limited to the management level of Japanese financial firms.

As bar charts differ from point and figure charts, the three-line break, renko, and kagi charts differ from candle charts. With candle charts, a new candle line is added to the chart at every session, whether the price of that session makes a new high, a new low, or is unchanged. With the charting techniques to be addressed in the rest of this book, prices must go to a new high or low before a line on the chart can be added. Since the market has to go to a *new* high or low, I have entitled Part 2 ''The Disparity Index and New Price Charts.''

Another difference between candle charts and the three-line break, renko, and kagi charts is that these new techniques ignore time and are dependent only on price changes. Since the market is not controlled by time, but by price movement in these charts, the traditional Japanese methodology of drawing them does not include time on the horizontal axis. However, in the charts in this second half of the book, I have included a rough measure of time on the horizontal axis to help provide reference points for my discussions.

The three-line break, renko, and kagi charts share similarities with one another, but there are discrete and interesting differences between each of these charting methods. Each chart and its related techniques will be described in detail later, in their respective chapters. For some of these new techniques, a trader will need to choose a pre-specified reversal amount in order to draw a reversal line. In others, it is the market action that will provide the signal to draw a new line. While the three-line break, renko, and kagi charts may be different from one another, they are all powerful weapons that should be part of a trader's technical arsenal. Some of the advantages of these new charts include:

1. Making support, resistance, and congestion areas more evident
2. Capturing the significant moves by filtering out irregular price fluctuations
3. Making the market's overall trend more apparent
4. Providing a broader view of the market by compressing the price action and offering a longer term perspective
5. Helping to determine the time to offset positions: Because the candles do not, as a general rule, provide a price target, the reversal signals sent out by these new techniques can be used to exit a market position

6. Providing a means of technical analysis for markets that supply only closes. This is because these techniques require only the closing prices. Thus, mutual funds and yields on financial instruments such as T-bonds can be analyzed using a three-line break, renko, or kagi chart.

Because three-line break, renko and kagi charts are slower to react than candle charts, they are frequently used by longer term investors. However, traders with shorter time frame orientations will find that these charting tools provide a practical and powerful method to determine trend direction. Once the trend is determined, candle signals can be used to trade in the direction of the prevailing trend.

As will be explained in the upcoming chapters, the sensitivity to the three-line break, renko, or kagi charts can be adjusted by changing reversal criteria. With each of these charts, I will show you how to adjust the chart's sensitivity. Short-term traders may want to make the charts more sensitive to the underlying price action. Those who are more concerned about a broader market perspective may want to use a chart with larger reversal amounts so as to get more information on a chart. This should help to obtain a historical perspective. This brings out another important advantage of these new charts; by changing the reversal criteria for these charts, a trader can adjust the sensitivity of the charts to his or her trading needs.

Generally, the more sensitive the chart, the greater the number of trading signals and the greater is the possibility of whipsaws, but the sooner it may get you into a new trend. A disadvantage of large reversal amounts is that by the time the trend reversal is made the market will be more distant from the top or bottom.

Choosing a reversal is subjective and dependent upon many aspects, including the market's volatility, the price of the underlying commodity or stock, a trader's trading style, and his or her time frame orientation and risk tolerance. Consequently, I will not attempt to find the optimum reversal amount, but I will let you know some of the more popular reversal criteria used by Japanese traders.

These new price charts are usually less flexible than are candle charts. This is because, with candle charts, there are more graduations of a reversal signal. For example, a small real body after an uptrend could be viewed as a slowing of upside momentum, but not necessarily as a price reversal. For the new techniques in Part 2, prices either do or do not provide reversal signals.

An important principle about trading with these new charts is that they are usually based on closing prices, so a reversal signal is not confirmed until the close. By that time, the reversal amount may well be exceeded. For example, if the reversal amount is $2, the market would have to close either higher or lower by $2, but by the time the market closes, it could be $4 higher or lower. As a result, a trader could lose $2 of a potential move. Some Japanese traders circumvent this problem by initiating a light position if the reversal amount is met or exceeded on an intra-session basis. If the market then closes by the reversal amount, they can either add more at the close or wait for a correction to add more. If the market fails to confirm the reversal by the close, the traders would offset the light position they had earlier added.

Most commonly the closing price of the day or week is used to construct the three-line break, renko, or kagi charts. Because of this, the focus of Chapters 6 through 8 will be on daily and weekly charts. However, some traders in Japan use intra-day kagi charts (three-line break or renko charts are not normally used on an intra-day basis—perhaps these charts have been less successful than intra-day kagi charts). Thus, for traders who have the time and the data, kagi charts can be constructed on an intra-day basis using tick-by-tick data.

Chapter 6 will discuss the three-line break chart, Chapter 7 the renko chart, and Chapter 8 the kagi chart. Each chapter will be segmented the same way. Each of these three chapters will begin with an *Overview* to give a flavor of the technique. Do not worry that if, after the overview, you do not have a grasp of the technique. That will come with each chapter's next section—*Construction*. This is where I provide a step-by-step written and visual guide to building the chart.

After completing the section on constructing the chart, you should have a full understanding of the underlying technique. The *Trading Techniques* section, at the conclusion of each chapter, will then show you the more popular trading techniques for that charting method. At the ends of Chapters 6, 7, and 8, I have supplied the data necessary for you to draw practice three-line break, renko, and kagi charts. The answer charts are provided on the pages following each of these sessions.

There are many ways to trade with these new charts. While I will focus on some of the more popular trading techniques used in Japan, these are by no means all of them. With almost every Japanese trader to whom I spoke, or every article or book that I had translated, I came away with a new trading technique. This tells me that the three-line break, renko, and kagi charts are limited only by your trading imagination. Consequently, my goal in Part 2 is to help you build a solid foundation upon which the scaffolding of your own ideas can be built.

Note

[1]Oyama, Kenji, p. 52.

CHAPTER 5

HOW THE JAPANESE USE MOVING AVERAGES

....

石の上にも三年

"Money Grows on the Tree of Patience"

In Japan, as in the West, moving averages are used as a valuable trading tool. Some of Japan's moving averages techniques include golden and dead crosses, the disparity index, and the moving average divergence. Based on my work and discussions with Japanese traders, it appears that the most popular moving averages are the 5-, 9-, or 25-day averages for shorter term traders, and for longer term traders, the 13-, 26-week or the 75- and 200-day moving averages. However, just as in the West, many Japanese traders have their favorite moving averages.

THE GOLDEN AND DEAD CROSS

The Japanese use dual moving averages in which they compare short- and long-term averages. For example, they will compare the 13- week and 26-week moving averages. As shown in Exhibit 5.1, if a shorter term moving average crosses over the longer term moving average, it is viewed as a bullish sign. The Japanese call such a crossover a *golden cross*. A *dead cross* is a bearish indication that occurs when a short-term moving average crosses under the longer term moving average.

In Exhibit 5.2, the 26-week moving average is shown as a solid line, and the 13-week moving average as a dashed line. When the shorter term moving average moved under the longer term average in July 1992 it

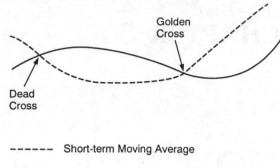

EXHIBIT 5.1. Golden and Dead Cross

------- Short-term Moving Average

——— Long-term Moving Average

created a bearish dead cross. In November 1992, the 13-week moving average went above the 26-week moving average, thus completing a bullish golden cross. Observe how the hanging man session in May 1993 (which, during the next session, became part of a bearish engulfing pattern) hinted at a correction, as did the dead cross a few session earlier.

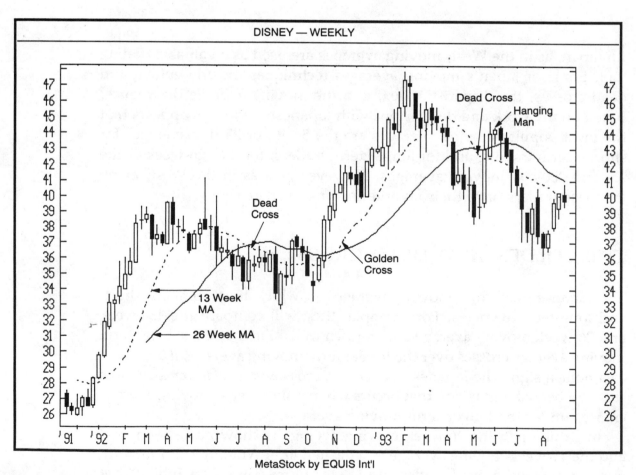

MetaStock by EQUIS Int'l

EXHIBIT 5.2. Golden and Dead Crosses, Disney–Weekly

THE DISPARITY INDEX

The disparity index (or disparity ratio), compares, as a percentage, the latest close to a chosen moving average. For example, when the 13-week disparity index is −25%, it means that the market, based on the close, is 25% under the 13-week moving average. A 200-day disparity index of +12% means that the current close is 12% above the 200-day moving average.

The Japanese will say, for example, that, "the separation between the price and the 13-week moving average expanded to 50%" or "that the market was an unusual 31% below its 13-week moving average." These are references to the disparity index in which the current price is compared to, in both of these cases, the 13-week moving average.

Exhibit 5.3 shows an example using a 9-day disparity index. Looking at that exhibit:

Area 1. When the disparity index is at 0 (shown at 1), it means that today's price is the same as the chosen moving average (in this case, the 9-day moving average).

Area 2. When the disparity line is under 0, it means that today's price is a percentage under the chosen moving average. At period 2, for instance, the current close is 12% below the 9-day moving average.

Area 3. When the disparity line is above 0, it means that today's price is a certain percentage above the chosen moving average. For instance, at point 3 in Exhibit 5.3, today's price is 15% above the 9-day moving average.

Trading with the Disparity Index

In much of the material I had translated there were often references that the market should be at a high- or low-price level before acting on a

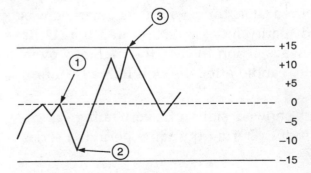

EXHIBIT 5.3.   The Disparity Index

candlestick reversal pattern. An example: "The probability is high that at a low-price level, a harami cross is a signal that the bottom is near and a harami cross at a high-price level is a signal that the market is close to a top."[1] Another example: "If the koma (this is the Japanese term for a spinning top or a small real body candle) appears after some indication that the market is at a low price, then to an extent, one can buy some and feel at ease."[2]

Of course, the question arises as to what constitutes a high- or low-price area. Some traders have their own methodology to determine whether the market is at a high or low price. They may, for example, consider it at a low area if the market is near a major support area, or if it is at a 50% retracement area. Other traders may gauge high or low levels on the relative strength index or stochastics, or on an Elliott wave count.

A method used by some Japanese to determine whether the market is at a high- or low-price is by using the disparity index. This is because the disparity index is an effective mechanism to show if the market is oversold or overbought. Remember that an oversold environment unfolds when prices descend too quickly. In theory, the more oversold the market, the more vulnerable it becomes to a bounce. An overbought market is when prices ascend too far too fast, thus making the market susceptible to a correction. In this regard, a high disparity index reading can show that the market is overbought and a low disparity index could reflect an oversold market.

Exhibit 5.4 typifies how the disparity index can offer value-added analysis to a candle chart. Note than an oversold or overbought indication based on the disparity index will depend on the individual market and the chosen disparity index. For this stock, when the 13-week disparity index reached the +10% area, the market became overbought. At a disparity index near −10%, the market becomes oversold. By using this extra information imparted by the disparity ratio in Exhibit 5.4, we can get more confirmation of candle signals. Specifically:

1. As touched upon in Chapter 2, a doji becomes a more viable signal if it appears in an oversold or overbought market environment. In this case, the doji at 1 emerged at a time when the market was oversold (as gauged by the disparity index). This hinted that Delta was ripe for a bounce or sideways action to ease the market's oversold condition. The long white candle after the doji helped confirm the bullish implications.

2. At time period 2, the market showed signs of overheating, as reflected by the high disparity index. During the same period, a series

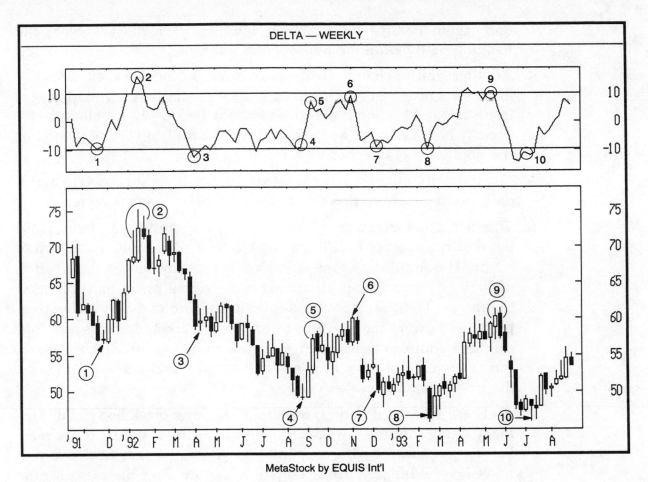

DELTA — WEEKLY

MetaStock by EQUIS Int'l

EXHIBIT 5.4.   The Disparity Index as Overbought/Oversold Indicator, Delta—Weekly and 13-Week Disparity Index

of long upper shadow candles demonstrated that the bears were aggressively dragging down prices from the $75 area.

3. The candle at session 3, with its long upper and lower shadow, was a high-wave candle. This candle was also the second session of a harami pattern. Both of these were signs that the market was losing its prior downward and directional bias. These candle patterns coincided with a low disparity index. This combination of candle signals and the oversold disparity index reading implied that either a bounce or sideways activity could be expected. An oversold condition can be relieved in one of two ways: either by a sharp bounce or by sideways action (the Japanese call sideways price activity *box action* since prices look like they are locked in a box). After this harami, the market traded laterally for two months. By this "box action," the disparity index moved off its low reading. This showed that the market was no longer oversold. As a result of not being oversold, the market

once again became vulnerable to another move lower. (Note the hanging man before the renewed price decline.)

4. Another doji appeared at the same time as the 13-week disparity index was near −10%. This should tell a trader that the market was in an oversold environment that should be closely monitored—especially because of the doji. The tall white candle on the session after the doji completed a morning doji star pattern.

5. The disparity index moving towards an overbought condition and a dark cloud cover warned that the upside drive was losing force.

6. This is a good example of how the disparity index can help avoid buying in a market that is vulnerable to a correction. A tall white candle at 6 implied a stronger market lay ahead. However, a +10% disparity index reading at that time showed that prices had ascended too far too fast (i.e., became overbought). The disparity index thus provided a warning sign not to buy the market. It turns out that candle 6 completed a last engulfing top pattern (in which a white candle envelops a black candle in an uptrend) that was confirmed by the next session's weaker close.

7., 8. These black real bodies, especially the long black body at 8, normally imply continued weakness. But the oversold nature of the market, as measured by the disparity index, hinted that further down moves were unlikely. Also, the white candle after the black candle at 7 had a long lower shadow. This also offset some of the bearishness of the black candle.

9. A classic combination of an overheated market (based on the elevated disparity index) and a bearish candle pattern (the bearish engulfing pattern). The fact that this bearish engulfing pattern appeared at the resistance area from October 1992 (at 6) further reinforced the outlook that Delta was at an important technical juncture.

10. Here we see how an oversold market joined with a bullish candle signal (the hammer at 10) strongly hinted of higher prices to come.

In this chart, the 13-week disparity index gave extreme readings in the ±10% area. However, the markets you follow will probably have different disparity zones that act as an overbought or oversold reading, so it pays to experiment.

As discussed above, the disparity index is a useful tool to weigh whether the market is overbought or oversold. As shown in Exhibit 5.5, the +15% and −15% readings on the 13-period disparity index reflect times when this market becomes overbought and oversold. Overbought

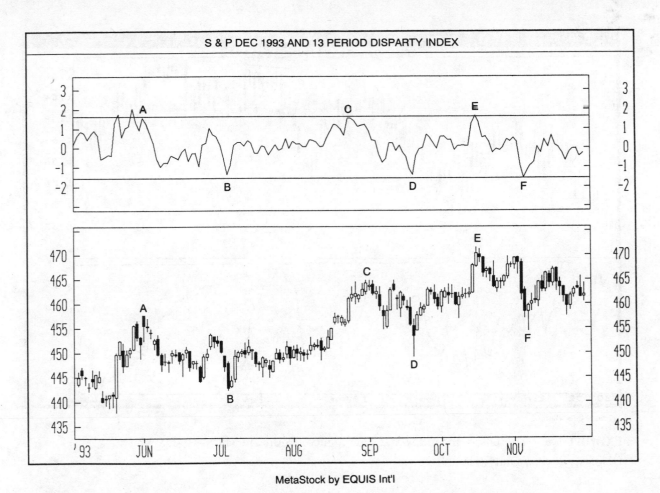

S & P DEC 1993 AND 13 PERIOD DISPARTY INDEX

MetaStock by EQUIS Int'l

EXHIBIT 5.5. The Disparity Index as a Trend Indicator, S & P December 1993, and 13-Day Disparity Index

readings occurred at time frames A, C, and E, while oversold indications arrived at time frames B, D, and F. However, in between these over-bought and oversold levels, the disparity index could be used as a tool of trend determination. In this context, while the disparity index is ex-panding, it conveys a bull trend. If the disparity index declines, it echoes a bear trend. In Exhibit 5.5, note that between the overbought reading at A and the oversold reading at B, the index was in a downtrend. This confirmed that the price trend was also down. This bearish confirmation with a falling disparity index came from C to D and from E to F. Bull trends were corroborated via an ascending disparity index from B to C and from D to E.

Exhibit 5.6 shows another use for the disparity index, that of a tool to monitor divergence. Note the downward sloping dashed line on the disparity index connecting the peaks at A and B. At the same time the disparity index was at B, prices had made a new high for the move—yet

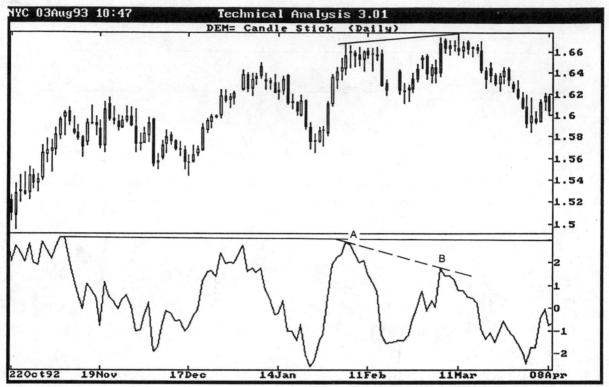

NYC 03Aug93 10:47   Technical Analysis 3.01
                    DEM= Candle Stick (Daily)

Reuters Graphics

EXHIBIT 5.6.   The Disparity Index and Divergence, Deutsche Mark—13-Day
Disparity Index, Daily Spot

the disparity index at B was lower than it was at A. This created a bearish
negative divergence in which prices reached a new high and the disparity
index did not.

THE DIVERGENCE INDEX

The Japanese also have a moving average oscillator called the *divergence
index*. The name is derived from the fact that this technique measures
how far the price diverges from the chosen moving average. The divergence is calculated by taking the current price and dividing it by the
chosen moving average. Thus, a 13-day divergence of 102% would mean
that the close today is 102% of the 13-day moving average. A 200-day
divergence of 97% would mean that today's price is 97% of the 200-day
moving average.

The divergence is the same as the disparity index; it is just scaled

3 line brk

date	future	long	short	in	out	profit/(loss)	current	points	$ amts
10/21/97	cch8		x	1665.00	0	0	1636.000	29.00	290
10/23/97	cdm8		x	72.63	0	0	71.840	0.79	790
10/23/97	cdh8		x	72.58	0	0	71.600	0.98	980
10/23/97	pbk8	x		63.50	63	-20	63.500	0.00	0
10/23/97	cu8	x		297.50	291.5	-300	297.500	0.00	0
10/23/97	suk8		x	11.80	0	0	11.760	0.04	44.8
10/23/97	sun8		x	11.66	0	0	11.660	0.00	0
10/23/97	lhm8	x		66.38	0	0	65.850	-0.53	-212
10/23/97	lcq8	x		70.15	0	0	69.800	-0.35	-140
10/23/97	cdz7		x	72.20	0	0	71.270	0.93	930
10/23/97	pbg8	x		64.40	63.15	-50	64.400	0.00	0
10/23/97	lcg8		x	69.20	0	0	68.700	0.50	200
10/24/97	lcz7	x		67.80	0	0	67.250	-0.55	-220
10/25/97	edz7	x		94.17	0	0	94.205	0.03	87.5
							2750.3		
							2380.3		30.85	2750.3

EMP# D# EMPLOYEE-NAME	TOTAL-HRS	REG-HRS	OVERTM-HRS	HOLDAY-HRS	SICK-HRS	VACATION (PAY-PERIOD)	GRAT-$	CTIPS-$	OTHER-$
106 04 JESSICA BORSARI									
106 05									
107 03 JAMES M CROWELL									
107 05									
107 07									
108 07 JOHATHAN T GRADY									
109 03 ERICA SMITH									
109 05									
110 07 MIGUEL FERNANDEZ									

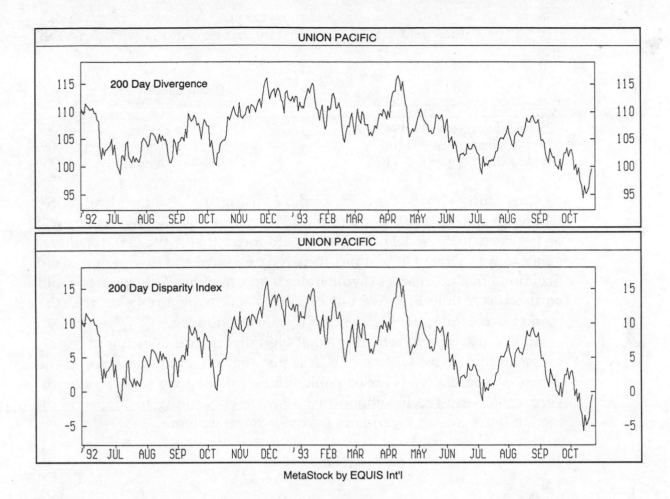

EXHIBIT 5.7. 200-Day Divergence and Disparity Index

differently. For example, a 13-day divergence of 102% means that the market is 2% above the 13-day moving average. A 13-day disparity reading of +2% also means that the market is 2% above the 13-day moving average. In other words, a divergence of 102% is the same as the disparity index being +2%. A divergence of 93% has the same implications as a −7% disparity index.

Exhibit 5.7 shows the disparity index and the divergence indicator on the same stock for the same time period. Note that the lines are the same; it is just the way the vertical scale reads that is different. Thus, all the techniques used for the disparity index would be the same as those used for the divergence index.

Just as many computer system traders experiment with moving averages, so you may want to consider experimenting with divergence. As an example of this, I have the following study done in the 1980s by the Japanese to statistically test the Nikkei with its divergence.[3]

All the values below are within 2 standard deviations (95% probability):

Divergence in a rising market:	Divergence in a falling market:
25-day divergence 99–104%	25-day divergence 96–101%
75-day divergence 100–107%	75-day divergence 93–100%
200-day divergence 102–110%	200-day divergence 90–99%

This study shows that, for example, using the 200-day divergence, when the Nikkei is rising, there is a 95% chance that the divergence will be between 102% and 110%. This would mean that if the 200-day divergence moves above 110%, it is considered excessive and there is increased likelihood that the market is vulnerable to a correction. This concept could be used as a time to move out of long positions in the belief that the market is reaching the high end of its current bull leg.

In this discussion, remember that high divergence does not necessarily mean that prices will reverse. It is just that the market may be in the throes of speculative fever or panic selling (in the case of low value divergences), and the likelihood of the move continuing in the same direction decreases as divergence becomes more extreme.

Notes

[1]Hoshi, Kazutaka, p. 107.

[2]Ishii, Katsutoshi, p. 52.

[3]*Analysis of Stock Price in Japan.* Tokyo, Japan: Nippon Technical Analysts Association 1986, pg. 104.

CHAPTER 6

THREE-LINE BREAK CHARTS

石橋をたたいて渡る

"Weigh the Situation, Then Move"

A Japanese trader described the three-line break chart as a "more subtle form of point and figure charts where reversals are decided by the market and not by arbitrary rules. That means we can gear it to the strength and dynamism of the market."[1]

As shown in Exhibit 6.1, the three-line break chart looks like a series of white and black blocks of varying heights. A new block is in a separate column. Each of these blocks is called a *line*. Using the closing price, a new white line is added if the previous high is exceeded and a new black line is drawn if the market reaches a new low for the move. If there is neither a new high nor a low, nothing is drawn.

If a rally (sell-off) is powerful enough to form three consecutive white lines (three black lines), then the low of the last three white lines (the high of the last three black lines) has to be exceeded before the opposite color line is drawn (this procedure is explained in detail later in this section). The term "three-line break" comes from the fact that the market has to "break" above (or below) the prior three lines before a new opposite color line is drawn. Here again, as discussed in my first book, we see the importance of the number "three" in Japanese technicals.

A major advantage of the three-line break chart is that there is no arbitrary fixed reversal amount. It is the market's action that will give the indication of a reversal.

Other names for the three-line break chart include:

1. three-step new price;
2. new price three-line break;

3. surpassing three lines;
4. the three-line turnaround method; and
5. new price three-step bars.

CONSTRUCTION OF THE THREE-LINE BREAK CHART

For the following explanation detailing construction of the three-line break chart, I use the data in Table 6.1. This data is used to construct the three-line break chart shown in Exhibit 6.1.

The three-line break chart is based on closing prices. The price at which the chart is started is called the base price.

OUR EXAMPLE: The base price is
135.

TABLE 6.1 Prices for the Three-Line Break Chart Displayed in Exhibit 6.1

Session	Closing Price	Session	Closing Price
1	135	21	165–
2	132↓	22	168↑
3	128↓	23	171↑
4	133–	24	173↑
5	130–	25	169–
6	130–	26	177↑
7	132–	27	180↑
8	134–	28	176–
9	139↑	29	170↓↓
10	137–	30	175–
11	145↑	31	179–
12	158↑	32	173–
13	147–	33	170–
14	143–	34	170–
15	150–	35	168↓
16	149–	36	165↓
17	160↑	37	171–
18	164↑	38	175–
19	167↑	39	179↑↑
20	156↓↓	40	175–

Legend
  ↑—New high: white line drawn.
  ↓—New low: black line drawn.
  (–)—Price within prior range: no line drawn.
  ↑↑—White: turnaround line.
  ↓↓—Black: turnaround line.

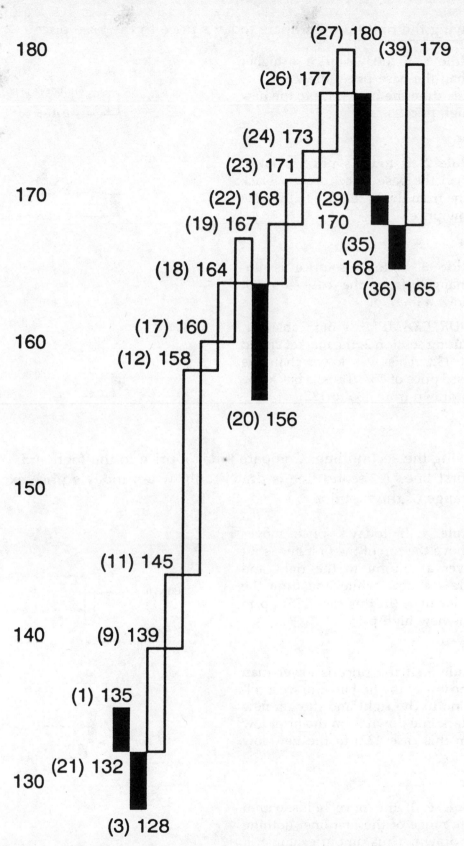

EXHIBIT 6.1. Example of a Three-line Break Chart Based on Prices from Table 6.1.
(Figures in Parentheses Refer to Session Number.)

Drawing the first line: Compare today's price to the base price.

Rule 1. If today's price is higher than the base price, draw a white line from the base price to the new high price.

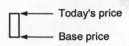

or

Rule 2. If today's price is lower than the base price, draw a black line from the base price to the new low price.

or

Rule 3. If today's price is unchanged from the base, do not draw a line.

OUR EXAMPLE: From Table 6.1, during session 2, the market closed at 132. This was lower than the base price of 135. Thus, a black line is drawn from 135 to 132.

Drawing the second line: Compare today's price to the high and low of the first line. A second line is drawn only when today's price exceeds the range of the first line.

Rule 4. If today's price moves above the top of the first line, shift over a column to the right and draw a new white line from the prior high (in this case 135) up to the new high price.

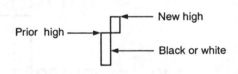

or

Rule 5. If the price is lower than the low of the first line, move a column to the right and draw a new black line down from the prior low (in this case 132) to the new low price.

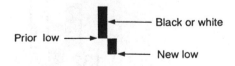

or

Rule 6. If the price holds within the range of the first line, nothing is drawn. Thus, in our example, if the price is between 135 and 132, no new line is drawn.

Note: Prices should exceed the prior high or low—not just touch the prior high or low—to draw a new line.

OUR EXAMPLE: Since the range of the first line is 135–132, the market would either have to move under 132 or above 135 for us to draw a new line. Session 3, at a price of 128, sets a new low. As a result, we make a new black line one column to the right. This line goes from the prior low of 132 to the new low of 128.

Drawing the third line: Compare today's price to the highest high and the lowest low of the prior two lines.

The concept here is the same as that of determining when to draw the second line. Only when the price moves to a new high or a new low for the move is a white or black line drawn. In our example, the market would have to go under 128 for a black line or above 135 for a white line.

Rule 7. If the market makes a new high by exceeding the high of the prior lines, shift a column to the right and draw a new white line up to the new high.

or

Rule 8. If today's price is lower than the low of the prior lines (i.e., makes a new low), shift a column to the right and draw a new black line down to the new low price.

or

Rule 9. If prices are in the range of the first two lines, nothing is drawn. In this example, as long as the price remains between 128 and 135 (the prior low and high), we do not draw a line.

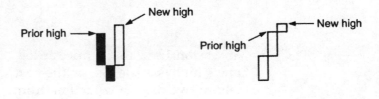

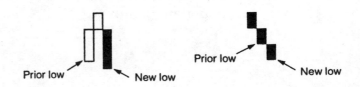

OUR EXAMPLE: In session 4, the price was 133. Since this was within the price range of the prior two lines (128–135), there is no new line drawn. The next time a line is drawn is session 9, when prices moved to a new high to 139. Since this was above the prior high (at 135), we shift a column to the right and a new white line is drawn from the top of the prior line up to 139. The new range of lines is now from a low of 128 to a high of 139.

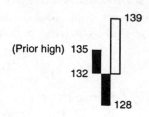

The next price outside of this 128–139 range is at price 11 at 145. At that time, a white line is drawn from the prior 139 high to the new high at 145. We now have two consecutive white lines. The new range is 128–145.

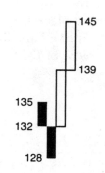

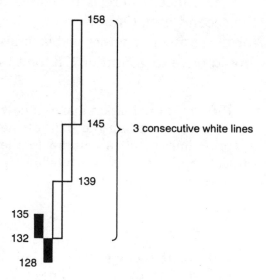

At session 12, with the price at 158, a new high is made. So, on the next column we draw a white line from 145 to 158. We now have three successive white lines. As shown in the following discussion, this is an important occurrence.

Drawing a line after three consecutive white or black lines: If there are three successive white or black lines, it confirms a trend (a series of three white lines confirms a bull trend; three black lines confirm a bear trend). Remember that this technique is called the *three-line break*. Its name is derived from the fact that today's price must exceed the low of the *three* successive white lines, or the high of the *three* consecutive black lines, to get a reversal line.

Rule 10. If there are three consecutive white lines, a new white line can be drawn whenever a new high is made (even if this high is as little **as** one tick). However, the price must move under the lowest price of the last three consecutive white lines to draw a black reversal line. Such a black reversal line is called a *black turnaround line*. A black turnaround line is drawn from the bottom of the highest white line to the new low price.

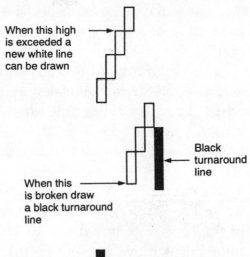

When this high is exceeded a new white line can be drawn

Black turnaround line

When this is broken draw a black turnaround line

Rule 11. If there are three consecutive black lines, a new black line can be drawn with any new low. However, if there are three consecutive black lines the price must exceed the high of the prior three black lines to draw a *white turnaround line*. A white turnaround line is drawn from the top of the lowest black line to the new high price.

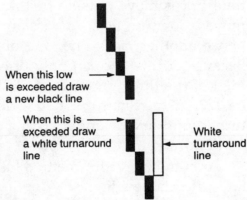

When this low is exceeded draw a new black line

When this is exceeded draw a white turnaround line

White turnaround line

For the rest of this discussion, see Table 6.1 and Exhibit 6.1.

By session 12 there are three consecutive white lines. As a result, the market has to move under the low of the third white line (at 132) to draw a black turnaround line. However, white lines continue to be drawn as long as a new high is made (that is, if prices move above 158). Thus, in our example, before a new line can be built, the market must either move under 132 (for a black line) or above 158 (for a white line).

The next price that exceeded our 132–158 range was price 17 at 160, a new high. Thus, a new white line is drawn from 158 to 160. Now, the bottom of the last three white lines is 139. Thus, the new price range to monitor is below 139 to get a black line and above 160 to draw a white line.

Price 18 is a new high, as is price 19. So, two new white lines are added. When we get to price 19 at 167, the low of the third white line is then 158. Thus, our price range is either under 158 for a black turnaround line or above 167 for a new white line.

Price 20 is 156. This is under the lowest low of the preceding three white lines (at 158), so we draw a black turnaround line from the bottom of the top white line down to the new low price at 156. Because there are not three white consecutive white lines (since the black line appeared), a new white line is added if a new high or low for the move is made.

The new range to exceed is the prior high at 167 and the recent low at 156. Price 22 makes a new high at 168. As a result, we add another white line. This white line starts at the top of the prior black line and goes up to the new high at 168. New highs are made (and new white lines are added for each higher session) up until session 27 at a price of 180.

At price 29 at 170, the market moved under the low of the third prior white line (at 171), so a black turnaround line is drawn from the bottom of the top white line down to 170. Our new range is 170–180. The next time prices move outside this range is at session 35, when the market moved down to 168. At session 36 there is another new low at 165—hence another black line. We now have three consecutive black lines. Because of this, we can only draw a white line if the price exceeds the high of the three previous black lines. In our example, this price would be 177. As a result, our new price range is above 177 for a new white turnaround line or under 165 for a new black line. At price 39 at 179, a white turnaround line is drawn up to 179.

To summarize the method: If there are one or two black or white lines, then a new line is added if the market reaches a new high or low. However, if there are three consecutive white lines, the market must move under the low of these white lines to draw a black turnaround line. If there are three consecutive black lines, the high of these lines must be exceeded to draw a white turnaround line.

TRADING TECHNIQUES WITH THE THREE-LINE BREAK CHART

White and Black Lines as Buy and Sell Signals

A series of alternating white and black lines, as shown in Exhibit 6.2(A), reflects a trendless market. However, once three consecutive white or black lines appear, as displayed in Exhibit 6.2(B), the market is in a trending mode. A basic trend reversal signal is produced when a turnaround line moves under three consecutive white lines or above three consecutive black lines. This is shown in Exhibit 6.2(C).

The most basic method of using the three-line break is buying on a white line and selling on a black line. Remember that if there are three consecutive white (black) lines, the market has to move under (above) the low (high) of these three lines for a black (white) line to be con-

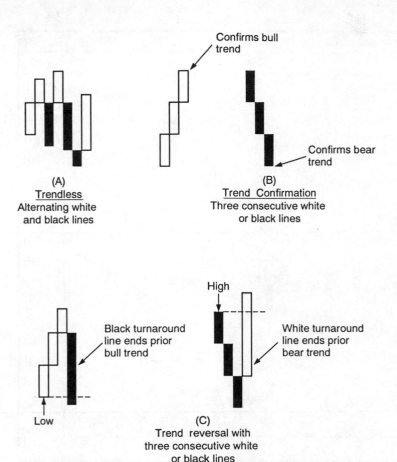

Confirms bull
trend

(A)
Trendless
Alternating white
and black lines

(B)
Trend Confirmation
Three consecutive white
or black lines

Confirms bear
trend

High

Black turnaround
line ends prior
bull trend

White turnaround
line ends prior
bear trend

Low

(C)
Trend reversal with
three consecutive white
or black lines

EXHIBIT 6.2. (A) Alternating White
and Black Line. (B) Three Consecutive
Same-Color Lines. (C) Turnaround
Lines.

structed. Exhibit 6.3 shows buy and sell signals based on these criteria. As can be seen from this example, some reversal signals in the three-line break chart are sent well after the new trend has started. However, many traders are comfortable with this insofar as they believe that it is safer to be in for the major part of the trend rather than trying to pick a top or bottom. The three-line break tries to accomplish this.

The three-line break chart requires a close to confirm a turnaround line. However, by the time this confirmation is completed, the market may have moved substantially away from where there may have been an attractive buy or sell. A means around this problem is to use an intra-session reversal signal as the time to lightly buy or sell. Then, if desired, add more to the position if the turnaround line is confirmed. For example, looking at Exhibit 6.3, B_1 became a turnaround line once it closed above $31 (the high of the three prior black lines). However, by the time the turnaround line was corroborated, the market had closed near $33. A trader could have bought lightly on an intra-day basis on the break above $31 and then added on the close near $33. Of course, if the market had failed to close above $31, then there would have been no turnaround line formed. In such a scenario, the prudent action would be for the intra-

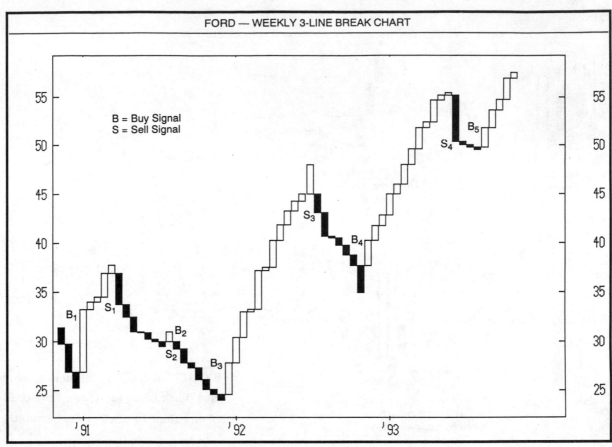

EXHIBIT 6.3.   White and Black Lines as Buy and Sell Signals, Ford—Weekly

day buyer to liquidate the long he or she had bought earlier that session. For traders who prefer to wait for the validation of a turnaround line formed on a close before initiating any long position, they could wait for such a confirmation and then, over the next few sessions, hope for a correction that would favor a buy.

Three-Line Break Charts and Candle Charts

In Chapter 4, I examined the value of monitoring the market's prevailing trend when using the candles. Since the three-line break chart defines whether the market is in a bull or bear trend, it can be employed as an adjunct to candle charts. The three-line break chart can help define the prevailing trend, and the candles can be used as an entry mechanism to trade in the direction of the prevailing trend. For example, if there are three white consecutive lines, the major trend (as defined by the three-line break) is up. Based on this, bullish candle signals could be used as a buy signal, and bearish candle signals within this bull trend could be used to cover shorts. Since candles rarely help set price targets, a white or black turnaround line can also be used as a signal to exit a trade originally based on a candle signal.

In Exhibit 6.4(A), a three-line break chart shows that a black turnaround line occurred after the price touched $29.50 (the candle chart in Exhibit 6.4(B) shows that there was another indication of a top with a bearish engulfing pattern). The black turnaround line meant that the trend had turned down. Based on the theory that a new position should be placed in the direction of the major trend, traders should look for a candle signal as a time to go short in the bear trend. However, bullish candle signals in this bear market should either be ignored or used to cover shorts.

In this case, I will show how to use the three-line break chart in Exhibit 6.4(A) to fine tune trading with the candle chart in Exhibit 6.4(B).

In the candle chart in Exhibit 6.4(B), a hammer appeared on September 3. The fact that the hammer came after a falling window was an indication that the hammer should not have been a buy signal. A few

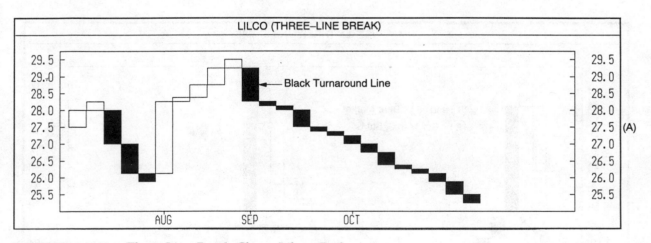

EXHIBIT 6.4(A). Three-Line Break Chart, Lilco—Daily

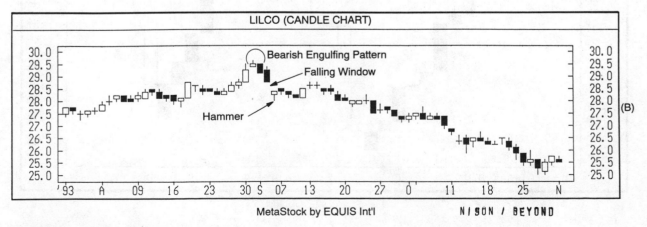

EXHIBIT 6.4(B). Candle Chart, Lilco—Daily

days after the hammer (on September 8), the market had weakened enough to form the black turnaround line shown in Exhibit 6.4(A). At that time, with a bear trend confirmed via the three-line break chart, the rally into the window's resistance area a few days later could be used as a selling opportunity.

Three-Line Break Charts and Trend

Exhibit 6.5(A) is a three-line break chart and Exhibit 6.5(B) is a candle chart. Using these Exhibits, I will show how the insights about the overall trend provided by the three-line break charts refine trading based on candle signals.

From Exhibit 6.5(A), the trend turned bearish beginning at the black turnaround line of 1 (which formed the first week of August). It is interesting that before this black turnaround line appeared, the candle charts gave a hint of a top with the hanging man line in June. Throughout the

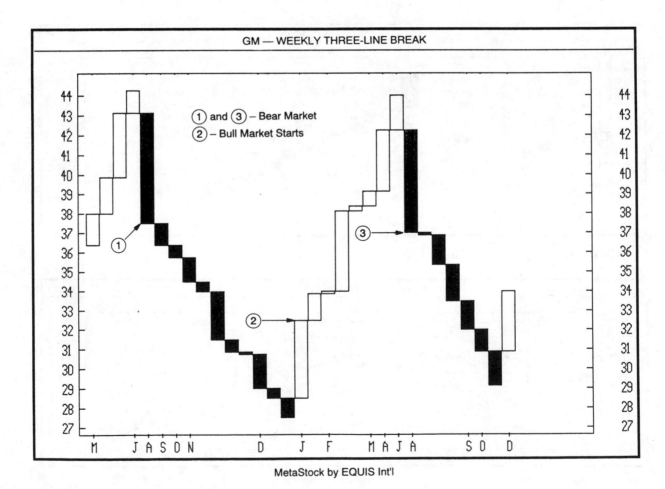

MetaStock by EQUIS Int'l

EXHIBIT 6.5(A).   Three-Line Break Chart, GM—Weekly

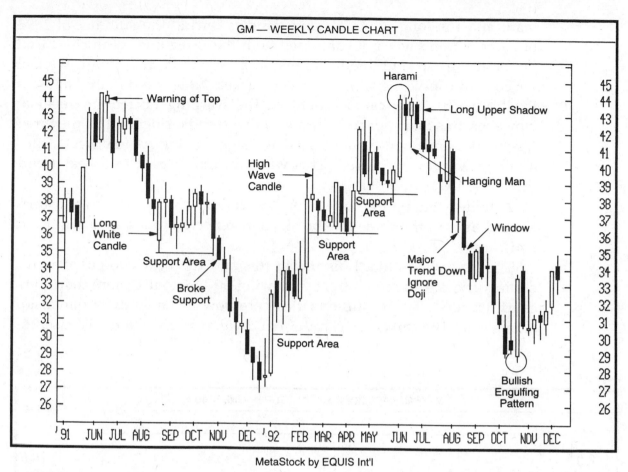

GM — WEEKLY CANDLE CHART

MetaStock by EQUIS Int'l

EXHIBIT 6.5(B). Candle Chart, GM—Weekly

rest of the year, the market remained in a bear mode, as shown by the continuous series of black lines in the three-line break chart. In this environment, candle signals to sell short should be acted upon since there was a prevailing downward trend. A long white candle during this period gave a temporary respite to the selloff, but once the support area at the bottom of this white candle was broken, it was a signal for lower prices.

At white turnaround line 2, the market transformed into a bull mode. This means that bullish candle signals should be used as a buying opportunity. The bull trend lasted from January until the black turnaround line in August. During this bull mode, observe how the market held support near the midpoint of the tall white real bodies. February's high-wave candle was an indication that the prior uptrend was in transition. However, with the major trend still higher, and the long white candle as support, we could view sell-offs after the high-wave candle as corrections in a bull trend. Another tall white candle in April became support and provided a base for another upleg.

Hints of a bearish turnaround came with the harami, the hanging man, and the long upper shadow candles during the summer of 1992, but a bear trend was not confirmed with the three-line break chart until the black turnaround line in August at line 3. From that point, we look for bearish candle signals to sell the market. Note the doji in August in Exhibit 6.5(B). This candle could be the warning of a trend reversal. However, this doji appeared during a downtrend (as defined by the three-line break), and should not be used as a signal to buy. A few weeks later, a falling window appeared. This was a bearish signal in a bear trend; thus, a sell was in order.

A bullish engulfing pattern on the candle chart and a white turnaround line on the three-line break chart reflected that a new bull trend had begun.

The new charts that I discuss in this and the next two chapters use closing prices. Consequently, by allowing traders to use more than a line chart, traders who use these markets are now given an extra dimension of analysis. The three-line chart of bond yields in Exhibit 6.6 is based on

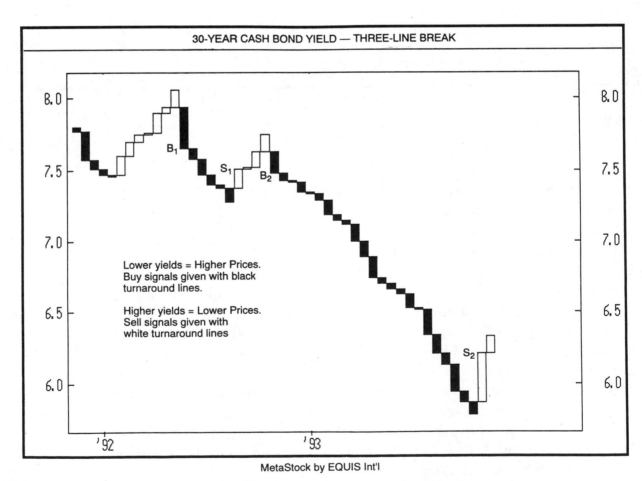

EXHIBIT 6.6.   Using Three-Line Break Charts in Markets with Only Closing Prices, 30-Year Cash Bond Yield—Weekly Close Only

closing price only. Yet, notice all the information this chart provides as it signals reversals with the emergence of a white or black turnaround line. Remember that when looking at three-line break charts in terms of yield, the black lines are bullish since lower yields translate to higher prices. This is why the buy signals on the chart are given with the black turnaround line and sell signals on the white turnaround lines (a white turnaround line means higher yields and lower prices).

Other Break Charts

Japanese traders often adjust the sensitivity of the three-line break chart by changing the number of lines that the market has to break before a turnaround line is drawn. The three-line break requires the breaking of the last three white or black lines to get a reversal. As displayed in Exhibit 6.7(A), we see that a two-line break follows the same concept, except that it uses two white or black lines as its reversal criterion. Such a chart is termed a two-line break chart. As displayed in Exhibit 6.7(B), for a four-line break chart, the last four consecutive and same color lines have to be exceeded for a new turnaround line to be drawn.

Shorter time frame traders would usually use shorter reversal amounts (such as a two- or three-line break). Traders and investors who are looking for major moves and are long-term oriented could use the five- or even ten-line breaks. The most popular break chart in Japan is the three-line break chart; that is why my examples are based on the three-line break chart. However, all the trading tools used in the three-line break charts can be applied in the same way to any other break chart.

In Exhibit 6.3, shown earlier in this chapter, I highlighted the buy and sell signals for Ford using a three-line break chart. Using the same date as on Exhibit 6.3, I made a two-line break chart (Exhibit 6.8) and a five-line break chart (Exhibit 6.9). Note how the frequency of buy and sell

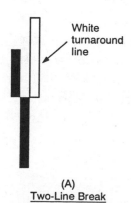

(A)
Two-Line Break
Must exceed the high of
two consecutive
black lines

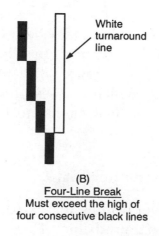

(B)
Four-Line Break
Must exceed the high of
four consecutive black lines

EXHIBIT 6.7. Two- and
Four-Line Breaks

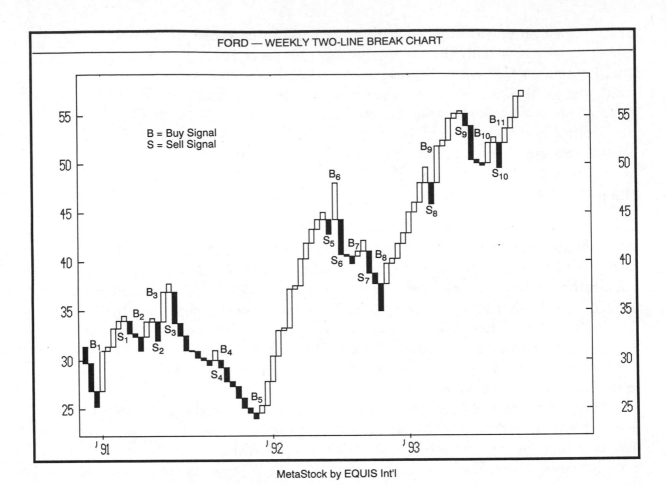

EXHIBIT 6.8. Two-Line Break Chart, Ford—Weekly

signals increases with the two-line break charts as compared to the three-line or the five-line break charts. This is because the fewer the number of lines that have to be exceeded to get a turnaround line, the greater the sensitivity of the chart. Consequently, a two-line break is more sensitive and will be more volatile than a three-line break chart. A five-line break chart will be less sensitive and have fewer reversals than a three-line break.

Exceeding one, two, or three lines may be compared to using a shorter term moving average. Using the three- to five-line break charts can match the intermediate term moving average, while the ten-line break is like a long-term moving average. Which of these break criteria work best is found through trial and error. It is similar to finding a moving average that works best in your markets.

Extra Confirmation of a Trend Reversal

Some Japanese traders prefer waiting for an extra confirmation of a trend reversal, even after a turnaround line. They get this confirmation by

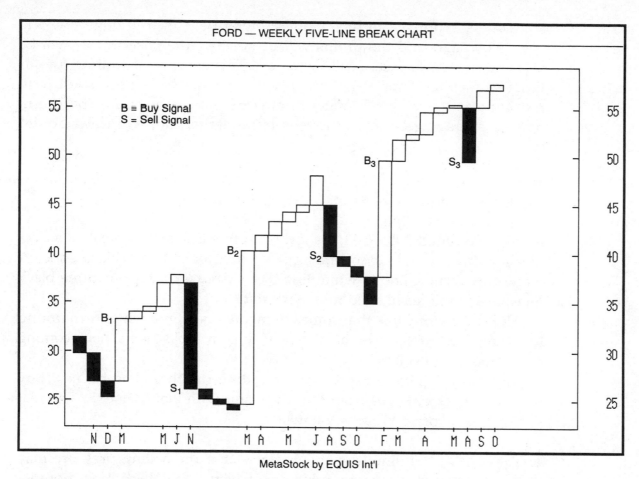

EXHIBIT 6.9. Five-Line Break Chart, Ford—Weekly

waiting for the line after a turnaround line to confirm the new trend. For example, as shown in Exhibit 6.10, a trader could wait for the white line after the white turnaround line before buying. (Looking back at Exhibit 6.3, traders using this concept would not have bought at B₂ since there was only a white turnaround line.)

This idea of waiting for extra confirmation would, of course, involve a tradeoff between risk and reward. The longer a trader waits for a confirmation of a trend reversal, the greater the likelihood of being correct, but the lower the profit potential since more of the new trend had already

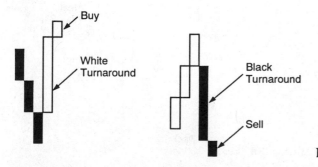

EXHIBIT 6.10. Waiting for Extra Confirmation

started. As expressed in the Japanese literature, ''even though one will get a slow start and the profits will be smaller, the false moves will be less and the safety factor will increase.'' This concept of waiting for additional lines to confirm the new trend is similar to using a short-term moving average versus a longer term one. Those who use a short-term moving average get aboard the new trend earlier, but whipsaws are increased.

Black Shoe, White and Black Suits, and a Neck

As displayed in Exhibit 6.11, a short black line is sometimes called a *black shoe* for the obvious reason that such a line looks like a black shoe. A white turnaround line (a white line that surpasses the prior three black lines) is sometimes likened to a *white suit*.

The short white line that comes immediately after a white turnaround line (i.e., a white suit) is called a *neck* since it looks like a neck coming out of the white suit.

There is a Japanese expression regarding the three-line break: ''Buy when the neck emerges from the white suit with black shoes.'' The reason for this expression is as follows:

1. The small black line (the shoe) shows that the selling pressure may be easing since the move towards lower prices is becoming more lethargic.

2. The white turnaround line is a bullish reversal signal.

3. The neck is the buy signal. The neck's short white line is viewed as the market taking a breather after its prior advance (i.e., after the prior white turnaround line). A short white line could also reflect that the bears may have not yet covered their shorts (these who sold during the series of black lines that came before the white turnaround line). This could mean higher prices once these shorts decide to cover. Since the neck is also the second white line after the white turnaround line,

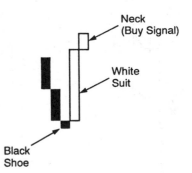

EXHIBIT 6.11. Black Shoe, White Suit, and a Neck

it serves as extra bullish confirmation. As discussed previously, some traders prefer waiting for the second white line as a buy signal.

In Exhibit 6.12, I show an example of a neck, a black suit, and a black shoe. This black turnaround line is sometimes called a *black suit*. The small black line after the black suit is the sell signal.

There is a saying that a trader should ''sell if the black shoe comes out of a black suit after a neck.'' The meaning of this expression is explained below:

1. The diminutive real body at the top of the rally (i.e., the neck) shows that either the buying pressure is slackening or the selling pressure is enough to slow the bulls' advance.
2. The black turnaround line (the black suit) is a reversal signal that tells us that the bears have gained control.
3. The small black line (the shoe) means that the market is weak, but not oversold. Also, it shows that the buyers on the way up (during the series of white lines before the black turnaround line) may not have liquidated as yet. This could mean that there is still more selling likely to come when these existing longs decide to liquidate. The black shoe after the black turnaround line also provides bearish confirmation for these who prefer to wait for a second black line to get a reversal signal.

I show in Exhibit 6.13 a bottom reversal signal in September and into October that is based on the saying, ''buy when the neck emerges from a white suit with black shoes.'' The small black line, i.e., a black shoe, emerged near $42 in September. The white suit (another name for the white turnaround line) came after this black shoe. Following the black shoe, a white line, because of its small size, was a neck, and hence a buy signal. A top reversal pattern, grounded on the dictum, ''sell when black shoes are under a black suit after a neck,'' appears at the price peak near $59. The small white line after the rally was a neck, the black turnaround line after this neck was a black suit, and the confirmation of a sell came with the small black shoe.

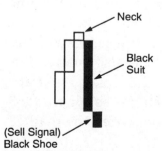

EXHIBIT 6.12. Neck, Black Suit, and a Black Shoe

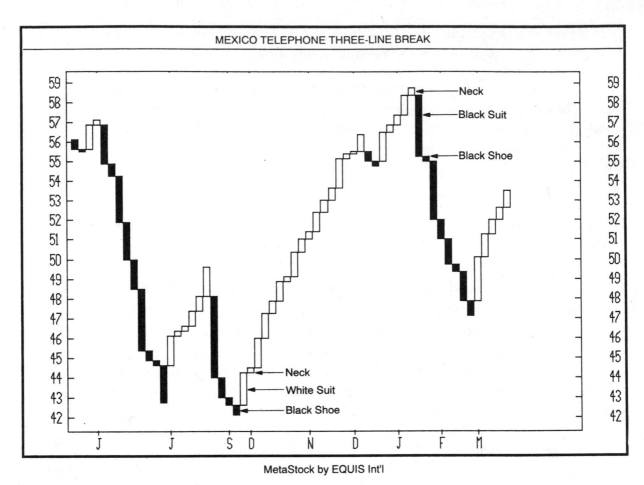

MEXICO TELEPHONE THREE-LINE BREAK

Neck
Black Suit
Black Shoe
Neck
White Suit
Black Shoe

MetaStock by EQUIS Int'l

EXHIBIT 6.13. Buy When the Neck Emerges from a White Suit with Black Shoes; Sell When Black Shoes Are Under a Black Suit After a Neck, Mexico Telephone— Daily

Record Sessions and Three-Line Break Charts

Just as record sessions are important in candle charting, so this technique is useful for some of the new charting techniques such as the three-line break chart, and as we'll see later, kagi charts. When there are 8 to 10 consecutive or almost consecutive white lines, the market is viewed as being overextended to the upside. When there are 8 to 10 black lines during a downtrend, the market becomes vulnerable to a bounce.

One of my important sources of information has been the Nippon Technical Analysis Association. I sent the NTAA member a copy of Exhibit 6.14 with some questions about the three-line break chart. This gentleman graciously addressed my questions, and he also placed the numbers shown on each of the falling black lines. He did this to illustrate how he uses record session counts as one of the techniques for trading with the three-line break chart. We see in this chart that when the market

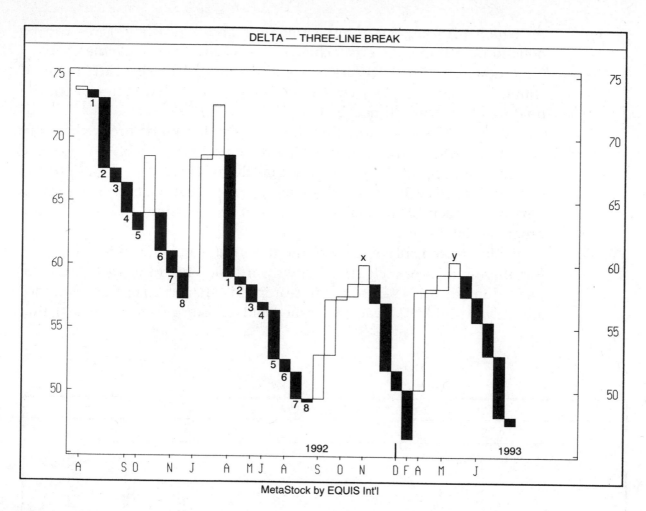

EXHIBIT 6.14. Three-Line Break Chart Record Sessions, Delta—Weekly

reached eight record sessions low, prices bounced. Another interesting aspect of this chart was that the NTAA member also placed an X and a Y on the chart at the price peaks shown. He mentioned that this area was resistance on any rebounds. Although it is not shown on this chart, a rally in late 1993 failed near this $60 resistance area and fell to near $45. Thus, we can see that using an obvious resistance area, such as the dual highs near $60, should be used with three line-break charts.

Western Patterns and Three-Line Break Charts

Techniques that apply to candle or bar charts, such as support and resistance or double tops and trendlines, also apply to three-line break charts.

The uptrend support line and the resistance zone in the $49.50 area in Exhibit 6.15 illustrate how a trendline and a resistance area can be defined on a three-line break chart just as easily as on a candle chart.

A double top or tweezers top is also sometimes called a two-paired chimney. In Exhibit 6.16, we see an example of such a pattern with the dual highs at A and B near $74.

Exhibit 6.17 shows how trendlines on the three-line break chart can be used as effectively as on a traditional bar chart. The breaking of the uptrending support lines signaling that the uptrend was in the process of changing. In addition this chart also displays that the bulls were losing force since each of the major price peaks at shoulders 1, 2 and 3 were progressively lower.

Exhibit 6.18 displays some of the tools that can be used to trade with the three-line break chart. A downward sloping resistance line was pierced in early 1993. Also of interest in this chart is the prior resistance area from mid-1992 near $68 (called old resistance on the chart) that

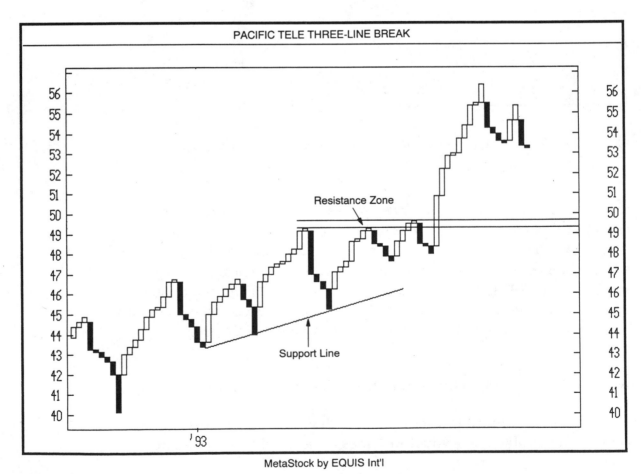

MetaStock by EQUIS Int'l

EXHIBIT 6.15.   Trendlines and Resistance with Three-Line Break Charts, Pacific Telephone—Daily

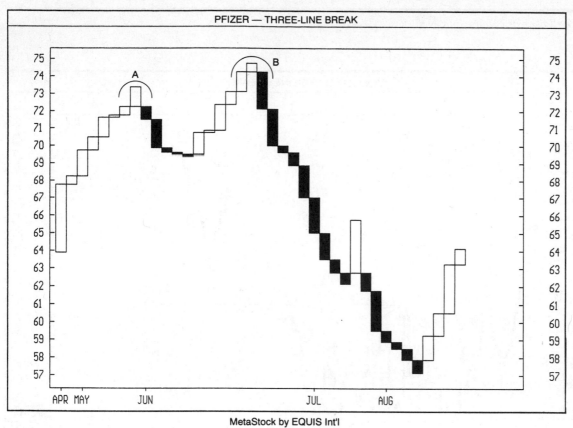

EXHIBIT 6.16. Double Top with Three-Line Break Charts

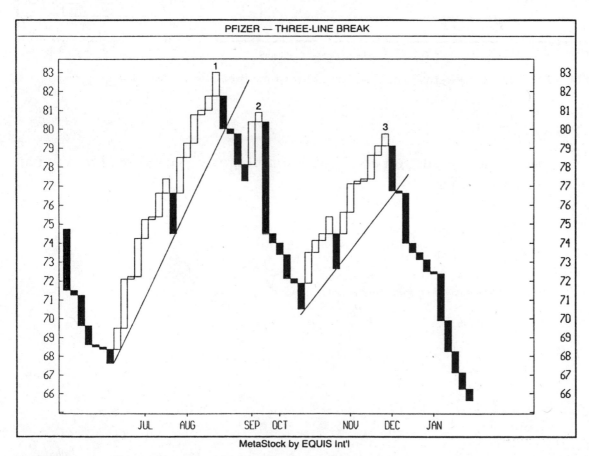

EXHIBIT 6.17 Three-Line Break Chart Trendlines, Pfizer—Daily

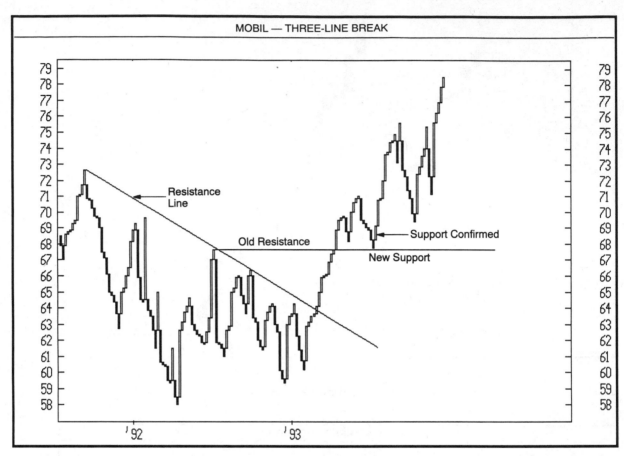

MetaStock by EQUIS Int'l

EXHIBIT 6.18. Classic Western Techniques on a Three-Line Break Chart, Mobil—
Daily

became a new support area. This support area was confirmed by a white
turnaround line.

Note

[1]*Equity International Magazine*, July/August 1991.

PRACTICE SESSION FOR THE THREE-LINE BREAK CHART

To reinforce your understanding of the three-line break chart, use the closing prices in Table 6.2, on the following page, to construct a three-line break chart. The scale on the vertical axis should be set up from $23 to $30. You may photocopy and use the supplied graph shown on page 193 or draw a rough scale on plain paper. The exact size of the white or black lines is not important. The meaningful aspect of this practice is to use your chart as a gauge to see how well you understand when a new white or black line should be drawn.

After you construct the chart, compare it to Table 6.3 and Exhibit 6.19 (on the pages following the exercise) where the actual chart and the days on which new lines were constructed are shown.

TABLE 6.2 Data for Three-Line Break Chart Practice Session

Date	Closing Price	Date	Closing Price
02/18/94	25.156	04/29/94	27.000
02/22/94	25.250	05/02/94	26.875
02/23/94	26.375	05/03/94	26.625
02/24/94	26.500	05/04/94	27.687
02/25/94	26.875	05/05/94	28.000
02/28/94	27.750	05/06/94	27.125
03/01/94	27.375	05/09/94	25.875
03/02/94	27.375	05/10/94	27.250
03/03/94	27.125	05/11/94	25.500
03/04/94	28.750	05/12/94	24.875
03/07/94	28.125	05/13/94	24.875
03/08/94	27.875	05/16/94	24.125
03/09/94	28.250	05/17/94	25.000
03/10/94	28.250	05/18/94	26.250
03/11/94	28.375	05/19/94	27.375
03/14/94	28.250	05/20/94	27.500
03/15/94	27.500	05/23/94	28.000
03/16/94	28.500	05/24/94	27.625
03/17/94	29.125	05/25/94	27.125
03/18/94	29.250	05/26/94	26.250
03/21/94	28.750	05/27/94	26.250
03/22/94	28.500	05/31/94	26.250
03/23/94	28.625	06/01/94	26.375
03/24/94	28.250	06/02/94	26.625
03/25/94	27.125	06/03/94	27.375
03/28/94	27.500	06/06/94	28.500
03/29/94	26.250	06/07/94	27.250
03/30/94	25.875	06/08/94	26.250
03/31/94	26.500	06/09/94	26.500
04/04/94	26.375	06/10/94	26.125
04/05/94	27.375	06/13/94	25.750
04/06/94	26.375	06/14/94	26.000
04/07/94	26.062	06/15/94	26.625
04/08/94	25.750	06/16/94	26.125
04/11/94	26.125	06/17/94	26.250
04/12/94	25.875	06/20/94	25.750
04/13/94	25.750	06/21/94	25.375
04/14/94	25.250	06/22/94	25.375
04/15/94	24.375	06/23/94	24.750
04/18/94	24.000	06/24/94	23.500
04/19/94	23.625	06/27/94	24.062
04/20/94	23.875	06/28/94	23.250
04/21/94	26.500	06/29/94	23.500
04/22/94	26.750	06/30/94	24.125
04/25/94	27.375	07/01/94	24.625
04/26/94	27.375	07/05/94	24.625
04/28/94	26.875		

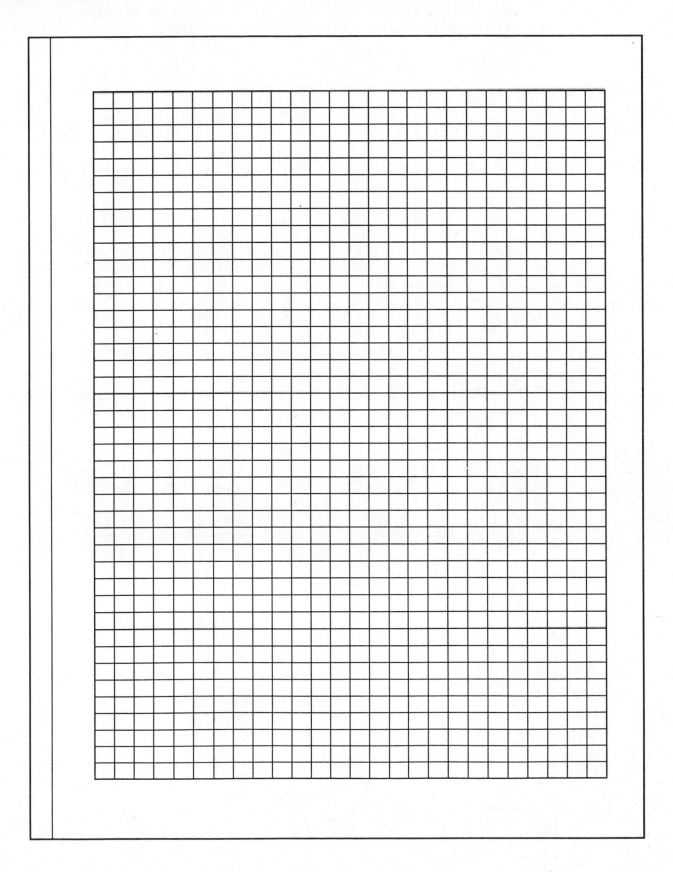

TABLE 6.3 Data for Answers to Three-Line Break Chart Practice Session. Numbers in Parentheses Refer to Line Numbers in Exhibit 6.19

Date	Closing Price	Date	Closing Price
02/18/94	25.156	04/29/94	27.000
02/22/94	25.250(1)	05/02/94	26.875
02/23/94	26.375(2)	05/03/94	26.625
02/24/94	26.500(3)	05/04/94	27.687(20)
02/25/94	26.875(4)	05/05/94	28.000(21)
02/28/94	27.750(5)	05/06/94	27.125
03/01/94	27.375	05/09/94	25.875(22)
03/02/94	27.375	05/10/94	27.250
03/03/94	27.125	05/11/94	25.500(23)
03/04/94	28.750(6)	05/12/94	24.875(24)
03/07/94	28.125	05/13/94	24.875
03/08/94	27.875	05/16/94	24.125(25)
03/09/94	28.250	05/17/94	25.000
03/10/94	28.250	05/18/94	26.250(26)
03/11/94	28.375	05/19/94	27.375(27)
03/14/94	28.250	05/20/94	27.500(28)
03/15/94	27.500	05/23/94	28.000(29)
03/16/94	28.500	05/24/94	27.625
03/17/94	29.125(7)	05/25/94	27.125
03/18/94	29.250(8)	05/26/94	26.250
03/21/94	28.750	05/27/94	26.250
03/22/94	28.500	05/31/94	26.250
03/23/94	28.625	06/01/94	26.375
03/24/94	28.250	06/02/94	26.625
03/25/94	27.125(9)	06/03/94	27.375
03/28/94	27.500	06/06/94	28.500(30)
03/29/94	26.250(10)	06/07/94	27.250(31)
03/30/94	25.875(11)	06/08/94	26.250(32)
03/31/94	26.500	06/09/94	26.500
04/04/94	26.375	06/10/94	26.125(33)
04/05/94	27.375	06/13/94	25.750(34)
04/06/94	26.375	06/14/94	26.000
04/07/94	26.062	06/15/94	26.625
04/08/94	25.750(12)	06/16/94	26.125
04/11/94	26.125	06/17/94	26.250
04/12/94	25.875	06/20/94	25.750
04/13/94	25.750	06/21/94	25.375(35)
04/14/94	25.250(13)	06/22/94	25.375
04/15/94	24.375(14)	06/23/94	24.750(36)
04/18/94	24.000(15)	06/24/94	23.500(37)
04/19/94	23.625(16)	06/27/94	24.062
04/20/94	23.875	06/28/94	23.250(38)
04/21/94	26.500(17)	06/29/94	23.500
04/22/94	26.750(18)	06/30/94	24.125
04/25/94	27.375(19)	07/01/94	24.625
04/26/94	27.375	07/05/94	24.625
04/28/94	26.875		

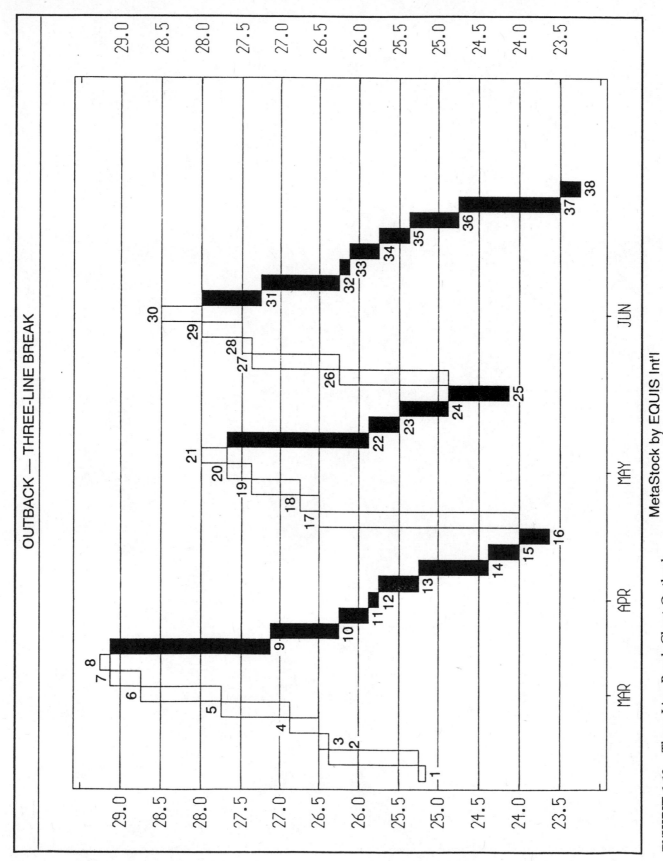

EXHIBIT 6.19. Three-Line Break Chart Outback

CHAPTER 7

RENKO CHARTS

....

故きを温ねて新しきを知る

"Consider the Past and You Will Know the Future"

The renko chart, shown in Exhibit 7.1, is also termed a neri, training, or zigzag chart. The renko charts looks similar to the three-bar break chart since they both have lines that look like blocks. The individual blocks that form the renko chart are sometimes referred to as *bricks* (the term renko may come from ''renga,'' which is the Japanese word for bricks).

As we saw in Chapter 6, in a three-bar break chart, another line is added as the market moves in the direction of the prevailing trend, no matter how small the move. For example, if the market closed today by even one tick higher, a new white line would be added to the three-line break chart if the prior line was white.

However, for a renko chart, a line is drawn in the direction of the prior move only if a fixed amount has been exceeded. For example, if there is a white brick on the renko chart, the market has to advance by a predetermined fixed amount before a new white brick can be drawn.

Another difference between the renko and three-line break chart is that the lines in the three-line break chart are of different sizes, while the bricks in a renko chart are all the same size.

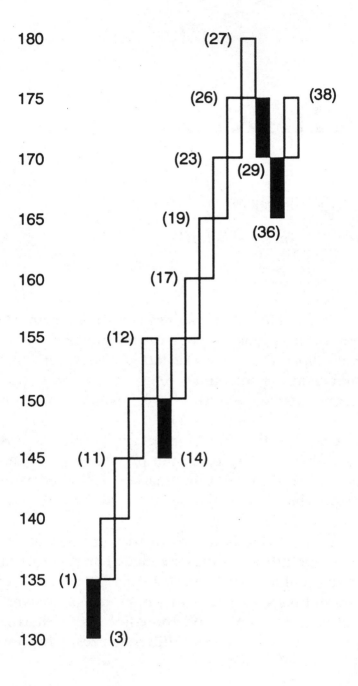

EXHIBIT 7.1. Example of Five-Point Renko Chart Based on Prices from Table 7.1

CONSTRUCTION OF RENKO CHARTS

Table 7.1 shows the price data used to draw the example of the renko chart in Exhibit 7.1.

The renko chart uses closing prices. The first step is to choose a price range unit. This price range point is the minimum amount the market must move before a renko brick is drawn. The price range point also serves to set the height of the brick. Thus, a five-point renko chart would have bricks that are five points tall. This will become clear after I go through the following detailed example. An important aspect of the renko chart is that rising lines are denoted by equal size white bricks and falling lines are denoted by equal size black bricks. Thus, no matter how large the move, it is shown on the renko chart as equal sized bricks. For example in a five-point renko chart, a 20-point rally is displayed as four five-point-high renko bricks.

TABLE 7.1 Data for the Five-Unit Renko Chart Displayed in Exhibit 7.1

Session	Closing Price	Session	Closing Price
1	base price 135	21	165<
2	132<	22	168<
3	128↓(1)	23	171↑(1)
4	133<	24	173<
5	130<	25	169<
6	130<	26	177↑(1)
7	132<	27	180↑(1)
8	134<	28	176<
9	139<	29	170↓(1)
10	137<	30	175<
11	145↑(2)	31	179<
12	158↑(2)	32	173<
13	147<	33	170<
14	143↓(1)	34	170<
15	150<	35	168<
16	149<	36	165↓(1)
17	160↑(2)	37	171<
18	164<	38	175↑(1)
19	167↑(1)	39	179<
20	156<	40	175<

Legend
(<)—Move is less than fixed amount. No brick is drawn.
↑—Where the price exceeds the prior brick by the fixed amount.
　( ) Shows how many white bricks are drawn.
↓—Where the price moves under the prior brick by the fixed amount.
　( ) Shows how many black bricks are drawn.

OUR EXAMPLE: We will use a five-point renko chart. This means each brick will be five points high. Our base, or starting price, is 135.

Drawing the first brick: Compare the base price to the current close.

Rule 1. If the market rallies from the base price:

A white brick (or a series of white bricks) is drawn only if the market moves above the base price by the fixed amount or more. Thus, if there is a base price of 100 and we are using a five-point renko chart, then the market has to move up to at least 105 before a white brick is drawn.

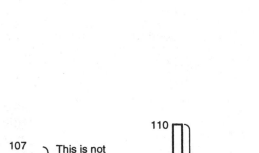

Note: Prices should touch or exceed the prior high or low by the point amount for a brick to be drawn. This is different from the three-line break chart, where the price should exceed the prior high or low.

If the market moves up by more than what would be required to draw one brick, but less than needed to draw two bricks, only one brick is drawn. For example, in a five-point renko chart, if the base price is 100 and the market moves to 107, then one white renko brick is drawn from the base price of 100 up to 105. The rest of the move—from 105 to 107—is not shown on the renko chart. However, if the market had moved up to 110, then there would be two five-point-tall white bricks. A move to 112 would also have two white bricks. The portion of the rally from 110 to 112 would not show.

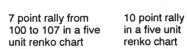

or

Rule 2. If the market falls from the base price:

Draw a black brick only when the price declines from the base by the fixed amount or more (in this example, five points). Thus, with a base price of 100, the market has to decline to 95 or lower before a black brick is drawn. The first black brick starts from the base price and goes down by the fixed point amount.

If the decline is more than the fixed point, but less than twice the minimum amount, then draw only one black brick. As an example, a decline from a base price of 100 down to 92 on a renko chart would have one five-point black brick from 100 to 95.

However, if there was a decline of, for example, 13 points, then two black bricks would be drawn. If the market fell by 15 points, there would be three black bricks, with each brick in a separate column.

or

Rule 3. If the market moves up or down by less than the minimum fixed point (in this case, five points), then no bricks are drawn. For example, for a five-point chart and a base price of 100, until the market goes up to 105 or down to 95, there is no brick shown.

OUR EXAMPLE: In Table 7.1, the base price is at 135. Since this example is a five-point renko chart, to draw a black brick the market has to move to 130 or lower (i.e., five points under the 135 base price). For a white brick, the market would have to ascend to 140 or higher (i.e., five points above the 135 base price). At session 2, the market fell to 132 or three points (135 to 132). This was not enough to draw a black brick since it was less than the minimum five points needed. By session 3, prices had

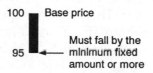

100 — Base price

95 — Must fall by the minimum fixed amount or more

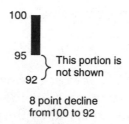

100
95
92

This portion is not shown

8 point decline from 100 to 92

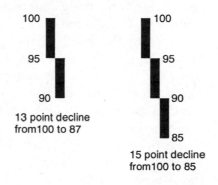

100
95
90

13 point decline from 100 to 87

100
95
90
85

15 point decline from 100 to 85

135 (Base price)

130 (Session 3)

moved down to 128. This was now seven points under the base price of 135. This seven-point fall is enough to draw one black brick. Thus, at session 3, we draw one five-point black brick from 135 to 130.

Drawing the next brick: Compare today's close with the high and low of the last brick.

Rule 4. If today's close is above the top of the last brick (whether that brick is white or black) by the point amount or more, move a column to the right and draw one or more white equal height bricks. The brick starts from the high of the prior brick. Thus, if the top of the latest brick was at 100, in our five-point renko chart, the market would have to move to 105 or higher for a white brick to be drawn. This white brick would go from 100 to 105. If the market goes to 113, then there would be two white bricks, with each brick in a separate column.

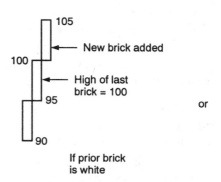

or

Rule 5. If today's price closes under the bottom of the last brick (white or black) by the minimum amount or more, then move a column to the right and draw one or more black bricks with each equal size brick in its own column. This means that if the bottom of the last brick is 95, the market would have to go to at least 90 before a black brick is drawn. Such a brick would go from the low of the previous brick at 95 down to 90.

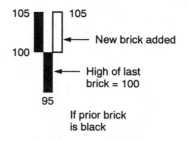

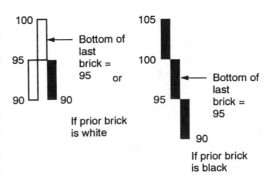

or

Rule 6. If the price is under the high or above the bottom of the last brick, then nothing is drawn.

OUR EXAMPLE: The high of the first brick is 135 and the low is 130. To draw a new brick in our five-point renko chart, the price has to move to 140 (i.e., five points above the 135 high) or higher for a white brick, or 125 (i.e., five points under the 130 low) or lower for a black brick. If the market remains under 140 or above 125, then nothing is drawn.

The next time the market reached either 140 or higher or 125 or lower was at session 11, with a price of 145. At that time, we drew two five-point white bricks from the prior high of 135 to the new high at 145.

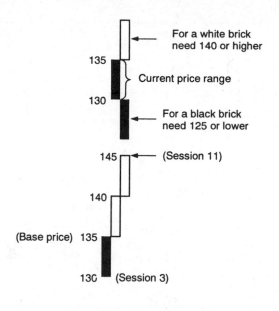

Drawing the next bricks: Using the data from Table 7.1 draw the rest of the chart shown in Exhibit 7.1 by the same process just discussed. For example, let's look at session 12 on Table 7.1. At that session the price was 158. The prior high, at session 11, was 145. We thus draw two five-point white bricks from the high of the prior renko brick at 145 up to 155 (the rest of the move from 155 to 158 is not shown on the renko chart). With the high of the last brick (at session 12) at 155 and the low of that brick at 150, we need the market to move either to 160 or higher for a white brick, or 145 or under for a black brick. Thus, at session 14 the market fell enough (to 143) to draw a new black brick down to 145.

TRADING TECHNIQUES WITH RENKO CHARTS

Unlike the varied trading techniques applicable with three-line break charts and kagi charts (discussed in the next chapter), the renko charts are more limited. The only trend reversal signals with renko charts are with the emergence of a bullish white brick or bearish black brick. Buy and sell signals based on this technique are shown in Exhibit 7.2.

As shown in that exhibit, buy signals (shown by the letter B) are generated with the appearance of a white brick. Sell signals (shown by S) are produced when a black brick appears. Since the renko chart is a trend-following technique, there will be times when the market is in a lateral trading band. In such an environment there may be whipsaws (see B_1-S_1, B_3-S_3, and B_4-S_4). However, the expectation with a trend-following technique such as this is that it allows traders to ride on the

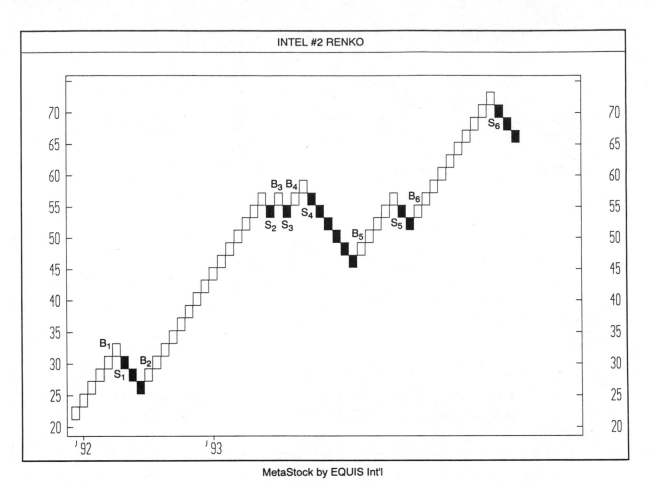

MetaStock by EQUIS Int'l

EXHIBIT 7.2.   Basic Buy and Sell Signals Generated with a Renko Chart, Intel—$2
Renko, Daily

major portion of the trend. This is shown by the buy and sell signals
produced at B_2–S_2, B_5–S_5, and B_6–S_6.

Exhibit 7.3 shows the advantages offered by a renko chart in a trending market. The buy signals come with the arrival of a white renko brick
and the sell signals with a black brick. Only when the market shifted into
a lateral range at L did the renko chart induce in and out trading.

In Exhibit 7.4 we take a longer term bond chart to see how the renko
chart could be used as a technical tool to buy. When the market shifts
into a neutral band, as it did at areas 1 and 2 on the chart, then the renko
chart may induce more volatile trading. However, this chart did allow a
long to enter and capture the bulk of the 1993 rally while keeping him
out of the market for most of the late 1993– early 1994 selloff.

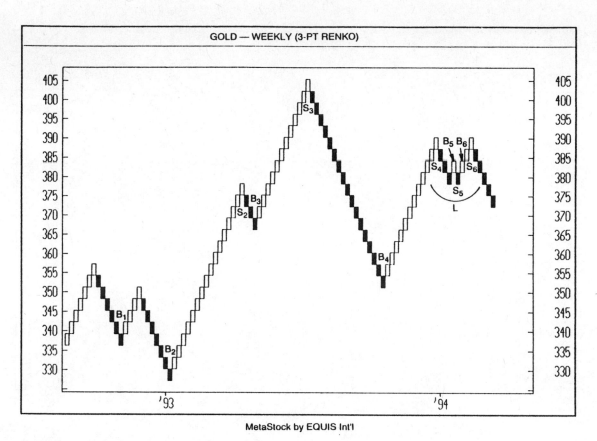

MetaStock by EQUIS Int'l

EXHIBIT 7.3. Basic Buy and Sell Signals, Gold—Weekly—$3 Renko

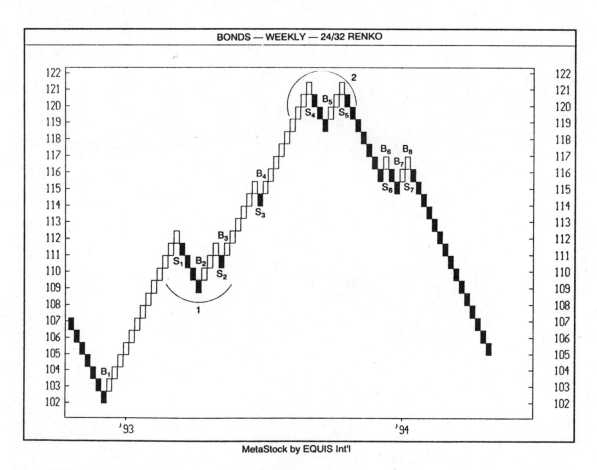

BONDS — WEEKLY — 24/32 RENKO

MetaStock by EQUIS Int'l

EXHIBIT 7.4. Bond Futures—Weekly—24/32 renko Buying Long

PRACTICE SESSION FOR THE RENKO CHART

Using the data from Table 7.2 (on the following page), build a $1 renko chart. The scale should be from $40 to $50. You may photocopy and use the supplied graph on page 209 or use plain paper. When finished, compare your answer to that shown in Exhibit 7.5 and Table 7.3 found on the following pages.

TABLE 7.2   Data for Construction of $1 Renko Practice Chart

Date	Close	Date	Close
03/24/94	47.625	05/16/94	43.750
03/25/94	47.750	05/17/94	44.000
03/28/94	47.500	05/18/94	44.875
03/29/94	46.125	05/19/94	44.625
03/30/94	45.125	05/20/94	45.250
03/31/94	45.250	05/23/94	45.250
04/04/94	44.500	05/24/94	45.250
04/05/94	45.000	05/25/94	45.125
04/06/94	45.250	05/26/94	45.500
04/07/94	44.875	05/27/94	45.625 W_7
04/08/94	44.250	05/31/94	45.500
04/11/94	43.375	06/01/94	45.625
04/12/94	42.500	06/02/94	45.000
04/13/94	42.750	06/03/94	44.750
04/14/94	42.000	06/06/94	44.875
04/15/94	41.375	06/07/94	45.250
04/18/94	40.000	06/08/94	45.250
04/19/94	39.875	06/09/94	45.125
04/20/94	40.125	06/10/94	45.125
04/21/94	41.250	06/13/94	45.625
04/22/94	42.250	06/14/94	45.500
04/25/94	42.625	06/15/94	45.375
04/26/94	43.375	06/16/94	46.500
04/28/94	45.250	06/17/94	47.000
04/29/94	47.500	06/20/94	46.125
05/02/94	47.625	06/21/94	45.125
05/03/94	46.500	06/22/94	45.375
05/04/94	46.125	06/23/94	45.875
05/05/94	46.250	06/24/94	45.250
05/06/94	45.750	06/27/94	45.250
05/09/94	45.125	06/28/94	44.625
05/10/94	45.250	06/29/94	45.125
05/11/94	43.500	06/30/94	45.250
05/12/94	43.625	07/01/94	46.125
05/13/94	44.125	07/05/94	46.750

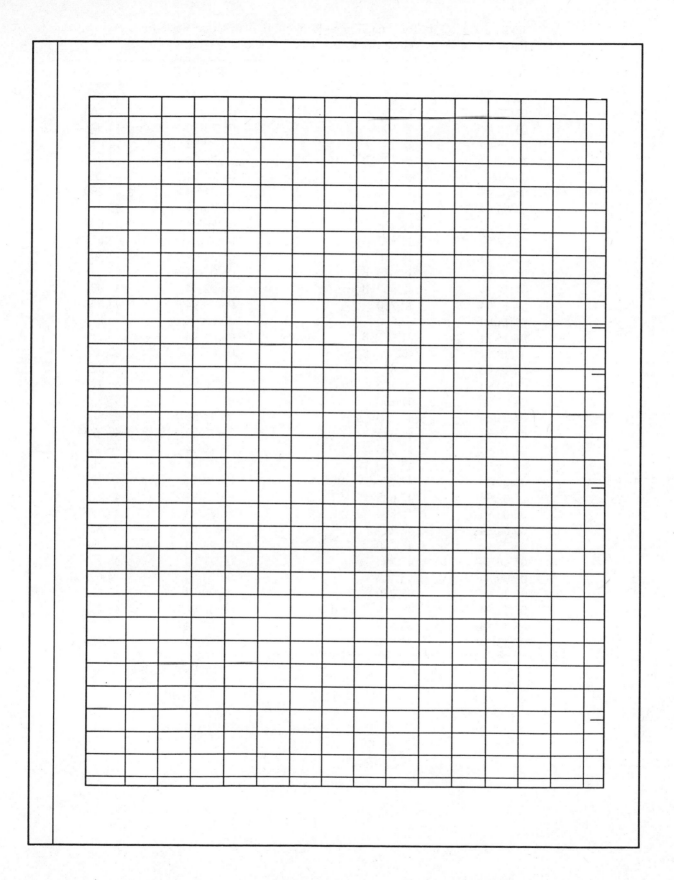

TABLE 7.3 Data for Answers to Renko Chart Practice Session Shown in Exhibit 7.5. W = White Brick, B = Black Brick.

Date	Close	Date	Close
03/24/94	47.625 base price	05/16/94	43.750
03/25/94	47.750	05/17/94	44.000
03/28/94	47.500	05/18/94	44.875
03/29/94	46.125 B_1	05/19/94	44.625
03/30/94	45.125 B_2	05/20/94	45.250
03/31/94	45.250	05/23/94	45.250
04/04/94	44.500 B_3	05/24/94	45.250
04/05/94	45.000	05/25/94	45.125
04/06/94	45.250	05/26/94	45.500
04/07/94	44.875	05/27/94	45.625 W_7
04/08/94	44.250	05/31/94	45.500
04/11/94	43.375 B_4	06/01/94	45.625
04/12/94	42.500 B_5	06/02/94	45.000
04/13/94	42.750	06/03/94	44.750
04/14/94	42.000	06/06/94	44.875
04/15/94	41.375 B_6	06/07/94	45.250
04/18/94	40.000 B_7	06/08/94	45.250
04/19/94	39.875	06/09/94	45.125
04/20/94	40.125	06/10/94	45.125
04/21/94	41.250	06/13/94	45.625
04/22/94	42.250	06/14/94	45.500
04/25/94	42.625 W_1	06/15/94	45.375
04/26/94	43.375	06/16/94	46.500
04/28/94	45.250 W_2 and W_3	06/17/94	47.000 W_8
04/29/94	47.500 W_4 and W_5	06/20/94	46.125
05/02/94	47.625 W_6	06/21/94	45.125
05/03/94	46.500	06/22/94	45.375
05/04/94	46.125	06/23/94	45.875
05/05/94	46.250	06/24/94	45.250
05/06/94	45.750	06/27/94	45.250
05/09/94	45.125 B_8	06/28/94	44.625 B_{11}
05/10/94	45.250	06/29/94	45.125
05/11/94	43.500 B_9 and B_{10}	06/30/94	45.250
05/12/94	43.625	07/01/94	46.125
05/13/94	44.125	07/05/94	46.750 W_9

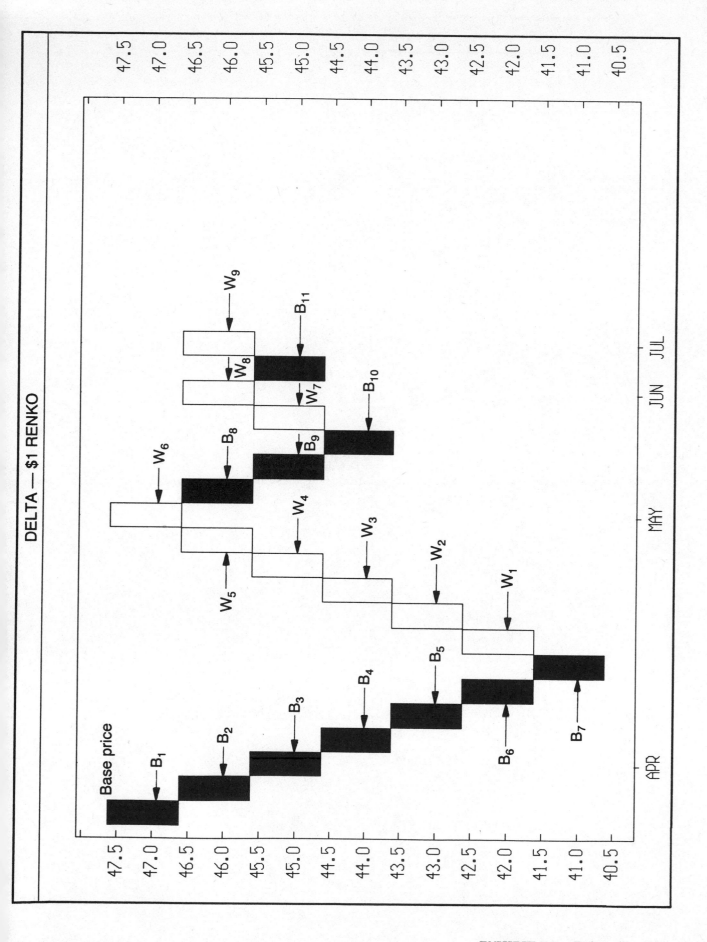

EXHIBIT 7.5. Delta—$1 renko

CHAPTER 8

KAGI CHARTS

. . . .

以心伝心

"Like the Right Arm Helping the Left"

The Kagi chart is thought to have been created around the time that the Japanese stock market started trading in the 1870s. A kagi chart is shown in Exhibit 8.1. The name kagi chart comes from the Japanese word "kagi," which was an old fashioned key that had an L-shaped head. This is the reason that kagi charts are also called key charts by some Japanese. Other names for the kagi chart include the price range chart, the hook chart, the delta chart, and the string chart.

A Japanese book on kagi stated, ". . . just as candle charts are superior to bar charts, so key charts are superior to point and figure charts"[1] I am not enough of an expert on point and figure charts to agree or disagree with that statement. What I can state with certainty, however, is that kagi charts will open new and rich methods of analysis that are unavailable with any other chart.

The basic premise of the kagi chart is that the thickness and the direction of the kagi lines are dependent on the market's action. If the market continues to move in the direction of the prior kagi line, that line is extended. However, if the market reverses by a predetermined amount, a new kagi line is drawn in the next column in the opposite direction. An interesting aspect of the kagi chart is that when prices penetrate a prior low or high, the thickness of the kagi line changes. The thick kagi line is called a *yang* line and the thin kagi line is called a *yin* line. Later in this chapter, I will detail how to construct and interpret the yang and yin lines. The short horizontal line on the kagi chart is labeled the *inflection* line.

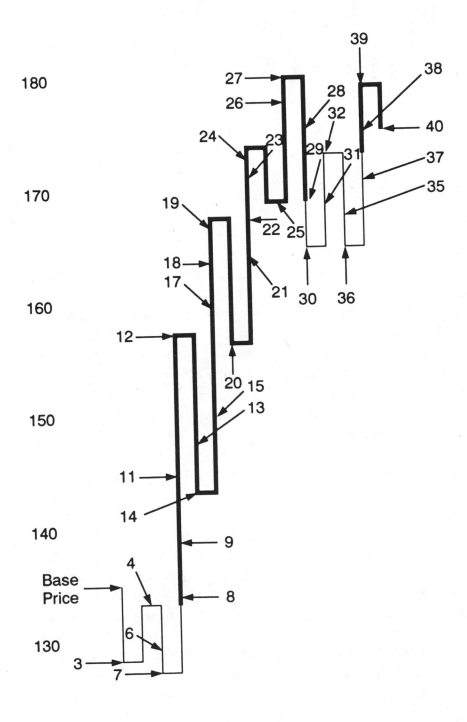

EXHIBIT 8.1.   Example of a Kagi Chart Using Table 8.1

CONSTRUCTION OF KAGI CHARTS

Kagi charts are most commonly based on closing prices. Before starting the kagi chart, a turnaround (i.e., or reversal) amount must be chosen. This is the minimum price movement that is needed before a new reversal line can be drawn in the next column. For instance, if the turnaround amount is $3, and if there is a rising line, today's price must close lower by at least $3 before a falling turnaround line can be drawn. This will be become clear when I get into more detail about the construction of the kagi chart. For kagi charts, the turnaround amount can be touched or exceeded for a reversal line to be drawn.

OUR EXAMPLE: The starting price, as shown at session 1 in Table 8.1, is 135. The turnaround amount in this example will be four points.

TABLE 8.1 Data Used for Four-Point Kagi Chart in Exhibit 8.1

Session	Closing Price	Session	Closing Price
1	135 base price	21	165↑
2	132<	22	168↑
3	128↓	23	171↑
4	133↑	24	173↑
5	130<	25	169↓
6	129↓	26	177↑
7	127↓	27	180↑
8	134* (prior high–133)	28	176↓
9	139↑	29	170↓
10	137<	30	165* (prior low–169)
11	145↑	31	169↑
12	158↑	32	173↑
13	147↓	33	170<
14	143↓	34	170<
15	150↑	35	168↓
16	149<	36	165↓
17	160↑	37	171↑
18	164↑	38	175* (prior high–173)
19	167↑	39	179↑
20	156↓	40	175↓

Legend
(<)—Move is less than reversal amount. No line is drawn.
*—Where the price exceeds the prior high or low (line changes thickness).
↑ ↓—Up and down arrows—show direction of the current line on Exhibit 8.1.

<u>Drawing the first line</u>: Compare today's price to the base price.

Rule 1. If today's price is higher than the base price by the turn-around amount or more (in our ex-ample, this would mean four or more points from the starting price), then a thick (yang) line is drawn from the starting price to the new high closing price.
Note: To draw a line, the change in price should be the same or greater than the turnaround amount.

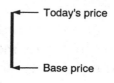

Rule 2. If today's price is lower than the base price by the prede-termined turnaround amount or more, then draw a thin (yin) line from the starting price down to to-day's price.

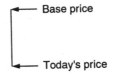

Rule 3. If the difference between the current close and the base price is less than the minimum turn-around amount (in our case, four points), no line is drawn

OUR EXAMPLE: The starting price is 135. During the next session, the market moved down to 132. This is less than the predetermined turn-around amount of four points, so we cannot yet draw a line. At ses-sion 3, the price had fallen to 128. Now, the market had dropped more than the four points needed to draw the first line (from session 1 to session 3, prices fell seven points). Thus, we draw a thin yin line (because the market moved down) from the starting price of 135 down to 128.

<u>Drawing the second line</u>: Compare today's price to the tip (i.e., the bot-tom or the top) of the last kagi line. In our example, the bottom of the line is 128 and the top is 135, so we would compare the more current price to 135 and 128.

Rule 4. If the price continues in the same direction as the prior line, the line is extended in the same direction, no matter how small the move. Thus, in our example, if the price fell to 127, we would then extend the yin line down from 128 to 127. However, if the first line is a thick yang line (instead of yin line), the thick line would then be extended higher if there is a new high close.

or

Rule 5. If the market changes direction by the turnaround amount or more (this could take a number of sessions), then we go the next column, draw a short horizontal line (called an *inflection line*) to the next column and draw a vertical line in the new direction to the new price. In our example, the low of the last line was at 128. Since we need a four-point turnaround, the market would have to close at 132 or higher to draw a new line in the opposite direction.

or

Rule 6. If the market moves in the opposite direction to the preceding trend *by less than the turnaround amount*, then that session is ignored.

OUR EXAMPLE: With the bottom of the last kagi line at 128, we compare the price at session 4 to that at 128. With session 4 at 133, it means prices had risen by five points (from 128 to 133). This was enough of a move (since the turnaround amount was four points) to draw a new line in the opposite direction to the prior line. As a result, we move a column to the right by drawing a short horizontal line (the inflection line) and then draw a line going up. This line starts at 128 and goes up to 133.

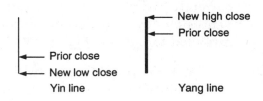

Yin line   Yang line

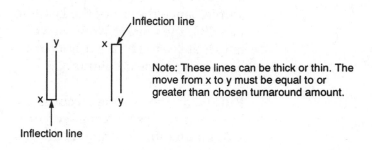

Note: These lines can be thick or thin. The move from x to y must be equal to or greater than chosen turnaround amount.

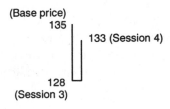

<u>Drawing the third line</u>: We again compare the most recent kagi line with today's price. Using our example, the last kagi line stopped at 133. So we now compare today's price to 133.

Rule 7. Because the kagi line is currently rising, if the price advances by any amount, the line is extended to the new high price.

Rule 8. If the price declines by the turnaround amount or more (in our case, four points), then a new line is drawn down. Based on our example, since the tip of the last line was 133, the market would have to fall to at least 129 for a line to be drawn in the next column.

Rule 9. If the market declines by less than the predetermined turnaround amount, nothing is drawn.

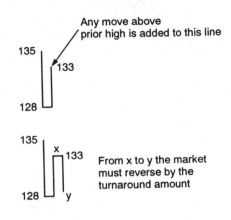

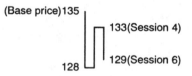

OUR EXAMPLE: The tip of the last kagi line, from session 4, is at 133. We compare session 5's price of 130 to this price at 133. Although prices reversed as the market went down from 133 to 130, the decline was less than the four points needed to draw a turnaround line on our kagi chart. Thus, session 5 is ignored. The next time a new line is added is at session 6. At session 6, the price is at 129 or four points under the bottom of the prior kagi line at 133. We move to the next column and draw a turnaround line from 133 down to 129.

At session 7, the price declines to 127. We extend the line down from 129 to 127 (since the move lower from 129 to 127 was in the direction of the prior kagi line, we do not need the four-point move that would be needed for a rising turnaround line).

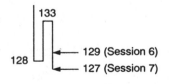

At session 8, the price has moved up to 134. This is a seven-point rally from the low of the prior kagi line at 127—more than enough to draw a rising turnaround line. We then shift to a new column, and draw a line up from 127 to 134. Note how this line changed from narrow to thick once the price exceeded the prior high at 133. This brings out one of the major features about kagi charts. Specifically:

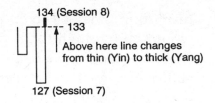

Rule 10. If a narrow line in a kagi chart exceeds the prior high, at the point where the previous high was exceeded, the line becomes thick. The preceding high is called a *shoulder*.

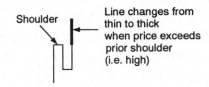

Rule 11. If a thick kagi line breaks a previous low, the line becomes narrow at the price where the low was penetrated. The preceding low is called a *waist*.

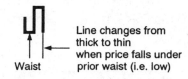

OUR EXAMPLE: For the rest of this discussion, see Table 8.1 and Exhibit 8.1.

As described in Rule 11 above, the line changes from thick to thin when a prior low is broken. Note how in Exhibit 8.1 there were times when the market reversed price action, but these reversals were not enough to break a preceding low (for example, from session 19 to 20). Thus, the line's thickness did not change. However, at session 30, the price at 165 broke under the prior low at 169 (at session 25). Consequently, when the kagi line for session 30 is drawn, once the price of that line moves under the prior low of 169, it changes from thick to thin (from a yang to yin line). Observe how at session 38 the market broke a prior high and, as such, went from a thin yin line to a thick yang line.

Using Percentage Kagi Charts

A problem in using a fixed price turnaround amount is that the reversal amount may have to be adjusted depending on the stock's price. A $1 turnaround may be acceptable for a $20 or $30 stock, but a $1 turnaround would be too high for a $5 stock and too low for a $100 stock. The kagi chart has a unique and powerful approach to this problem—it offers the ability to use a fixed percentage reversal amount instead of a fixed price. For example, in a 3% kagi chart, if the chart starts at $50, the first turnaround price will be $1.50 (3% of $50). If the stock rises to $70, the turnaround price would be $2.10 (3% of $70). Thus, as the stock's price rises, the turnaround price would automatically increase, and if the price falls, the turnaround price would decrease.

Using percentage kagi charts is not as common as the fixed price kagi in Japan. This is because many Japanese traders prefer to draw the kagi charts by hand, and doing percentage changes is relatively time consuming. However, with computer software now available for kagi charting (see the EQUIS, MetaStock software information at the end of this book), traders can now easily use percentage turnarounds.

Whether a trader uses a fixed price or a fixed percentage unit as a reversal, the amount chosen for the turnaround lines is an individual preference depending on a trader's time frame and trading style. An expert in kagi from the Nippon Technical Analysts Association passed on to me that, as a general rule, he uses a 3% turnaround level for stocks. The 5% kagi also appears popular for longer term traders.

TRADING TECHNIQUES WITH THE KAGI CHART

Buy on Yang, Sell on Yin

The are many ways to use kagi charts, but the most basic is to buy when the kagi line goes from thin to thick, and to sell when the kagi line changes from thick to thin. Remember that the kagi line becomes thick (i.e., becomes a yang line) when the prior high is exceeded. The kagi line converts to a thin yin line when a prior low is broken.

In Exhibit 8.2, I show basic kagi buy and sell signals. The buys occur with the emergence of a yang (thick) line, and sell signals unfold when the kagi line converts to a yin line (i.e., thin). As can be seen, when the market trades sideways, the buy and sell signals can induce losses (for example, from B_2 to S_2 and from B_3 to S_3). This is because kagi charts, like renko and three-line break charts, are trending tools, and in non-trending markets can cause traders to frequently move in and out of the market. (There are ways to circumvent this, for example, by adjusting the sensitivity. This will be discussed later.) However, the goal of the kagi chart is to catch longer term trends. This was accomplished between the buy at B_4 and the offsetting sale at S_4. A constructive aspect of this

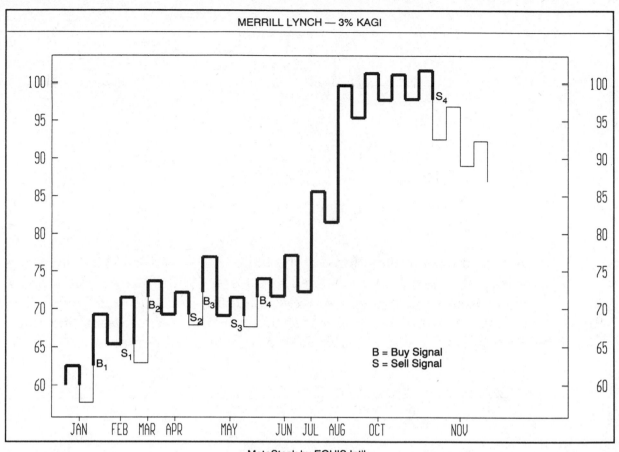

EXHIBIT 8.2. Basic Buy and Sell Signals, Merrill Lynch—3% Kagi, Daily

Merrill Lynch chart was that, since January, there was a series of higher highs and higher lows. This conveyed an underlying strength to the market. Since S_4, however, there have been lower highs and lower lows. This aspect of comparing highs and lows is discussed below.

Shoulders and Waists

A shoulder is a prior high and a waist is a former low. A series of shoulders and waists with ascending highs or descending lows can relay much information about the underlying tone of the market. As shown in Exhibit 8.3(A), a series of rising shoulders (denoted by S_1, S_2, and S_3) and waists (W_1, W_2, and W_3) underscores the market's vitality insofar as the bulls are able to maintain a cycle of higher highs and higher lows. In Exhibit 8.3(B), falling shoulders S_1, S_2, and S_3 and declining waists W_1, W_2, and W_3 echo a market in which the bears have the greater control.

In Exhibit 8.4, we see how a sequence of higher shoulders (S_1–S_5)

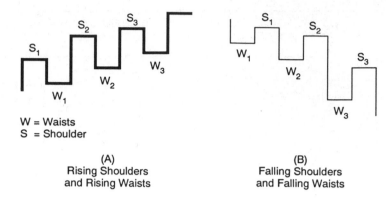

W = Waists
S = Shoulder

(A)
Rising Shoulders
and Rising Waists

(B)
Falling Shoulders
and Falling Waists

EXHIBIT 8.3.   Shoulders and Waists

showed the underlying force of the bulls. The chart also shows how the waists, at W_1–W_4, formed ascending lows. While this combination of higher highs and higher lows was unfolding, the kagi chart reflected a healthy environment. A hint that the bulls' force was dissipating came at waist 5 (W_5). That waist broke the prior cycle of higher lows since W_5

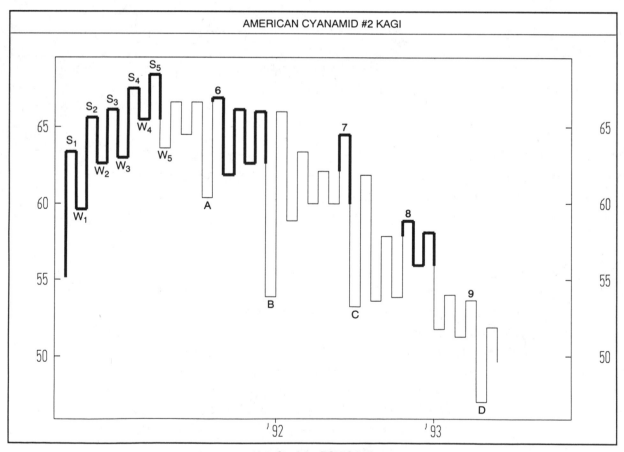

MetaStock by EQUIS Int'l

EXHIBIT 8.4.   Importance of Highs and Lows, American Cyanamid—$2 Kagi, Daily

made a lower low (it was lower than W_4). From a long-term perspective, this market has shown continuing weakness, as evidenced by the series of lower major highs at 6–9 and the lower major lows at A–D.

Stock mutual funds prices are based only on the close. Because candlestick charts require the open, high, low, and closing prices, they cannot be used to analyze stock mutual funds. Now, however, we can technically analyze mutual funds with three-line break, renko and kagi charts, since these techniques only require the close. In Exhibit 8.5 I show that comparing the heights of the shoulders and waists can be used to gauge the underlying strength of a mutual fund. In this chart I show a group of rising shoulders (S_1 through S_5) and rising waists (W_1 to W_5). The first sign of a slackening in demand came when shoulder S_6 was lower that the prior shoulder and waist W_5 was lower than the former waist W_5. After this, area S_5 became resistance.

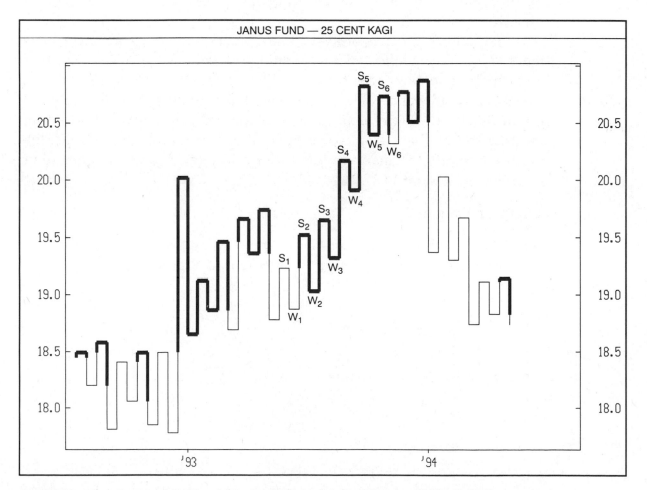

EXHIBIT 8.5.   Comparing Shoulders and Waists, Janus Fund—.25 Kagi, Daily

Multi-Level Breaks

In Chapter 6, I discussed how Japanese traders may wait for extra confirmation in the three-line break chart by waiting for an additional white or black line. The same strategy can be used with kagi charts. In the kagi chart, this entails waiting for two or more prior highs or lows to be penetrated. In Exhibit 8.6., I illustrate how each former high or low is referred to as a *level*. As illustrated in Exhibit 8.6(A), the thick yang line converts to a thin yin line when the first level (i.e., the previous waist, W_1) is broken. However, some traders may wait for a two-level break, meaning that the two prior lows at W_1 and W_2 are broken before a sell signal is confirmed. Exhibit 8.6(B) shows a three-level break. This means that the rally has to exceed the prior three highs (the prior three shoulders S_1–S_3) before a buy is confirmed.

As is the case with any technique where extra confirmation requires extra time, there is less profit potential once the trend is confirmed since this confirmation takes longer. However, the extra confirmation should mean greater probability that the trend has changed. We come back to the immutable law of risk and reward. The less the risk, the less the reward.

In Exhibit 8.7, a series of lower highs (marked S_1–S_5) and lower lows (marked W_1–W_5) manifested a weakening market. However, this cycle of lower highs and lows was broken with the higher high at S_6. Area S_6 was also a two-level break since it moved above the prior two highs (at S_4 and S_5). Further reinforcing the view that this market was bottoming was that the pullback from S_6 stopped above the prior low at W_5. This was the first time in many months that a low (at W_6) was higher than the previous low (at W_5).

Length of Yang and Yin

Just as the length of a white or black candle line reflects whether it is the bulls or bears who are in charge, so it is with a kagi line. By viewing an

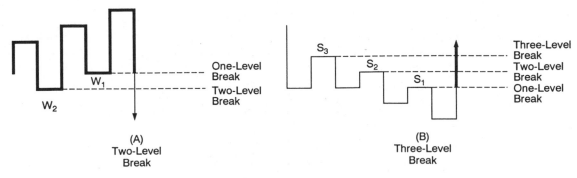

EXHIBIT 8.6. Two- and Three-Level Breaks

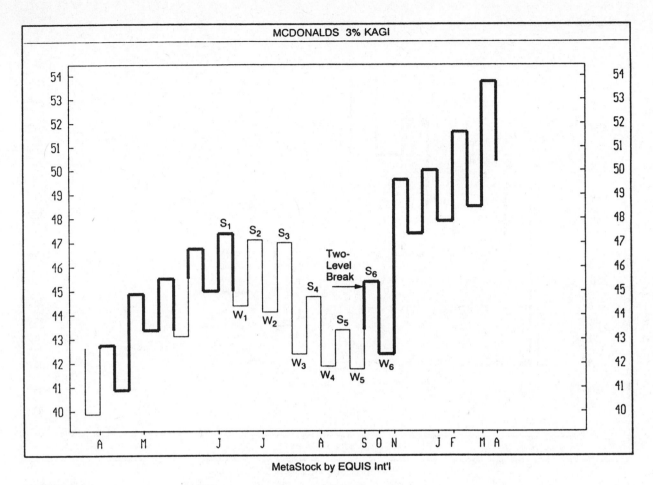

EXHIBIT 8.7. Two-Level Break, McDonald's—3% Kagi, Daily

individual kagi line and comparing the yin (thin) and yang (thick) sections of that line, we can obtain insight into who has the balance of power— the bulls or the bears. Exhibit 8.8 graphically displays this concept of yang and yin lengths. If the yin and yang sections are the same size, then it is viewed like a doji, where the market is in balance. If the yang section is longer, it is the bulls who dominate. A longer yin section means that the bears are in control.

In Exhibit 8.9, kagi lines 1 through 3 have longer yang sections than

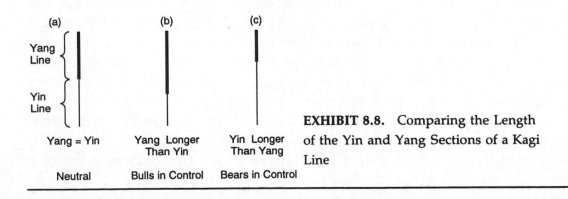

EXHIBIT 8.8. Comparing the Length of the Yin and Yang Sections of a Kagi Line

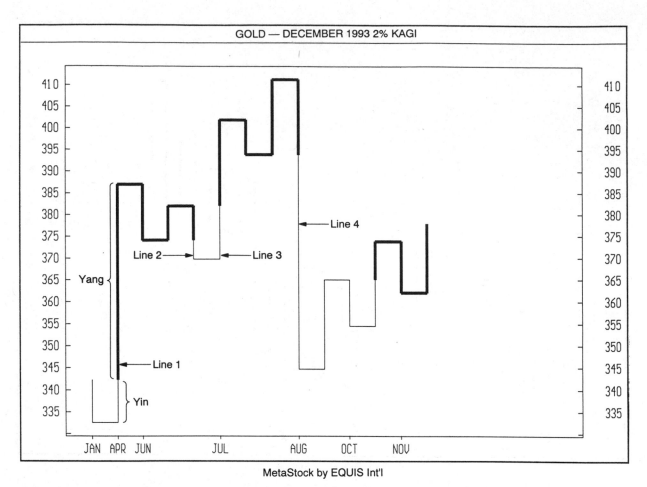

EXHIBIT 8.9. Yin and Yang Portions of a Kagi Line, Gold—December 1993, 2% Kagi, Daily

yin sections. This means that the bulls had a stronger grip on the market than did the bears. In kagi line 4, the longer height of the yin line as compared to the yang line kept a bearish undertone to the market.

Where Corrections Stop Within the Prior Kagi Line

Where a correction stops within a kagi line can be used as a gauge of the market's health. Specifically, in kagi charting, the center of a long kagi line is important. If, as shown in Exhibit 8.10(A), the market corrects after a rally, and this correction stops before touching the center of a prior long kagi line, it is bullish. Such a scenario displays that the bulls kept the bears from progressing steeply into the bulls' domain. If, in this scenario, the market then exceeds the prior shoulder, it is a buy signal since it is a time when the bulls have regained full control of the market.

If, during a downtrend, a rally fails to pierce the midway point of a

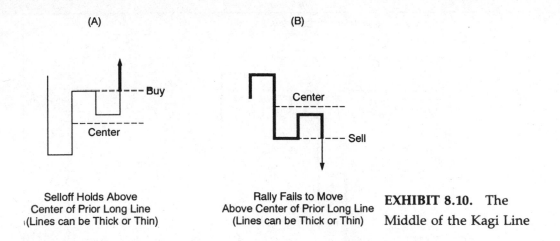

(A)   (B)

Selloff Holds Above
Center of Prior Long Line
(Lines can be Thick or Thin)

Rally Fails to Move
Above Center of Prior Long Line
(Lines can be Thick or Thin)

EXHIBIT 8.10. The Middle of the Kagi Line

prior long kagi line, then it is a negative signal insofar as the bulls were not aggressive enough to push prices above the midway point of the prior line. This is shown in Exhibit 8.10(B). Once the market declines past the previous low, it is viewed as a sign to sell since it is at that point where the bears have wrested control of the market.

Note that it is usually in the longer kagi lines that the midpoint becomes important. This is similar to the middle of long white or black candles taking on significance.

In Exhibit 8.11, I display the middle of some long kagi lines by the letter M. We see how M_1 became a support area as the low of kagi line 1 held above M_1. Midpoint M_2 had extra importance since M_2 was also above the prior highs made from March through May in the 109–110 area. The fact that the pullback via kagi line 2 held above these old highs and also held above M_2 relayed the underlying strength of the market. Area M_3 became support on the correction made with the selloff at kagi line 3. Kagi line 4 broke the support area set up by M_3. Thus far, not only has the market failed to push above the new resistance area set up by M_4, but it has not even managed to push above the lows set by kagi line 3 (remember the technical axiom that old support can convert to new resistance).

Double Windows

Double windows can be top or bottom reversal patterns. (Note: a double window in kagi charting is different from a window in candle charts.) As illustrated in Exhibit 8.12(A), a double window bottom is formed when:

1. during a downtrend, the market bounces and forms a shoulder (at S_1). This shoulder's high is less than the prior waist's low (W_1).
2. the following waist (shown as W_2) is also above shoulder S_1.

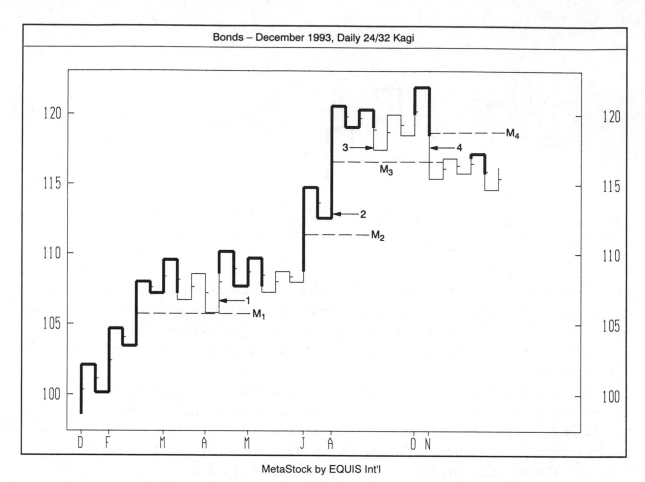

EXHIBIT 8.11. Kagi and Halfway Points, Bonds—December 1993, 24/32nd Kagi

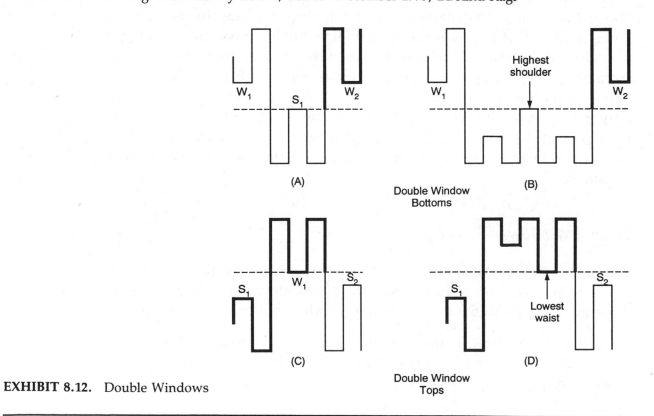

EXHIBIT 8.12.   Double Windows

This is called a double window because both waists W$_1$ and W$_2$ are above the intervening shoulder (i.e. S$_1$). It is like having a price gap (i.e. an open window) between the high at shoulder S$_1$ and the lows at waists to the left and right of this shoulder. If there is more than one shoulder, it would still be considered a double window if the highest shoulder does not overlap the waists to the left and right. This is shown in Exhibit 8.12(B).

Double window tops are shown in Exhibits 8.12(C) and 8.12(D). The double window top is formed when:

1. during an uptrend the left shoulder (shown by S$_1$) is below the following waist (shown by W$_1$) and
2. the next shoulder (at S$_2$) is also below W$_1$.

In other words, the shoulders at S$_1$ and S$_2$ that surround the intervening waist (W$_1$) are both under W$_1$. Exhibit 8.12(D) illustrates how it is also a double window top if the lowest waist in a group of waists is still higher than the two shoulders at S$_1$ and S$_2$.

Exhibit 8.13 shows how a double window bottom unfolds in a three-

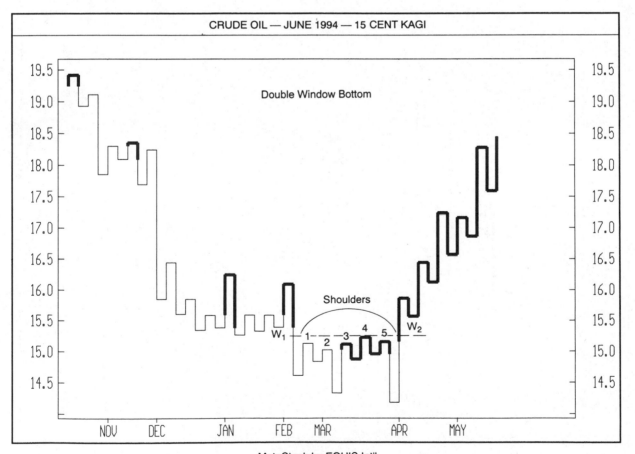

MetaStock by EQUIS Int'l

EXHIBIT 8.13. Double Window Bottom, Crude Oil—June 1994, 15 Cent Kagi

step process. First, we see a low waist at W_1. The next step is to compare the waist (W_1) to the next shoulder or group of shoulders. In this chart, a series of shoulders marked 1 through 5 was built during February and March. Note how waist W_1 was above the highest shoulder S_4. Finally, after the highs of these shoulders are exceeded, we see if the next waist (W_2) is higher than the highest shoulder (which was shoulder 4). Since this criterion was met, we have a double window bottom. In this chart it is also interesting to see how the support from December through January became converted to resistance, as evidenced by shoulders 1 through 5. The market breaks this resistance area, and the double windows are two bullish signals.

In Exhibit 8.14, in late 1993, we see a double window top. This pattern was formed since the lowest waist (at 2) was above the surrounding shoulders at 1 and 3. Another double window top unfolded in early 1994. For that window we can easily see how shoulder A was below the next group of waists (at B and C) but it is not as clear that shoulder D is below B. However, the low at B was 114-6/32nds and the high at D was

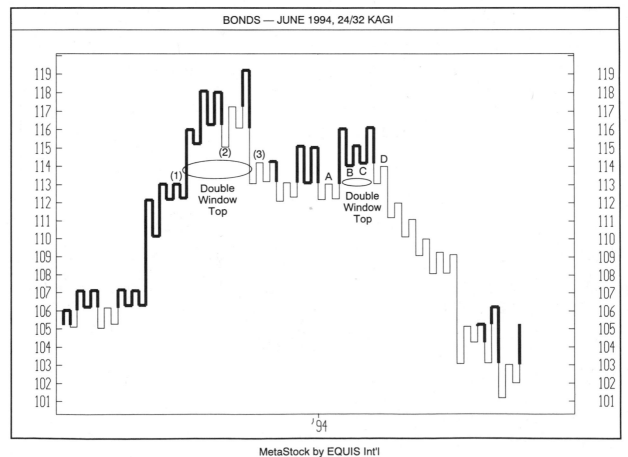

EXHIBIT 8.14. Double Window Tops, Bonds—June 1994, 24/32 Kagi

114-1/32nd. Thus, there was a 5/32nd price gap between the lowest waist at B and the next shoulder at D. As a result, a double window top was completed. The ovals that I used to illustrate the two double windows in this chart are the traditional method used by the Japanese to show double windows.

Trendlines

As shown in Exhibit 8.15, the highs during the decline that began in late 1992 were defined by a downward sloping resistance line. Of interest during this decline is that the rebounds (shown by S_1 through S_5) pushed up halfway or less into kagi lines 1 through 6. This showed that the counterattacks by the bulls were relatively feeble. The first sign that the bulls were starting to get a grip on this market was that the low at Y was not lower than the low at X. This was the first time in many months that a lower low was not formed. Areas X and Y formed a double bottom.

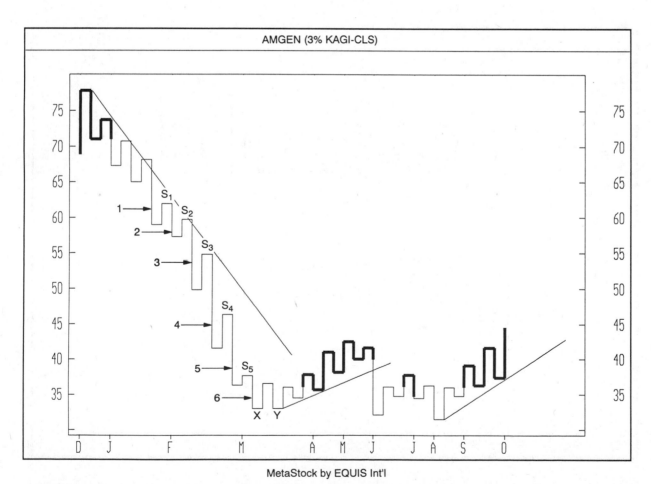

MetaStock by EQUIS Int'l

EXHIBIT 8.15. Support and Resistance Lines, Amgen—3% Kagi, Daily

This provided enough of a base for a minor rally. This rally's support area was a rising trendline that started at Y. Another rising trendline was formed with the ascending lows from August.

The change of polarity principle can be used (where prior support becomes resistance and vice versa) with kagi charts since a prior support of resistance area is so evident on a kagi chart. For example, in Exhibit 8.16, we can see how resistance areas near $45 and $50 became converted to support areas.

Tweezers

As discussed above, support and resistance areas often become very clear on the kagi chart. Exhibit 8.17 shows a double top, or what the Japanese call a tweezers top. Of interest is that, as annotated on the candle chart of Wal-Mart, there was also a series of topping patterns based on the candles. Note how confirmation of the double top on the kagi chart did

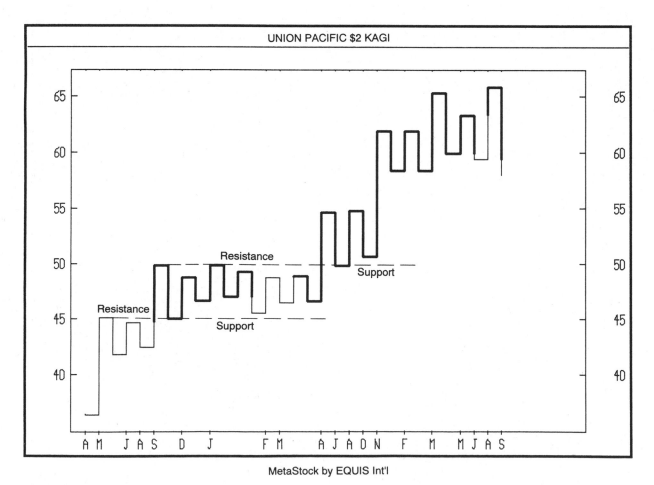

MetaStock by EQUIS Int'l

EXHIBIT 8.16.   Change of Polarity Principle, Union Pacific—$2 Kagi, Daily

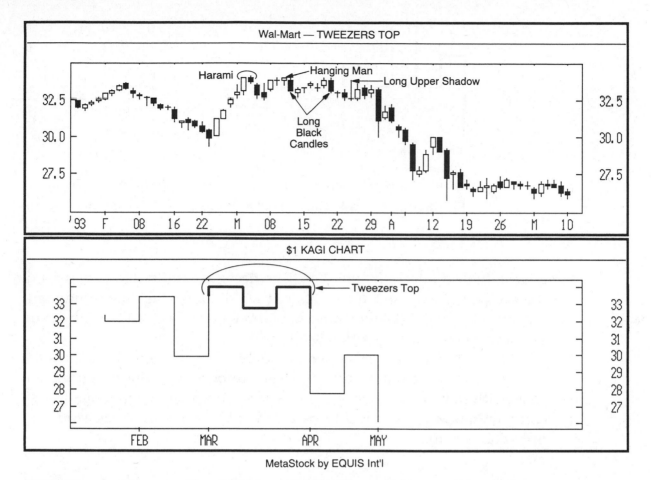

EXHIBIT 8.17.   Tweezers Top, Wal-Mart—Candle Chart and $1 Kagi Chart, Daily

not come until early April, whereas the candle signals gave earlier clues of a topping out process. This reflects a limitation of the kagi chart insofar as trend reversals are usually given later in the move. Kagi charts (like the three-line break and renko charts) are not for those who are trying to pick exact tops or bottoms, but who are interested in catching the "meat" of the move.

Three-Buddha and Reverse Three-Buddha

The basic three-Buddha and reverse (or inverted) three-Buddha patterns are illustrated in Exhibit 8.18. These patterns are the same as the Western head and shoulders and inverted head and shoulders patterns. The sell signal is sent when the "right shoulder" of the three Buddha is pierced.

In Exhibit 8.19, I show some ways traders can determine if the three-Buddha top can be more bearish or a reverse three-Buddha more bullish. For example, Exhibit 8.19(A) illustrates how the rebound from the right Buddha stalled under the center of the prior long kagi line. This reflected

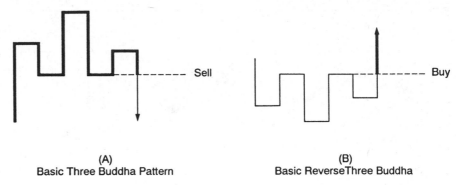

(A)
Basic Three Buddha Pattern

(B)
Basic ReverseThree Buddha

EXHIBIT 8.18.   Basic Three Buddha and Reverse Three Buddha Patterns

a weak bullish attack. Exhibit 8.19(B) reflects the underlying strength of the market since the selloff held above the prior long kagi line's midpoint. Exhibit 8.19(C) and (D) illustrates how three Buddha's can have the extra importance obtained by a two-level break.

A three-Buddha top is shown in Exhibit 8.20. The first bearish signal was given with the break of the uptrend support line. More confirmation came with the one-level break. For traders who prefer even more bearish corroboration, the two-level break could have been viewed as extra confirmation of a top.

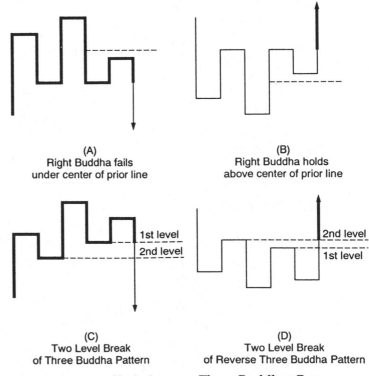

(A)
Right Buddha fails
under center of prior line

(B)
Right Buddha holds
above center of prior line

(C)
Two Level Break
of Three Buddha Pattern

(D)
Two Level Break
of Reverse Three Buddha Pattern

EXHIBIT 8.19.   Variations on Three Buddhas Patterns

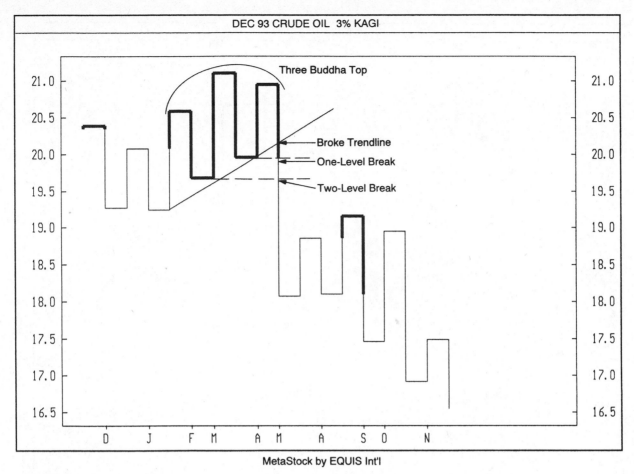

EXHIBIT 8.20. Three-Buddha Top, December 1993 Crude Oil

Exhibit 8.21 displays a classic inverted three-Buddha pattern where the two waists at W_1 and W_2 are about the same price. By breaking above shoulders S_1 and S_2 (shown at the arrow) the inverted three-Buddha pattern was confirmed with a two-level break. Note how the old resistance area at shoulders S_1 and S_2 became support and the market continued to advance with a series of higher waists and higher shoulders.

Record Sessions

A key element used by Japanese traders in candles and kagi charts is the concept of record sessions. These are the same record sessions as discussed in Chapter 3, on candlestick patterns. In the context of kagi charts, record sessions are the counting of the shoulders or the waists. As shown in Exhibit 8.22, a sequence of nine higher shoulders (not necessarily consecutive) is called nine record session highs. Likewise, a group of nine lower waists is called nine record session lows. The Japanese view a market that has about nine record highs or lows as a time to look for a countertrend move.

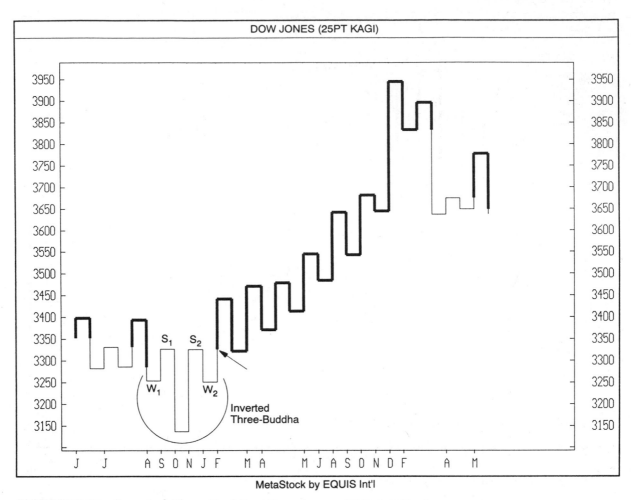

EXHIBIT 8.21.   Inverted Three-Buddha, Dow Jones—25 Point Kagi

As shown in Exhibit 8.23, in early 1992, the market formed an inverted three-Buddha pattern. From there, the bulls took the market from near $30 to $43. The rally unfolded with nine record session highs. After the ninth record high, prices stalled, and in early 1993, they formed a double top near $43.

Although most Japanese traders use Kagi charts built from daily or

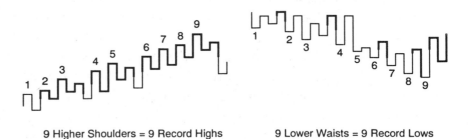

9 Higher Shoulders = 9 Record Highs   9 Lower Waists = 9 Record Lows

EXHIBIT 8.22.   Record Session High and Lows

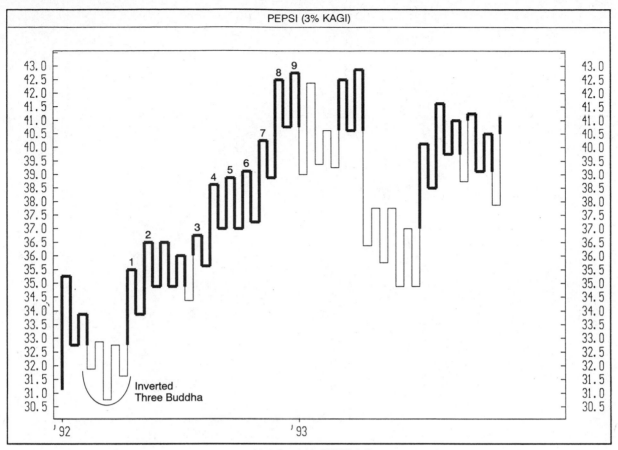

MetaStock by EQUIS Int'l

EXHIBIT 8.23. Record Session Highs, Pepsi—3% Kagi, Daily

weekly closes, kagi charts can be used on an intra-day basis just as point and figure charts can be used on a daily or intra-day basis. Exhibit 8.24 shows a five minute kagi chart. This means that the close of each five minute segment during the day is used to compose the kagi chart. All the rules to draw the kagi chart and any of the trading techniques previously addressed can be used on an intra-day kagi chart. In this chart we see an evident resistance area near 453 in late April and early May. An ascending support line was punctured on May 6th. Just before the break of this support line the market reached a new high for the prior move (at X) and from there a series of nine lower lows emerged. This formed 9 record session lows and increased the likelihood of a bounce. In addition, the lows made on May 9 and 10 formed a double window bottom.

Exhibit 8.25 shows one of the key advantages of kagi charts—it allows a more detailed analysis of markets, such as mutual funds, that have only closing prices. In this example of the Magellen Fund there various kagi techniques that could have been used to signal a top towards the end of 1993. These signals included:

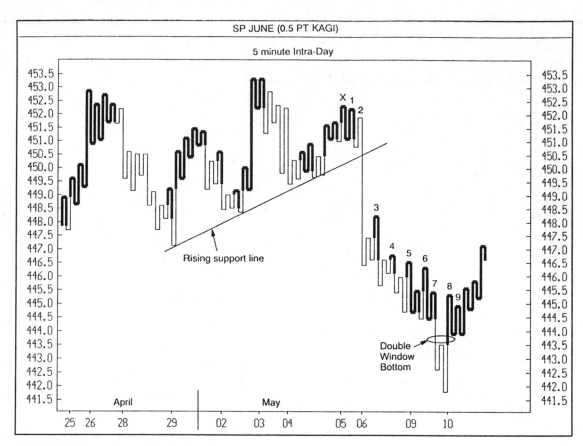

EXHIBIT 8.24. Intraday Kagi charts, S & P June 1994—5 Minute Kagi Chart

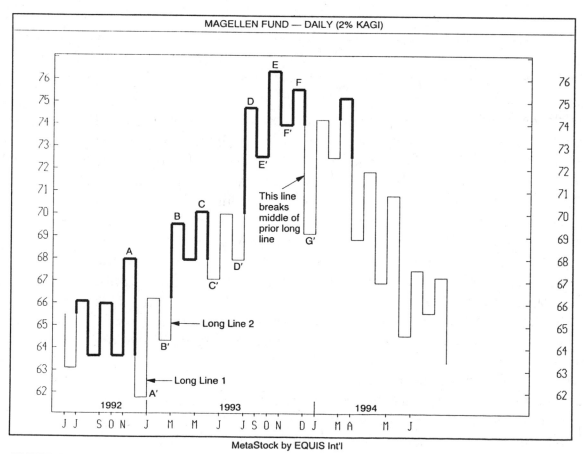

EXHIBIT 8.25. Magellen Fund—2% Kagi, Daily

1. The market relayed its underlying strength when price retracements held above the middle of long kagi lines marked by 1, 2 and 3. However, when the bears were aggressive enough to drag prices under the middle of long kagi line 3 (at the arrow) it was a clue that the underlying market condition had changed.

2. The series of ascending highs at A through E and rising lows A' to F' represented a firming market. Warning of a loss of upside drive came via the lower high at F and the lower low at G'.

3. From late 1992 to late 1993 the length of the yang portion of the kagi lines was longer than the yin portion of those lines. This represented that the bulls were more in control of the market than were the bears. But with long kagi line 3 (the same line that broke under the middle of the prior long kagi line), the longer yin portion of the kagi line, relative to the yang line, reflected a time when the bears had grabbed control of the market.

[1]Oyama, Kenji. *Hanawa Kurenai Yanagiwa Midori*, pg. 51.

PRACTICE SESSION FOR THE KAGI CHART

....

On a photocopy of the graph supplied on page 243 or on a piece of plain paper, create a kagi chart from the data shown in Table 8.2. The chart's scale should be from a low of $34 to a high of $40. The session numbers on the right side of Table 8.2 show where the new kagi line is extended as described in the answer chart (Exhibit 8.26, following the practice pages). Be sure you try to draw this practice kagi chart on your own, before looking at the answer chart.

TABLE 8.2 Data for Construction of Kagi Chart

Session	Date	Close	Session	Date	Close
1	04/04/94	35.750	33	05/19/94	39.500
2	04/05/94	37.250	34	05/20/94	38.875
3	04/06/94	39.000	35	05/23/94	38.500
4	04/07/94	38.375	36	05/24/94	39.000
5	04/08/94	37.750	37	05/25/94	38.500
6	04/11/94	37.750	38	05/26/94	38.500
7	04/12/94	37.375	39	05/27/94	39.000
8	04/13/94	36.250	40	05/31/94	39.000
9	04/14/94	35.750	41	06/01/94	40.000
10	04/15/94	35.250	42	06/02/94	39.875
11	04/18/94	36.250	43	06/03/94	39.875
12	04/19/94	35.250	44	06/06/94	38.875
13	04/20/94	34.500	45	06/07/94	38.500
14	04/21/94	35.625	46	06/08/94	38.250
15	04/22/94	35.500	47	06/09/94	38.875
16	04/25/94	36.625	48	06/10/94	39.375
17	04/26/94	36.375	49	06/13/94	39.375
18	04/28/94	36.250	50	06/14/94	39.750
19	04/29/94	36.875	51	06/15/94	39.500
20	05/02/94	37.250	52	06/16/94	39.375
21	05/03/94	36.875	53	06/17/94	38.500
22	05/04/94	36.500	54	06/20/94	37.750
23	05/05/94	37.125	55	06/21/94	37.625
24	05/06/94	36.375	56	06/22/94	37.500
25	05/09/94	35.875	57	06/23/94	36.500
26	05/10/94	36.625	58	06/24/94	35.000
27	05/11/94	37.125	59	06/27/94	36.625
28	05/12/94	36.250	60	06/28/94	36.000
29	05/13/94	37.000	61	06/29/94	35.875
30	05/16/94	37.250	62	06/30/94	35.000
31	05/17/94	37.500	63	07/01/94	35.250
32	05/18/94	38.500	64	07/05/94	35.125

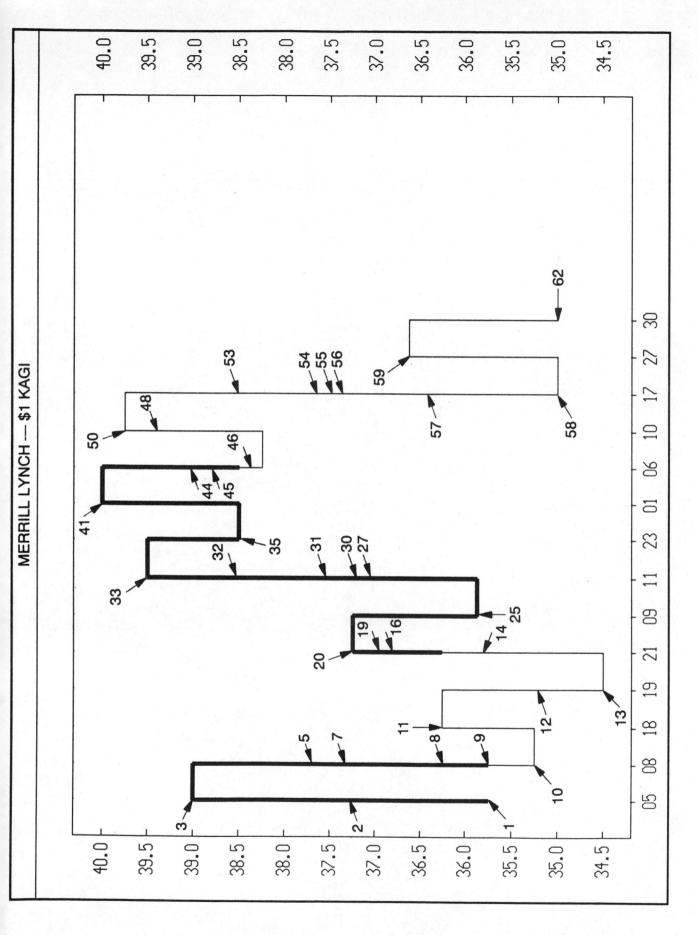

EXHIBIT 8.26. Merrill Lynch—1 Point Kagi

245

CONCLUSION

In this book, I have discussed candlestick charts, the disparity index, three-line breaks, and renko and kagi charts. With all of these techniques, the question that may arise is: Which is the best? I cannot say that kagi charts are better than three-line break or candle charts. They each have their advantages and uses. For example, kagi, three-line break, and renko charts are useful for providing a view of the market on a macro scale. Candlestick charts can be used on a micro scale by providing early clues about market reversals. For example, a member of the Nippon Technical Analysts Society told me that he uses kagi charts and other Japanese tools, but waits for a candle signal before placing a trade.

In the Introduction to this book, I quoted a samurai who said that, "Learning is the gate, not the house. You first have to go through the gate to get to the house." Now, I have taken you through the gate and up to the door of the house. However, as a Japanese proverb states, "Your teacher can lead you to the door; acquiring of learning then rests on you."

With the help of this book, I hope that you have learned enough to lay the foundation of basic concepts on which you can build. The techniques I examined should be viewed as basic tools that you can adjust to your individual trading needs and style. There are so many ways to use these exciting and powerful tools.

Each trader will find that experimenting with the three-line break, renki, and kagi charts will depend on individual factors such as trading style, risk adversity, and trading time frame orientation. There are no right or wrong ways to use the new price charts and I am sure many of you will come up with your own trading ideas.

As one of my contacts in the Nippon Technical Analysts Association wrote to me: ''All my friends use different techniques to confirm their ideas.'' The tools discussed in this book are the plants that, when joined with the fertile soil of your own ideas, should help you reap a rich harvest of valuable trading concepts.

GLOSSARY

TECHNICAL TERMS WITH VISUAL REFERENCES

....

This is a glossary of the patterns and the new charting methods discussed in this book. Since I do not discuss all the candle patterns in this book, for those who want a more complete glossary of the candle patterns, please see my first book, *Japanese Candlestick Charting Techniques.*

Boldface, Italicized terms are cross-referenced glossary items.

Anchor chart—this was probably the first chart to graphically display the importance of the relationship between the open and close. The top and bottom of the anchor's vertical line are the high and low of that session. The horizontal line of the anchor line is the open. The arrow of the anchor line is the close. If the close is higher than the open, the arrow points up. If the close is lower than the open the arrow points down.

Anchor Chart (High-Low-Close-Open)

Bar chart—the common chart used in the West. The top and bottom of the vertical line are the high and low of the session. The horizontal line on the right of the vertical line is the close and the horizontal line to the left is the open. The Japanese used bar charts before the more evolved *anchor chart* and *candle chart* replaced the bar chart. In essence the bar chart is a less evolved form of charting than the candle chart. See also *anchor chart, pole chart,* and *stopping chart*

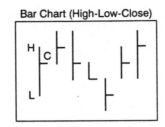

Bar Chart (High-Low-Close)

Base price—the starting price in a *kagi chart, renko chart,* and *three-line chart*.

Bearish engulfing pattern—a bearish candle pattern in which during a rally there is a black real body that envelopes the prior white real body. The larger the second candle in relation to the first candle, the more effective the pattern should be. A bearish engulfing pattern should act as resistance.

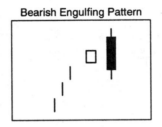

Bearish Engulfing Pattern

Black shoes—see "*buy when the neck emerges from the white suit with black shoes*" and "*sell if the black shoe comes out of a black suit after a neck*"

Black suit—see "*sell if the black shoe comes out of a black suit after a neck*"

Black turnaround line—the black line in a *three-line break chart* that breaks the low of the prior three consecutive white lines. See also *white turnaround line*.

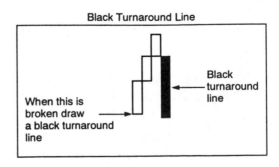

Black Turnaround Line

Blended candle—a single candle line built by combining two or more candle lines of a candle pattern. The blended candle can be used to help determine whether a group of candle lines is bullish or bearish. To construct the blended candle:

1. The open of the blended candle is the open of the first session of the candle pattern.
2. The top of the upper shadow of the blended candle is the highest high of the candle pattern (i.e., the top of the highest upper shadow).
3. The low of the blended candle's lower shadow is the lowest low of all the sessions of that pattern (i.e., the bottom of the lowest lower shadow).
4. The close of the blended candle is the close of the candle pattern's last session.

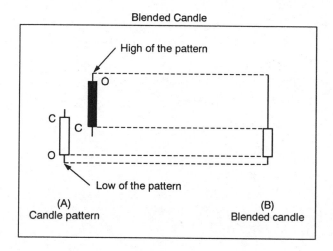

Blended Candle

High of the pattern

Low of the pattern

(A) Candle pattern

(B) Blended candle

Bullish engulfing pattern—a bottom reversal signal that is composed of two candle lines, the first is black and the second is white. The white real body of this pattern wraps around, or engulfs, the prior black real body. The second real body of this pattern (that is the white candle) should be much larger than the first (i.e., black) real body. A bullish engulfing pattern should act as support.

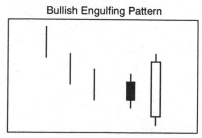

Bullish Engulfing Pattern

"Buy when the neck emerges from the white suit with black shoes"—an expression used by Japanese technicians to describe a bullish *three-line break chart* pattern. A short black line is sometimes called a black shoe, a

white turnaround line (a white line that surpasses the prior three black lines) is sometimes likened to a white suit and a small white line that follows a ***white turnaround line*** is called a neck since it looks like a neck coming out the white suit.

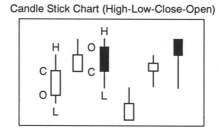

"Buy When the Neck Emerges
from the White Suit with Black Shoes"

Neck
(Buy Signal)

White
Suit

Black
Shoe

Candlestick chart (also called *candle chart*)—the most popular method of charting by the Japanese. Used since the 19th century, a candlestick chart uses the same data as a bar chart (the open, high, low, and close). However, the candle chart gives more graphic information about the market's health by segmenting individual candle lines into the ***real body*** and ***shadows.***

Candle Stick Chart (High-Low-Close-Open)

Change of polarity—a term used to describe the technical principle by which old resistance should be converted to new support and old support should be transformed to new resistance.

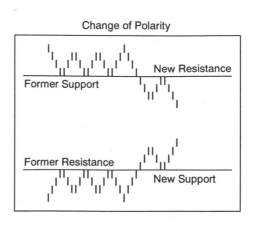

Change of Polarity

Former Support

New Resistance

Former Resistance

New Support

Collapsing doji star—a top reversal signal made up of three lines. The first is a tall white candle after which the market gaps lower via a falling *doji*. The third candle of this pattern is a black real body session that gaps under the doji's session. The three candles that make up this pattern are the same three as those needed for an evening doji star (See *evening Star*). The difference is that the evening doji star has the doji above the tall white real body while the collapsing doji star has the doji gapping under, instead of above, the first white candle.

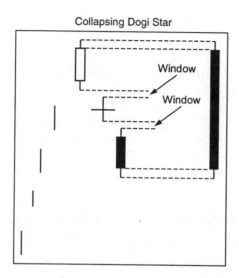

Collapsing Dogi Star

Dark cloud cover—during an uptrend there is a tall white candle followed by a session that opens at a new high. But by the end of that session the market closes as a black candle with a close well inside the prior long white candle's real body. The classic dark cloud cover's second session should close under the midpoint of the prior white candle. As a general rule, the deeper the close of the dark cloud cover's second session pushes into the white candle, the more bearish the signal. In the stock market, it could still be viewed as a dark cloud cover if the second session's open is above the prior session's close

Dark Cloud Cover

(instead of the prior session's high). Dark cloud covers should also be resistance.

Dead cross—a bearish indication formed when a short-term moving average crosses under a long-term moving average. See also *golden cross*.

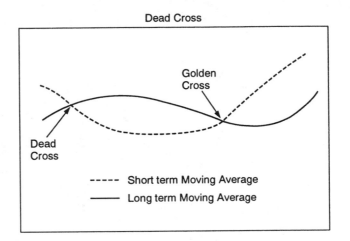

Disparity index or disparity ratio—an oscillator that compares the close of the current session to a moving average on a percentage basis. For example, a 25-day disparity index of −10% means that today's price is 10% under the 25-day moving average. Some of the ways the disparity index can be used include: as an overbought/oversold indicator, as a signal of trend direction, and as a tool to gauge divergence. See also *divergence index*.

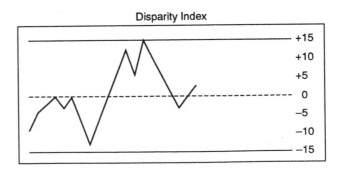

Divergence index—a percentage oscillator calculated by taking the current price and dividing it by the chosen moving average. Thus, a 25-day divergence of 110% would mean that the close today is 110% of the 25-day moving average. The divergence is the same as the *disparity*

index, it is just scaled differently. That is, a 25-day divergence index reading of 110% is the same as a 25-day disparity index of +10%.

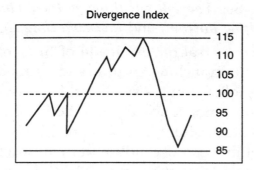

Doji—a session in which the open and close are the same. It reflects indecision and is a clue that the force behind the prior trend may be dwindling, especially if the doji comes after a tall white real body or after an extended move. Doji can also be used as a resistance area.

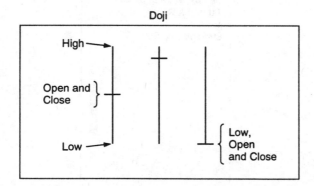

Double windows—a pattern in **kagi charts.** Double windows can be top or bottom reversal patterns. A double window bottom is constructed when the market forms a left *waist* (shown as W_1) that is above the next *shoulder* (shown as S_1) and the following waist (shown by W_2) is also above shoulder S_1. A double window top is completed when, during an uptrend, the left shoulder (shown by S_1) is below the fol-

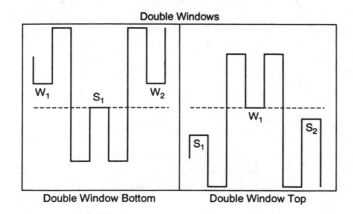

lowing waist (shown by W_1) and the next shoulder (at S_2) is also below waist W_1.

Engulfing patterns—See **bearish engulfing pattern, bullish engulfing pattern, last engulfing bottom,** and **last engulfing top**

Evening star—a top reversal pattern made of three candle lines. The criteria for this pattern include an up-trending market in which a long white candle is followed by a small real body (which can be black or white) that should not touch the real body of the first candle. The third candle of this pattern is a black real body that does not touch the real body of the second candle and then closes well into the white candle line that made up the first candle of this pattern. If the second candle of the evening star is a doji instead of a small real body then the pattern is an evening doji star.

Evening Star

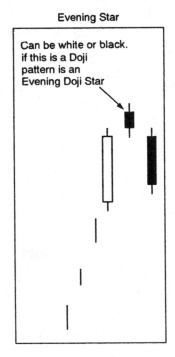

Can be white or black.
if this is a Doji
pattern is an
Evening Doji Star

Gapping doji—a **doji** session that gaps lower during a declining market.

Gapping Doji

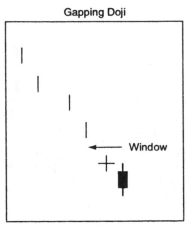

Window

Golden cross—the Japanese term for when a short-term moving average crosses above a long-term moving average. See also ***dead cross***.

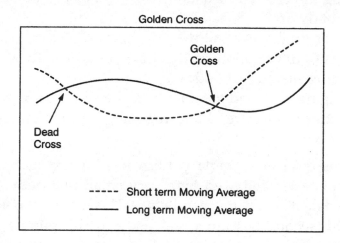

Hammer—a bullish candle line. The hammer has four criteria:
1. the prior trend must be down
2. a small real body (black or white) that is near the upper end of the trading range
3. a long lower shadow usually three times or more the length of the real body
4. little or no upper shadow

The ***hanging man*** and hammer have the same shape. What differentiates one from the other is that the hammer follows a downtrend while the hanging man is after an uptrend.

Hanging man—a bearish candle line with confirmation of the next session. The hanging man has five criteria:
1. the prior trend must be up

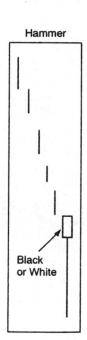

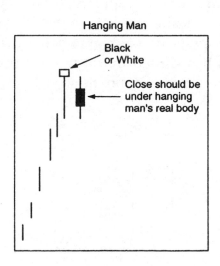

2. a small real body (black or white) that is near the upper end of the trading range
3. a long lower shadow usually three times or more the length of the real body and
4. little or no upper shadow
5. bearish confirmation of the next session with a close under the hanging man's real body.

The hanging man and *hammer* look the same. However, the hammer comes after a downtrend and the hanging man emerges after an uptrend.

Harami—this dual line candle pattern has an unusually long real body (white or black) followed by a very small real body (black or white) that holds within the first candle's real body. The classic harami should have the second session's real body in the middle of the first real body. See also *harami cross, high price harami,* and *low price harami.*

Harami

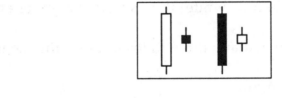

Harami
Cross

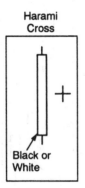

Black or
White

High Price
Harami

Either
candle
can be
black
or white

Harami cross—if the second candle of a *harami* is a doji instead of a small real body, the pattern is called a harami cross.

High price harami—a *harami* in which the second real body of the harami is near the upper end of the first real body. See also *low price harami.*

High-wave candle—a candle line with usually long upper and lower *shadows.* The high-wave candle's long lower shadow shows buyers enter (or sellers retreat) as the market moves lower, but the long upper shadow indicates a rejection of higher price levels. A high wave candle shows the trend has shifted into a neutral posture since it reflects a market that is in a state of confusion.

High-Wave Candles

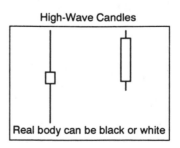

Real body can be black or white

Inflection line—the short horizontal line in a *kagi chart.*

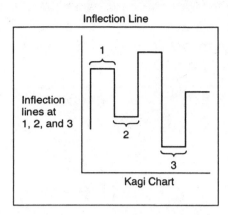

Kagi chart—One of the three types of Japanese charts (see also *renko* and *three-line break* charts) that does not have time on the horizontal axis. The basic premise of the kagi chart is that the thickness and the direction of the kagi lines are dependent on the market's action. If the market continues to move in the direction of the prior kagi line, that line is extended. However, if the market reverses by a predetermined amount, a new kagi line is drawn in the next column in the opposite direction. When prices penetrate a prior low or high, the thickness of the kagi line changes. The kagi chart can be constructed using percentage or fixed amount reversals. See also *inflection line, yang line,* and *yin line.*

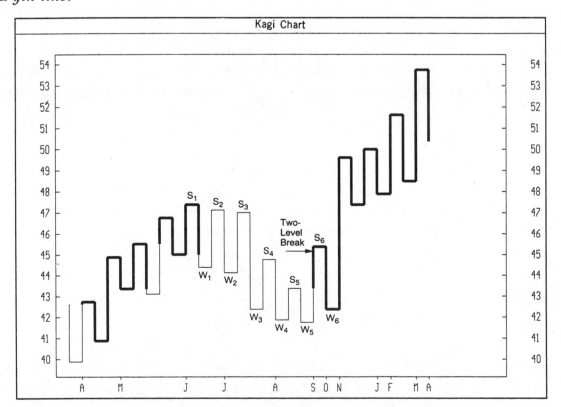

Last engulfing bottom—this a bullish candle pattern that has the same group of candle lines that form the **bearish engulfing pattern** (a large black candle that engulfs the prior white candle). However, the bearish engulfing pattern appears after a rising market while the last engulfing pattern appears after a falling market. See also **last engulfing top.**

Last Engulfing Bottom

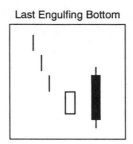

Last engulfing top—this bearish candle pattern has the same configuration as the **bullish engulfing pattern** (a large white candle that envelops a small black real body). However, the last engulfing top appears after an uptrend, whereas the bullish engulfing pattern appears during a price decline. See also **last engulfing bottom.**

Last Engulfing Top

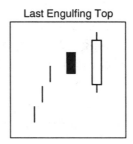

Long black candle—a candle line with an extended black **real body.** This means that the close is near the session's low and the open was near the high. A long black candle should have its real body at least three times larger than surrounding real bodies. Long black candles can be used as a tool to confirm a resistance area, as a confirmation of a break of support and the long black real body can be used as a resistance area. The resistance set up by a long black candle should be from 50% within the candle up to the top of the candle (including the upper shadow). See also **long white candle.**

Long Black Candle

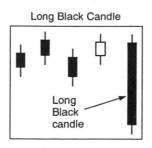

Long white candle—a candle with a tall white ***real body*** in which the open of the session is near the low, and the close is near the high. The length of the real body should be at least three times the length of recent real bodies. Some of the uses of long white real bodies include helping to confirm support and reinforcing the importance of a break-out from a resistance area. The long white candle can also be used as a support area. The support should be from midway of the white candle down to the bottom of the white candle (this includes the bottom of the lower shadow). See also ***long black candle.***

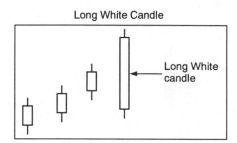

Long White Candle

Long White candle

Low price harami—a ***harami*** in which the second real body of the pattern is near the bottom end of the first real body. See also ***high price harami.***

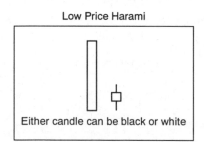

Low Price Harami

Either candle can be black or white

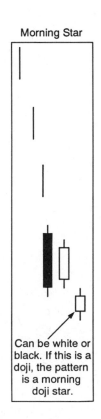

Morning Star

Can be white or black. If this is a doji, the pattern is a morning doji star.

Morning star—a bottom reversal pattern composed of three candle lines. During a downtrend there is a black real body. This is the first part of the pattern. The second session is a small real body candle that does not touch the first (i.e. black) real body. The second real body can be white or black. The last session of the morning star is a long white real body that ideally should not touch the second real body. This long white real body should close well into the first candle's black real body to complete this pattern. If the second candle of this pattern is a doji instead of a small real body then this pattern becomes a morning doji star.

Neck—see ***"buy when the neck emerges from the white suit with black shoes"*** and ***"sell if the black shoe comes out of a black suit after a neck'***

New Price Charts—used to describe a chart in which a new price, high or low, has to be reached before another line can be placed on the chart.

Japanese new price charts include the *kagi chart, renko chart,* and *three-line break chart.*

Piercing pattern—This is a two candle pattern that emerges after a downtrend. The first part of this pattern is a long black real body. In the next session the market opens at a new low for the move, but by the close of the session the market forms a white candle that closes 50% or more into the prior black real body.

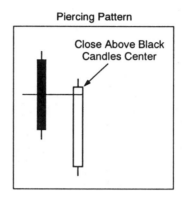

Pole charts—a chart constructed of the high and low of each session. It was the second type of chart used by the Japanese. See also *anchor charts, bar charts, candle charts, and stopping charts.*

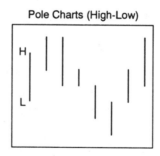

Real body—the rectangular portion of the candlestick line. The top and bottom of the real body represent the open and close of the session. If the sessions' close is under the open, the real body is filled in, with

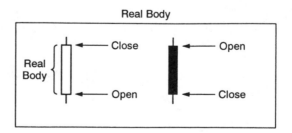

the top of the real body the open and the bottom of the real body the close. If the session's close is above the open, then the real body is empty with the top of the real body at the close and the bottom at the open. The size and color of the real body give important clues about the health of the market. See also *candlestick charts, long black real bodies, long white real bodies,* and *spinning tops.*

Record sessions—in Japan, a new high or a new low is referred to as a record session. In candle theory, a market that reaches eight to ten consecutive (or almost consecutive) record session highs or record session lows is a time when the market is overextended.

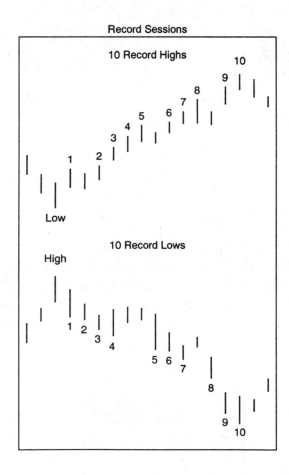

Renko chart—one of the three kinds of Japanese charts (see also *kagi* and *three-line break charts*) that does not take time into account for constructing the chart. Each line in a renko chart is called a brick. Rising bricks are shown as white and falling bricks are shown as black. A new white (black) brick is added when a rally (selloff) continues in the same direction once a fixed amount has been exceeded. In renko charts, the portion of the rally or selloff that does not exceed the fixed amount is not shown. In renko charts, each renko brick is the same size.

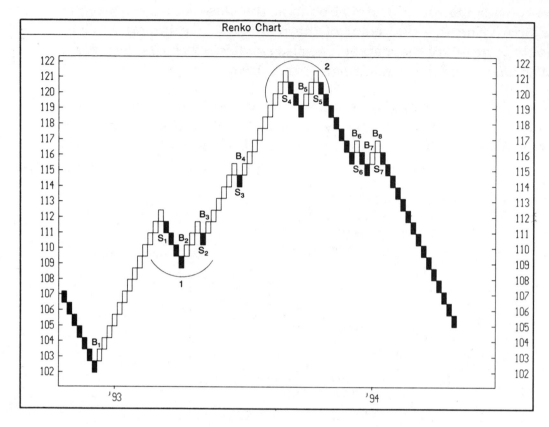

"Sell if the black shoe comes out of a black suit after a neck"—an expression used in Japan to denote a bearish *three-line chart* pattern. A short black line is sometimes called a black shoe, a *black turnaround line* (a black line that surpasses the prior three white lines) is sometimes called a black suit, and a small white line is sometimes called a neck, since it looks like a neck coming out the white suit.

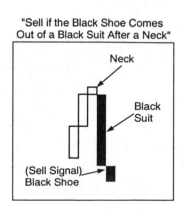

Shadows—The lines above and below the ***real body.*** The top of the upper shadow is the high of the session and the bottom of the lower shadow is the low of the session. Long upper shadows reflect that the market rejected higher prices. Long lower shadows show that the selling pressure evaporated (or the bears were overwhelmed by the bulls) at lower prices. See also ***candlestick chart*** and ***high wave candle.***

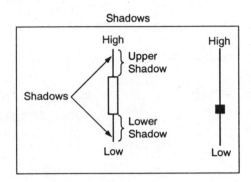

Shooting star—a bearish candle line with its long upper *shadow* candle with a small ***real body*** (black or white) that is near the bottom end of the trading range. Since the shooting star is a top reversal signal, it should appear after an uptrend.

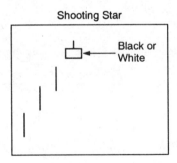

Shoulders—a prior high in ***kagi*** charting.

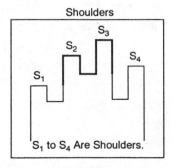

Spinning top—a candle line with a small **real body.** It is a sign that the prior move may be losing its momentum.

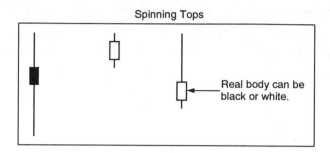

Spring—a bullish signal where the market breaks under an important support area and then ''springs'' back above the broken support area. See also **upthrust.**

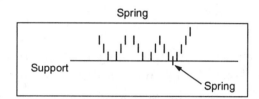

Stopping chart—a chart that uses only closing prices. It was the first type of chart used by the Japanese. See also **anchor chart, bar chart, candle chart,** and **pole chart.**

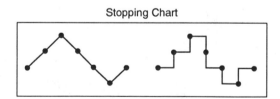

Three-line break—one of the three types of Japanese charts (see also **renko** and **kagi charts**) that does not consider time. In other words there is no time scale on the horizontal axis. Rising lines are shown as white and falling lines as black. When starting to draw a graph, the first line is a rising white line if it rises, or the first line is a black falling line if it declines. Then, if the price exceeds the first line, a new white line is drawn in the next column. If instead, the next price was below the first line, then a black line is drawn in the next column. A new line is only drawn when a new high or new low is touched. To determine if the market has started down, the low price of the last three rising lines must be broken on the downside during the fall. On the other hand, to determine if a decline has ended, the highest price of the last three declining lines must be exceeded on the upside. See also **black** and **white turnaround lines.**

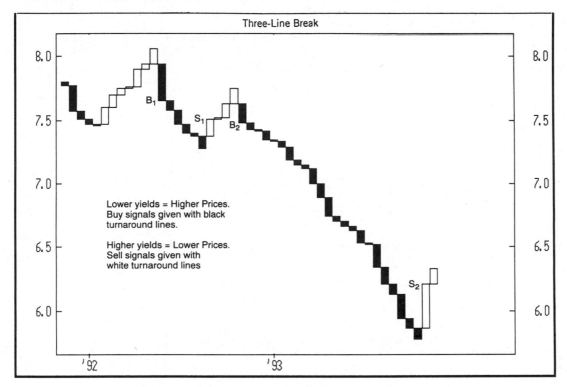

Trend—since most of the candle signals are reversals, there must be a prior trend to reverse for a candle pattern or candle line to have meaning. For instance a *doji* in the middle of a trading zone would not be an important trading signal since there is no trend to reverse. Another instance where trend is important is the **hammer** and **hanging man** lines. Both of these lines look the same, but one is a bullish hammer if it comes after a downtrend, and the other is a hanging man if comes after an uptrend.

Turnaround line—See **black turnaround line** and **white turnaround line.**

Two black gapping candles—two black real body candles that follow a *falling window.*

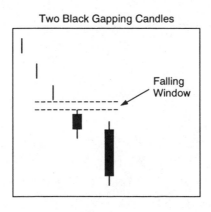

Upthrust—a bearish signal insofar as the market breaks through important resistance, but then fails to hold the new highs and pulls back under the previously pierced resistance area. See also *spring*.

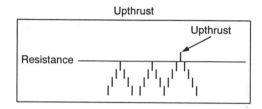

Waists—a prior low in *kagi charting.*

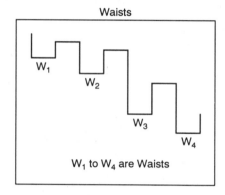

White suit—see *"buy when the neck emerges from the white suit with black shoes"* and *"sell if the black shoe come out of a black suit after a neck'*

White turnaround line—the white line in a *three-line break* chart that exceeds the high of the prior three consecutive black lines. See also *black turnaround line.*

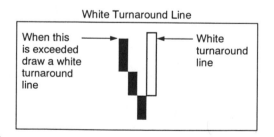

Windows—a continuation pattern in candle charts. A window is the same as a gap in Western technicals. There are rising and falling windows. A rising window is a bullish continuation pattern that is formed when the top of yesterday's upper shadow is under the low of the current lower shadow. A falling window opens when the prior session's low (i.e., the bottom of the lower shadow) is above the top of the current upper shadow.

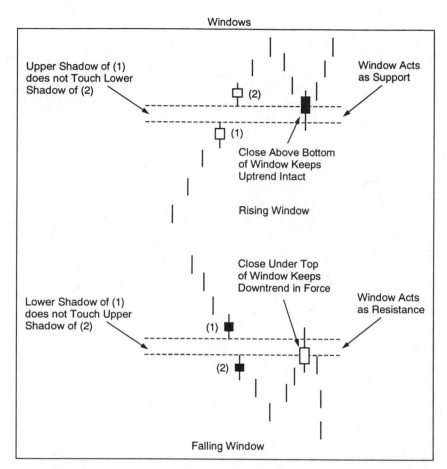

Yang line—in **kagi charts**, another name for the thick portion of the kagi line. See also *yin line*

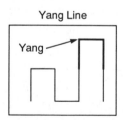

Yin line—in kagi charts, another name for the thin segment of the kagi line. See also *yang line.*

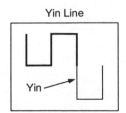

BIBLIOGRAPHY

Buchanen, Daniel Crump, *Japanese Proverbs and Sayings*, Oklahoma City, OK: University of Oklahoma Press, 1965.

Cleary, Thomas, *The Japanese Art of War*, Boston, MA: Shambhala, 1991.

Dilts, Marion May, *Pageant of Japanese History*, New York, NY: David McKay, 3rd edition, 1963.

Hiroshi, Okamoto, *Keisen no Mikata (The Way to Look at Charts)*, Tokyo, Japan: Nihon Keizai Shinbunsha, 1972.

Hoshii, Kazutaka, *Hajimete Kabuka Chato wo Yomu Hito no Hon (A Book for Those Reading Stock Charts for the First Time)*, Tokyo, Japan: Asukashuppansha, 1990.

Ikeda, Mamoru, *Kabushki Chato Nyumon (Introduction to Stock Charts)*, Tokyo, Japan: Diamondsha, 1978.

Ikutaro, Gappou, *Kabushikisouba no Technical Bunseki (Stock Market Technical Analysis)*, Tokyo, Japan: Nihon Keizai Shinbunsha, 1985.

Ishii, Katsutoshi, *Kabuka Chato no Tashikana Yomikata (A Sure Way to Read Stock Charts)*, Tokyo, Japan: Jiyukokuminsha, 1990.

Nippon Technical Analysts Association, *Analysis of Stock Price in Japan*, Tokyo, Japan, 1986.

Oyama, Kenji, *Hanawa Kurenai Yanagiwa Midori (The Flower is Red, the Willow is Green)*, Tokyo, Japan: Oyama Keizai Kenkyusho, 1977.

Sakata Goho Wa Furinkazan (Sakata's Five Rules are Wind, Forest, Fire and Mountain), Tokyo, Japan: Nihon Shoken Shinbunsha, 1969.

Seidensticker, Edward G, *Even Monkeys Fall from Trees and Other Japanese Proverbs*, Rutland, VA: **Charles** E. Tuttle, 1987.

Sun-Tzu, *The Art of War*, trans. Samuel B. Griffith, London, England: Oxford University Press, 1963.

Sun-Tzu, *The Art of Warfare*, trans. Roger Ames, New York, NY: Ballantine, 1993.

Shimizu, Seiki, *The Japanese Chart of Charts*, trans. Gregory S. Nicholson, Tokyo, Japan: Tokyo Futures Trading Publishing Co., 1986.

Technical Traders Bulletin, May 1991, Torrence Hills, CA: Island View Financial Group Inc., 1991.

Yasui, Taichi, *Kabushikikeisen no Shinzui (The Essence of Stock Charts)*, Tokyo, Japan, 1976.

INDEX

....

" The all-time heavyweight champion in the technical analysis field. "

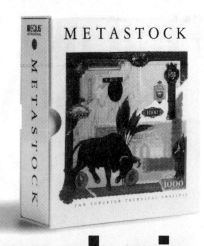

—*Stocks & Commodities Magazine, May 1994*

After ten years of developing investment software, we're still totally committed to just one thing—helping you become the best investor you can be.

That's why we add powerful analysis methods like the new Japanese charting techniques in this book. In fact, MetaStock™ is the only program which includes these three new charting methods. Plus, MetaStock is endorsed by guru Steve Nison.

As an EQUIS software user, you'll have access to a full range of help and support beyond the features you'll find in our programs.

When it comes to helping you become a successful computerized investor, we're here to help you every step of the way.

That's one of the reasons why MetaStock is the world's best-selling technical analysis software.

Here's what John Sweeney, Technical Editor at *Stocks & Commodities Magazine* discovered: "Most users I checked loved the relationship they had with EQUIS. Some had gotten unsolicited callbacks to see how they were doing. EQUIS was a company on which they could rely." (May 1994)

You can rely on us, too.

Order your FREE MetaStock Demo and a copy of *Maximizing Your Investments With MetaStock*, an information-packed booklet to help you get the most out of MetaStock.

Call Toll-Free:
1-800-882-3040 ext 44

equis ®

3950 South 700 East, Suite 100 · Salt Lake City, Utah 84107 · 801-265-8886 · FAX: 801-265-3999 · CompuServe: GO EQUIS (Section 14) Prodigy: Money Talk BB/Investment Tools/META · America Online: EQUIS ©1994 EQUIS International, Inc. MetaStock is a trademark of EQUIS International. A real-time trading version of MetaStock is also available. Please call for more information.

Find out how MetaStock helps you become a successful investor.

See how you can become a successful computerized investor by ordering a free MetaStock Demo and booklet, *Maximizing Your Investments With MetaStock*

You'll get a first-hand look at MetaStock, including the Japanese charting methods you've seen in this book.

MetaStock™ is the world's best-selling technical analysis software. Endorsed by Steve Nison, it's the only program which includes these three new charting methods.

Inside the booklet you'll find tips and ideas you can use with MetaStock to make better investment decisions:

- Get started with a Quick Tutorial

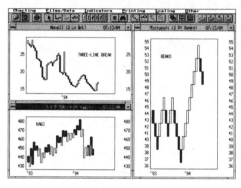

Only MetaStock lets you plot the new charting methods shown in this book: Kagi, Renko, and Three-Line Break. All with a click of the mouse.

- Learn shortcuts, tips, and tricks
- Learn about compatible third-party products
- See how to use our free customer support network
- Learn about other MetaStock features
- Get special discounts on MetaStock and other EQUIS investment products

You'll see why the readers of *Stocks & Commodities Magazine*

recently voted MetaStock #1 in its price category.

Investment software experts agree: "If you want to learn about technical analysis, this package is the place to start—and we guarantee that you'll never outgrow it. This may be the most well thought-out and easy-to-use package we reviewed."
—*Worth Magazine*, April 1994

With your own money on the line, you can trust MetaStock.

Order your FREE MetaStock Demo and a copy of *Maximizing Your Investments With MetaStock*

Call Toll-Free:
1-800-882-3040 ext 44